Bulls, Bears, Boers, and Brits

Afrika-Studiecentrum Series

VOLUME 44

The titles published in this series are listed at *brill.com/asc*

Bulls, Bears, Boers, and Brits

Finance and the Coming of War in Southern Africa, 1894 – 1899

By

Ian Phimister

BRILL

LEIDEN | BOSTON

Cover illustrations: Top: street view of London, in or before 1896. Left: Bank of England. Right: Royal Exchange. Creative Commons 1.0 Universal. Bottom: postcard, expressing French sympathy for the Boer cause. It depicts the British Colonial Secretary, Joseph Chamberlain as pickpocket, grabbed by Transvaal Boer President Kruger.

The Library of Congress Cataloging-in-Publication Data is available online at https://catalog.loc.gov
LC record available at https://lccn.loc.gov/2024054985

Typeface for the Latin, Greek, and Cyrillic scripts: "Brill". See and download: brill.com/brill-typeface.

ISSN 1570-9310
ISBN 978-90-04-69078-3 (paperback)
ISBN 978-90-04-69079-0 (e-book)
DOI 10.1163/9789004690790

This book is printed on acid-free paper and produced in a sustainable manner.

'… market valuations have been advanced to a preposterous level … – the utterly rotten, the indifferent, and the problematical shares … rising often more vigorously than the solid dividend-payers – it becomes evident that, however solid the Rand industry may be, much of the superstructure being raised upon it must come to grief.'

(*The Economist*, 12 October 1895)

• • •

'I may say that we are by no means ill disposed towards Kruger. We wish he could establish an honest executive, and then try [to] secure the observance of the provisions of the drink laws: but we don't think that the principle of taxing declared nett profits of mining Cos unfair, or that we are working under a crushing tyranny.'

(LORD HARRIS, acting chairman of Consolidated Goldfields, 20 November 1898)

Contents

Acknowledgements

I have been thinking about this subject for many years when not distracted by other projects and the demands of graduate supervision and postdoctoral mentorship. Its origins are rooted in endless discussions over the course of lengthy walks through Oxford's Port Meadow and along the banks of the Thames with Stanley Trapido.

But before the law of diminishing returns becomes too obvious, I must thank past and present members of the International Studies Group at the University of the Free State for their patient indulgence of this interest of mine. Ilse le Roux and Tari Gwena helped enormously with tables, diagrams, and the formatting of the manuscript. Andy Cohen, Kate Law, Lindie Koorts, Duncan Money, Admire Mseba, Tinashe Nyamunda, Rory Pilossof, Neil Roos, and Danelle van Zyl-Hermann were all extremely generous with their time and advice.

A conference at Oxford on global gold rushes convened by Ben Mountford and Steve Tufnell, and a seminar in Cambridge hosted by Gareth Austin and Duncan Needham, were invaluable for clarifying my arguments. Early versions of the manuscript benefitted greatly from comments by Alois Mlambo, Mucha Musemwa, Arrigo Pallotti, and Brian Raftopoulos. Going far beyond the call of duty, Tony Hopkins, Deryck Schreuder, Forbes Munro, Helen Bradford, Peter Cain, Gail Nattrass, Jan-Bart Gewald, Jeremy Mouat, and Charles van Onselen read successive drafts. Their critical scrutiny and consummate professionalism saved me from many errors of fact and interpretation.

Successive Rectors and Vice-Chancellors at the University of the Free State helped to create congenial research and writing environments, and I am most grateful to Jonathan Jansen and Francis Petersen for what they did to make these possible. From start to finish, Glen Taylor, UFS' Director of Research Development, displayed a keen awareness of the intellectual project and provided invaluable institutional support. I am greatly indebted to him.

My grateful thanks to Alessandro De Cola and Saskia Stehouwer for all their editorial interventions and assistance. Franca de Kort and Theo Joppe were the most gracious and patient of editors.

Throughout it all, Melanie Walker gritted her teeth and carried on. Her example was inspirational. This book is dedicated to her.

Ian Phimister
Bloemfontein
October 2023

Figures and Tables

Figures

Tables

CHAPTER 1

Introduction

Almost without exception, academic articles and books concerned with the Witwatersrand's gold mining history, of which there are hundreds, and to a lesser degree those of Southern Rhodesia's gold fields, have turned on the industry's assumed imperatives of cost minimisation and output maximisation. They have taken for granted the importance of working costs and production. The focus of *Bulls, Bears, Boers, and Brits* is very different. It looks instead at the prevalence of financial speculation, and how mining share markets were made and unmade in the last six years or so of the nineteenth century. It is a perspective that invites new ways of seeing the global making of southern Africa's violent past and the central part played by financial imperialism.

The aims, significance, and structure of *Bulls, Bears, Boers, and Brits* are set out below, including details of the sources on which it is based, as well as a section discussing the historiography of late-nineteenth-century gold mining in Southern Africa. The conclusion is followed by statistical appendices detailing company capitalisation and share price movements over time.

Its main body takes the form of successive substantive chapters, the first of which, 'Boom, 1894–1895', traces the frenzied trading in the sub-continent's gold mining and associated shares between August 1894 and September 1895. Centred on the Witwatersrand in the Transvaal, this spectacular boom soon expanded to sweep up similar market ventures north of the Limpopo River, in the territory that was becoming Rhodesia. By paying close attention to the structure and control of the London and Paris mining markets in particular, the chapter explores the dynamics of the boom and studies those best placed to take financial and political advantage of it. This is done in part through scrutiny of the Parliamentary Select Committee on British South Africa, and the evidence it chose not to consider. Particular attention is given to the role some contemporaries believed was played by Alfred Beit, one of the richest Randlords and a close confidant of Cecil Rhodes, even as the so-called 'Kaffir Boom' collapsed in fits and starts between October and December 1895.

The next chapter, 'Bust, 1896–1899', emphasises the systemic nature of the gold mining industry's speculative dimension. Market making was not confined to share pushing in boom times. Money was made by manipulating falling as well as rising markets. From 1896 onwards, the Southern African mining market was shaped more often by bears than it was by bulls. At all times, though, its financial operations were driven by the interests of the big controlling

 | DOI:10.1163/9789004690790_002

groups. For extended periods, these rarely coincided with British Imperial concerns. Arguably, the gold mining industry's profits were influenced less by the much-reviled concessions policy of the Transvaal Government than they were by overcapitalisation and market making.

In summary, this book argues that the part played by financial speculation is crucial to understanding the political economy of Southern Africa during the 1890s. More specifically, it suggests that the emphasis on production costs in almost every study of the history of gold mining is misplaced in a period when the predominance of speculative activity frequently rendered economic grievances largely unimportant if not entirely irrelevant. By examining the structure of international share markets for Southern African, particularly but not only Rand, mining shares, markets that lent themselves to manipulation by major mining houses and companies, this account scrutinises the unprecedented stock exchange boom and bust of the mid-1890s and its aftermath. Important sections of London's financial press and the City itself were perfectly content with the returns from the gold mining industry where these were not skewed by market making. There was considerably more criticism of speculative excesses by mining companies than there was of Kruger's Transvaal Government, at least until early 1899. Only then did key Randlords associate themselves with Imperial demands for Boer acceptance of British suzerainty.

Its starting point is an observation made by J.A. Hobson in the *Contemporary Review.* When dealing with international capitalism, he wrote, 'the forces and interests of the investor and of the financier are by no means always identical. … even were complete structural amalgamation of the gold mines otherwise advisable, such separation, real or apparent, as favoured the manipulation of and speculation in stocks might counteract the merely industrial economies, i.e., the shareholder might be sacrificed to the speculator'.[1] In the opinion of well-placed contemporaries, this was precisely what happened. The financially compromised spirit of the age was nicely captured in a speech by the Lord Chief Justice, Lord Russell of Killowen, in 1898, complaining about the abuses inflicted on shareholders and creditors by unscrupulous company promoters. The limited liability system, Russell thought, was being 'prostituted by the greed of unscrupulous persons in the hurry to obtain great wealth without being willing to put forth for its acquirement honest toils and honest endeavour'. Unchecked, this would seriously affect the 'public mind and conscience'. Deprecating the promotion of 'wild-cat' companies and the widespread prevalence of fraud, he warned against the pernicious practice of over-capitalisation

1 John Hobson, "Capitalism and Imperialism in South Africa," *Contemporary Review* 77 (1900): 4.

'to satisfy the greed of the middleman and promoter to cover extravagant advertising charges, extravagant fees for expert reports, gifts in money or in shares to procure directors, aye, and even to procure the introduction of directors'. 'Need I say that in such cases loss and failure are certain, and the public are called upon to pay fees for the deception which has been practiced upon them?'[2]

Celebrating this 'most important pronouncement' soon afterwards in the *National Review*, Hugh Stutfield, himself a member of the Stock Exchange and one of the City's most acute critics, similarly insisted that 'the art of making a market, as it is called, or artificially rigging the price of shares so as to tempt the public to buy, together with other forms of stock manipulation, puffing bribery of many subtle [sic], and secretly unloading on the public by means of sub-trusts and baby companies, has been brought to a high pitch of perfection'. In Stutfield's estimation, 'modern financial machinery' comprised little more than 'riggings, cornerings, liquidations, reconstructions, amalgamations, and share-splittings; the frequent bolsterings and patchings up of rottenness, and the multiplication of subsidiary … companies which hold up each other's shares'. The predatory spirit animating the City in general and its mining markets in particular was perfectly captured, he thought, in Ibsen's *Gabriel Borkman*, where company promoters were imbued with the 'morals of the higher rascality'. It was a fact, wrote Stutfield, that 'a very large proportion of the companies that appear nowadays are not honest trading concerns but simply devices for milking the investor'.[3] By failing to take any of this into serious consideration, accounts of Southern African history in the 1890s that focus on mining company complaints as the root cause of the Jameson Raid and the outbreak of war in 1899, are missing a key dimension of the past.

Of the archives investigated, the most useful were the Rothschild Archives in London; the Eckstein and Wernher/Beit Papers in the possession of Barloworld, Johannesburg; the Gold Fields Collection housed in the Cory Library for Historical Research, Rhodes University, Makhanda (Grahamstown); the Chamberlain Papers located in the University of Birmingham Library's

2 Geoffrey Searle, *Corruption in British Politics 1895–1930* (Oxford: Oxford University Press, 1987), 33, 38–40; and Sidney Webb and Beatrice Webb, *The Decay of Capitalist Civilisation* (London: George Allen and Unwin, 1923), 105, 106–107.

3 Hugh Stutfield, "The Company Scandal. A City View," *The National Review* 32 (1898): 581–82; and his "The Higher Rascality," *The National Review* 31 (1898): 181. This section first appeared in Ian Phimister, "Frenzied Finance: Gold Mining in the Globalizing South, c. 1886–1896," in *A Global History of Gold Rushes*, eds Benjamin Mountford and Stephen Tuffnell (Oakland: University of California Press, 2018), 156. For more on Stutfield, see David Kynaston, *The City of London. Volume II. Golden Years 1890–1914* (London: Chatto & Windus, 1995), 176–77; 182–83.

Manuscripts Collection in Birmingham; the Standard Bank Archives of Johannesburg; the National Archives of Zimbabwe, Harare; the Lyttleton Gell Papers kept in the Derbyshire Record Office in Matlock; the University of Southampton's Hartley Institute's collection of Carl Meyer's Letters; and the University of Cape Town's Jagger Library Special Collections in Cape Town, which hold the W.P. Schreiner Papers. Extensive use was made of financial periodicals and newspapers, particularly of *The Economist*, as well as *The Investors' Review*, easily the two most reputable financial journals of the day. *The Statist, The [African] Critic*, the *Financial Times*, the *Financial News* and the money columns in daily metropolitan papers such as the *Pall Mall Gazette* were frequently consulted. The *African Review* and Henry Labouchere's *Truth* were closely read, as were the *Standard & Diggers' News*, and the *Rhodesia Herald*. Specialist periodicals examined included the *Mining Journal, Engineering and Mining*, and *The British and South Africa Export Gazette*. Wider comment was sought from the *Nineteenth Century, Fortnightly Review* and the *Contemporary Review*.

CHAPTER 2

Historiography

Southern Africa's gold mining industry in the 1890s primarily comprised the Witwatersrand and De Kaap in the Transvaal, as well as scattered fields across the Limpopo River in what was becoming Southern Rhodesia. Discovered in 1886, the Witwatersrand gold field was by far the most important one in the region. Indeed, within seven years it was already responsible for one fifth of the world's total gold output. 'A chain of hills, fifteen miles to the south of Pretoria, separating the waters of the Orange River and the Limpopo, constitutes the Witwatersrand', reported a visiting expert in 1893. 'It stretches over about 45 miles from east to west, with a slightly southerly curve. Geologists found here gold deposits in a formation hitherto unknown'. In other parts of the world, not least Southern Rhodesia, he continued, gold was always discovered either in the beds of streams, in the shape of dust and nuggets, or in veins of quartz of very variable and uncertain nature. On the Rand, though, gold was 'contained in a conglomerate of sandstone, quartz, and other stone, intermixed with pebbles … [in] three principal, almost parallel, deposits, called the Main Reef, North Reef, and South Reef, which, with a few trifling interruptions, traverse the entire Rand from east to west, and sink into the ground with a dip towards the south'.[1] 'There have often been mines of short length [depth] far richer than these of the Rand', an American mining engineer concluded, 'but nothing approaching them has ever been seen so far as regularity and extent are concerned'.[2]

The Witwatersrand's unique combination of low-grade ore persisting at great depth was soon understood by mining engineers and managers to mean that its profitable working depended on obeying the iron laws of cost minimisation and output maximisation. Given stark formulation by Frederick Johnstone,[3] the playing out of this dynamic informs nearly every scholarly account of the Rand's mining history, most of them simply taking for granted that the

1 Felix Abraham, *The New Era of the Goldmining Industry in the Witwatersrand* (London: Effingham Wilson, 1894), 5. See also his *The Witwatersrand Gold Mines: A True and Unvarnished Account of their Origin and Progress* (London: Effingham Wilson, 1892); and John Hays Hammond, "The Gold Mines of the Witwatersrand, South Africa," *Engineering Magazine* XIV, no. 5 (February 1898): 733–51.

2 *The Times*, January 10, 1893.

3 Frederick Johnstone, *Class, Race and Gold. A Study of Class Relations and Racial Discrimination in South Africa* (Lanham: University Press of America, 1976), 19.

 | DOI:10.1163/9789004690790_003

industry's main aim from start to finish was the profitable production of gold. Differences between these many studies have turned on the weighting given by their authors to cost-driven factors, and the conclusions, economic and political, drawn from them. Heated as the ensuing debates often were, the centrality of the imperatives themselves was rarely questioned.

Contributions by Peter Richardson and Jean-Jacques van Helten emphasised that the 'low average grade of ore was a general feature of Rand properties'. This geological fact together with increasing depth and other practical mining issues had 'a decisive effect upon the character of the mining industry. Throughout the period under review ... the industry was forced to consider the prevalent level of costs as the *decisive* [their emphasis] factor in mining operations', especially as the price of gold was fixed by the Bank of England. More than this, once leading mining engineers realised that the gold-bearing reefs gradually descended southwards at right angles to the original outcrop discoveries, the first line or row of outcrop mines was followed by a second, and eventually a third, parallel line of deep-level mines for whom cost minimisation was essential if they were to be worked profitably. Not only did this influence the gold mining industry's emerging organisational structure, the 'Group System' whereby risks and costs were somewhat shared between the main mining houses, but it also meant that the industry's long-term future was bound up with deep-level mining.[4]

An economic explanation for the political consequences of this gradual transformation of the Witwatersrand 'from a field of outcrop workings to one where deep-level mining was the order of the day',[5] was first set out in a seminal article by Geoffrey Blainey in the 1960s. Convinced that the concessions policy and other taxes levied by the Transvaal government of Paul Kruger weighed most heavily on deep-level operations, Blainey identified the key conspirators behind the Jameson Raid, an abortive coup aimed at overthrowing the Boer status quo, as precisely 'the two big companies [Consolidated Gold Fields and Wernher, Beit & Company] that were heirs to the treasures and problems of the deep-levels'.[6]

4 Peter Richardson and Jean-Jacques van Helten, "The Gold Mining Industry in the Transvaal, 1886–1899," in *The South African War: The Anglo-Boer War, 1899–1902*, ed. Peter Warwick (Harlow: Longman, 1980), 25–26.

5 Peter Richardson and Jean-Jacques Van Helten, "The Development of the South African Gold-Mining Industry, 1895–1918," *Economic History Review* 37, no. 3 (1984): 322. See also, Alan Jeeves, *Migrant Labour in South Africa's Mining Economy. The Struggle for the Gold Mines' Labour Supply 1890–1920* (Johannesburg: Witwatersrand University Press, 1985), 37–38.

6 G. Blainey, "Lost Causes of the Jameson Raid," *Economic History Review* 18, no. 2 (1965): 364.

Although subsequent studies have been divided between the broadly political and the largely economic, only the latter are examined here.[7]

Amongst the scholars closely tracking Blainey's footsteps were Norman Levy and Shula Marks. For Levy, not only the Jameson Raid but also the start of the South African War in 1899 was best explained by the fact that 'the need of the deep-level owners to reduce costs was even greater [than previously]. Since Kruger's policies made the economies they desired impossible, the main deep-level concerns in particular accused the state of plundering the industry'. 'It is the deeper relationship of Wernher, Beit & Co. to the Chamber [of Mines] and the special needs of the deep-level mining houses, and the contradictions between these and the Transvaal state, which … provide the deepest insights into the causes of the war'.[8] No less emphatically, Marks insisted that 'leading companies like Consolidated Goldfields and Wernher, Beit and Company, with their main interests in the deep-level mines … [and] committed to a long-range mining programme … were particularly affected by the obstructive nature of the republican state'. In 1895, she added that, 'as the deep-level mines were just coming into operation, development costs were high and they calculated the expenditure of every penny. The state's taxation policies weighed more heavily on the deep-level than the outcrop mines; they were more dependent on state intervention to control their vast labour force and they complained bitterly that the Netherlands South Africa Railway Company's monopoly over the internal railway system and Kruger's concessions policies led to inefficiency and added considerably to their finely calculated costs'.[9]

Other historians were more or less critical of Blainey's findings. Least persuaded were Arthur Mawby and Elaine Katz. Mawby attacked Blainey's conclusions on two counts. 'The theory's greatest weakness', he wrote, 'is the

7 Most notably in a huge field, Andrew Porter, *The Origins of the South African War: Joseph Chamberlain and the Diplomacy of Imperialism 1895–1899* (London: Manchester University Press, 1980); Andrew Porter, "The South African War: Context and Motive Reconsidered," *Journal of African History* 31, no. 1 (1990): 43–57; Deryck Schreuder, *The Scramble for Southern Africa, 1877–1895* (Cambridge: Cambridge University Press, 1980); and Ian Smith, *The Origins of the South African War, 1899–1902* (London: Longman, 1996). The classic 'political' account predating Blainey's article is Johannes Marais, *The Fall of Kruger's Republic* (Oxford: Oxford University Press, 1961).

8 Norman Levy, *The Foundations of the South African Cheap Labour System* (London: Routledge and Kegan Paul, 1982), 108, 112.

9 Shula Marks, "Southern and Central Africa, 1886–1910," in *The Cambridge History of Africa*, vol. 6, eds G.N. Sanderson and Roland Oliver, (Cambridge: Cambridge University Press, 1985), 475. Minor variations aside, this interpretation is widely accepted as the subject's conventional wisdom; see most recently, Rob Skinner, *Modern South Africa in World History. Beyond Imperialism* (London: Bloomsbury, 2017), 38–39.

implication that the only significant variable in mining economics was the cost of operations ... [while overlooking] variations in the quality of the gold reef, and thus ... the amount of gold contained in any given amount of rock'. Nor was Blainey's clear distinction between deep-level and outcrop companies tenable. 'Eckstein's [Wernher, Beit & Company] were simply the *first* [his emphasis] mining houses to move into deep-level mining. As it became obvious during the later 1890s that the future of gold mining lay in deep-levels, so most mining groups acquired deep-level holdings'.[10]

To start with, Katz declared, Blainey's argument was wrong about production costs. 'The natural differences between the outcrop and the deep-level mines, especially the first row of deep-level mines ... were in no way as great as ... [claimed]: the two types were remarkably similar both geologically and from an engineering point of view'. Secondly, 'the impact of Kruger's policies on the production costs of the deep-level mines was by no means as drastic as Blainey assert[ed]'. These certainly 'angered all the mineowners whose resentment was exacerbated by the state's tardiness in enacting the necessary laws to provide the mines with a consistent and efficient African labour supply ... push[ing] up production costs at a time when the newly adopted economies of scale made reduced working costs imperative'. However, it was the poorer outcrop mines who suffered most, none of whose owners were involved in the Jameson Raid. By contrast, claimed Katz, Wernher, Beit & Company's holdings and those of Rhodes' Consolidated Gold Fields were barely compromised by Kruger's concessions policy. Pointing to the high dividends earned by Wernher, Beit & Company's flagship Rand Mines Ltd as evidence that the conspiracy was not motivated by a conflict of economic interests between the deep-level mines and the outcrop mines at the level of production, Katz's conclusion was unequivocal: 'The abandonment of the Blainey thesis is long overdue: the "outcrop / deep-level theory" has no validity "at the level" of either ownership or production'.[11]

Richard Mendelsohn, too, attempted to refine the Blainey thesis. In contributions before and after Katz's root and branch rejection of the thesis, he argued that Blainey's critics had overstated the extent to which Consolidated Gold Fields and Wernher, Beit & Company owned both outcrop and deep-level mining properties. Gold Fields, Mendelsohn noted, 'had made use of the

10 Arthur Mawby, "Capital, Government and Politics in the Transvaal, 1900–7: A Revision and a Reversion," *Historical Journal* 17, no. 2 (1974): 389, 392. See also his *Gold Mining and Politics – Johannesburg 1900–1907* (Lewiston: Edwin Mellen Press, 2000), 19–42.

11 Elaine Katz, "Outcrop and Deep Level Mining In South Africa before the Anglo-Boer War: Re-examining the Blainey Thesis," *Economic History Review* 158, no. 2 (1995): 325–26.

share market boom of 1894–5 to liquidate its outcrop holdings'. In the same way, 'deep-levels were of greater strategic importance to … [Wernher, Beit & Company] than its outcrops'. 'The chief difference between firms inside and those outside the [Jameson Raid] conspiracy', he concluded, 'was that the former were committed by 1895 to long-range mining programmes while the latter were either preoccupied with stock-jobbing or were content with modest holding operations. This meant that the conspirators stood to gain far more over the long-term than the rest from the replacement of a self-willed and frequently obstructive Boer government by one more easily manipulated by the mining industry'.[12]

Blainey's assumption that the mining industry generally, and deep-level operations particularly, suffered from the Transvaal's high taxes and poor administration, subsequently came in for direct and indirect criticism as scholars closely examined the nature of the Kruger state. While Duncan Innes maintained that the 'war clouds which built up and eventually erupted in 1899 thus had their origins in the contradiction between the political requirements of monopoly capitalism for an effective system of labour control and the capacity (or rather, incapacity) of a quasi-feudal / petty-bourgeois form of state to meet those requirements',[13] Jack and Ray Simons some 15 years earlier had concluded that hardly any agrarian societies were 'so richly endowed or well-equipped as the Transvaal for an industrial revolution. Far from being intractable, the burghers … built railways linking it [the Rand] to ports, enacted an excellent mining code, [and] kept order over unruly, rebellious fortune-hunters, [even as] the mining companies under republican rule produced in 1897, after barely ten years of effective development, more than three million ounces of gold valued at £10 ½ million and distributed £2,817,000 in dividends. … A war was neither inevitable nor necessary to modernise the republic'.[14]

Struck by the Kruger government's support for the gold mining industry's black labour needs, at least so far as supplies from Mozambique were concerned, Patrick Harries thought that 'mining capitalists had little reason to intrigue with British imperialists in a destructive war. By the end of the 19th century the mine-owners had no reason to regard the African labour supply

12 Richard Mendelsohn, "Blainey and the Jameson Raid: The Debate Renewed," *Journal of Southern African Studies* 6 (1980): 160, 170. See also his "Thirty Years' Debate on the Economic Origins of the Raid," in *The Jameson Raid. A Centennial Retrospective*, ed. Greg H. Cuthbertson (Johannesburg: The Brenthurst Press, 1996), 55–88.

13 Duncan Innes, *Anglo American and the Rise of Modern South Africa* (New York: Monthly Review Press, 1984), 63.

14 Jack Simons and Ray Esther Simons, *Class and Colour in South Africa, 1850–1950* (Harmondsworth: Penguin Books, 1969), 61–62.

as an obstacle to the development of the mining industry; even less was it a *casus belli*'.[15] For Dennis Bransky, what was at issue was not so much the Transvaal's ability to modernise itself, but whether or not it was done on terms that suited the mining industry.[16] Long dissatisfied with the tendency towards 'economic reductionism' in Blainey's article,[17] Charles van Onselen understood the Jameson Raid as having administered a 'severe political jolt' to what had previously been a 'weak government in an underdeveloped state'.[18] Compounded by an ensuing depression, the effect of the Raid caused the Kruger government to reconsider its attitude towards the gold mining industry's needs. Between 1896 and 1898, concluded van Onselen, Pretoria 'made serious, consistent and determined efforts to improve the quality of its administration, and to accommodate the mine owners' steadily escalating demands for a new order which could more effectively nurture the growth of industrial capitalism'.[19]

Historians also locked horns over the importance or otherwise of Britain securing direct control over the Rand's gold output. 'Fundamental to Britain's position ... was its place at the heart of the international money market', wrote Marks and Stanley Trapido. But as sterling's importance in the system was only 'assured by the preparedness of ... British banking institutions to defend it with gold', '... imperial statesmen could not afford to run the risk that the future of the South African [gold mining] industry would be jeopardized by a regime ... incapable of securing the long-term interests of the mines'.[20]

Objecting to the implication of their argument that 'Whitehall and the Bank of England regarded Transvaal gold as a major source for the augmentation of the nation's slender monetary reserves of gold', van Helten argued that the Bank could 'obtain gold more rapidly and in greater quantities by raising the Bank Rate and by using the gold devices [including, amongst others, the Bank's ability to raise its buying price of gold]; relying on gold from South Africa to augment the reserves was a lengthy and time-consuming affair and would not necessarily plug the gap in the reserves as the quantity of newly mined gold

15 Patrick Harries, "Capital, State, and Labour on the 19th Century Witwatersrand: A Reassessment," *South African Historical Journal* 18 (1986): 33.

16 D. Bransky, "The Causes of the Boer War. Towards a Synthesis," (unpublished, 1974), 33.

17 Charles Van Onselen, *The Cowboy Capitalist. John Hays Hammond, the American West, and the Jameson Raid* (Johannesburg: Jonathan Ball, 2017), 532.

18 Charles Van Onselen, *Studies in the Social and Economic History of the Witwatersrand 1886–1914, Volume 1. New Babylon* (Johannesburg: Ravan Press, 1982), 13; Van Onselen, *Cowboy Capitalist*, 530.

19 Van Onselen, *New Babylon*, 13.

20 Shula Marks and Stanley Trapido, "Lord Milner and the South African State," *History Workshop* 8 (1979): 56, 57.

might not be adequate'. Noting that the Bank of England 'regarded the use of the Bank Rate and other gold devices at the main methods to attract gold in large quantities from abroad in times of financial stress', and pointing to the 'prevailing *low* [his emphasis] Bank Rate' as evidence that the Bank had 'little difficulty in maintaining its gold reserves at acceptable levels whether or not newly-mined gold arrived from South Africa', he thought that it was 'questionable whether during the 1890s the British Government was motivated in its dealings with the Kruger regime by a desire to release the gold mines from the very considerable burdens and limitations imposed upon them by the Pretoria administration'.[21]

Finding such an interpretation too narrowly technical, Russel Ally suggested that examination of the broader geo-political context revealed 'a world characterised by intense international rivalries, and where the Bank of England's leadership of the international monetary system was coming under increasing challenge'. Under these circumstances, London 'could hardly have been indifferent to the fate of a country that supplied the international economy with its money commodity'.[22] Subsequently sharpened by Marks and Trapido to focus on the hugely increased demand for gold once the United States of America went off the silver standard, together with the India Office's growing preoccupation with Indian gold reserves, this perspective led them to reiterate their conviction that what was 'of the essence to Randlords and London alike' was 'ensuring the long-term continuation of efficient production'.[23]

What is striking about these long-running and fiercely contested exchanges, however, is not so much who was correct and who was mistaken, as the fact that for the past fifty years virtually every study of the Rand has gazed fixedly at production. Whether focused on the immediate constraints of workplace operations in outcrop and deep-level mines; the capacity of the Kruger state to modernise its administrative practices and policies; or the particular significance

21 Jean-Jacques Van Helten, "Empire and High Finance: South Africa and the International Gold Standard 1890–1914," *Journal of African History* 23 (1982): 544, 547.

22 Russell Ally, *Gold & Empire. The Bank of England and South Africa's Gold Producers 1886–1926* (Johannesburg: Witwatersrand University Press 1994), 27. See also his "Great Britain, Gold and South Africa – An Examination of the Influence Gold had in Shaping Britain's Policy towards South Africa, 1886–1914" (unpublished, 1992), 4, 14–15. An important exception to this line of thinking is "Breakdown into War," in *The Lion and the Springbok. Britain and South Africa since the Boer War*, eds Ronald Hyam, and Peter Henshaw, (Cambridge: Cambridge University Press, 2003), 48.

23 Shula Marks and Stanley Trapido, "Lord Milner and the South African State Reconsidered," in *Imperialism, the State and the Third World*, ed. Michael Twaddle, (London: British Academic Press, 1992), 84. See also, Shula Marks, "Rewriting the South African War," *H-SAfrica* (June 2003): 11.

of gold for Britain's central place in the global economy, the refrain has been much the same: 'costs as the decisive factor';[24] 'they calculated the expenditure of every penny';[25] 'conspirators stood to gain ... from the replacement of a ... frequently obstructive Boer government ... [and] the radical changes that could then be effected in the cost of dynamite, coal and labour';[26] and so endlessly on. Largely missing from this picture was the role played by financial speculation. Where its incidence was even noted, virtually every study treated it as a fleeting interlude to be skimmed over before returning to the imperatives of cost minimization and output maximization.[27] The possibility that most historians of Southern Africa's gold mining industry had been staring in the wrong direction was rarely considered.

At the time, only one scholar looked in detail at mining finance during the 1890s and beyond. Over the course of several articles, a book chapter and a monograph, Robert Kubicek examined the industry's capital formation and structure.[28] It was a starting point which made possible a quite different conclusion to the one reached by Blainey. 'The financial vulnerability of these various [mining] groups was not ... predicated exclusively upon whether or not

24 Richardson and Van Helten, "Gold Mining Industry in the Transvaal," 25–26.

25 Marks, "Southern and Central Africa," 475.

26 Mendelsohn, "Blainey and the Jameson Raid," 170.

27 Alan Jeeves, "The control of migratory labour on the South African gold mines in the era of Kruger and Milner," *Journal of Southern African Studies* 2 (1975): 8; and Alan Jeeves "Hobson's The War in South Africa: A Reassessment," in *Writing a Wider War. Rethinking Gender, Race, and Identity in the South African War, 1899–1902*, eds Greg Cuthbertson, Albert Grundlingh, and Mary-Lynn Suttie (Cape Town: David Philip 2002), 242.

28 Robert Kubicek, *Economic Imperialism in Theory and Practice. The Case of South African Gold Mining Finance 1886–1914* (Durham: Duke University Press, 1979). See particularly his "The Randlords in 1895: A Reassessment," *Journal of British Studies* 11, no. 2 (1972): 84–103; and his "Finance Capital and South African Goldmining 1886–1914," *Journal of Imperial and Commonwealth History* 3 (1975): 386–95; as well as his "Mining: Patterns of Dependence and Development 1870–1930," in *Studies in the Economic History of Southern Africa. Volume II. South Africa, Lesotho and Swaziland* eds Z. Konczacki, Jane L. Parpart, Timothy M. Shaw (London: Frank Cas 1991), 64–86. For discussion of speculation in the period immediately after the discovery of gold in 1886, see especially Arthur Webb, "Witwatersrand Genesis: A Comparative Study of Some Early Gold Mining Companies 1886–1894" (PhD diss., Rhodes University, 1981). Later studies include Wayne Graham, "The Randlord's Bubble 1894–6: South African Gold Mines and Stock Market Manipulation," *University of Oxford Discussion Papers in Economic and Social History*, no. 10 (August 1996): 2–32; Arthur Webb, "Blainey and Early Witwatersrand Profitability. Some Thoughts on Financial Management and Capital Constraints Facing the Gold Mining Industry 1886–1894," *South African Journal of Economic History* 12 (1997): 128–52; and Mariusz Lukasiewicz, "Gold, Finance and Speculation: The Making of the Johannesburg Stock Exchange, 1887–1899," (PhD diss., Graduate Institute, University of Geneva, 2017).

they were engaged in deep-level developments', wrote Kubicek. 'Nor can their financial position be determined, as it often has been, by studying the complaints of Randlords about restrictive and inefficient practices of the Transvaal government. How soundly the mine owners developed claims, built capital structures and took profits must be taken into account. On the basis of these criteria the Wernher, Beit & Company complex was by far the soundest and securest on the Rand and quite in a position to cope with market down turns, increased mining costs and obstructive government practice. Farrar's holdings, on the other hand, were the weakest and vulnerable on all three counts. Yet Beit, Phillips and Farrar were involved in the Johannesburg plot. Barnato and Robinson, who had erected shaky financial edifices, stood aloof from the plot. … no commonly shared financial problem distinguished Randlords who participated in subversive politics from those who did not'.[29]

A similar emphasis informed the monograph that followed the articles. 'The most glaring gap in the literature', Kubicek observed, 'is the absence of a full-scale study of capital formation'.[30] Each major mining group was examined in turn, from Wernher, Beit & Company, and its Johannesburg subsidiary, known variously as the Corner House Group, or Ecksteins, through Consolidated Gold Fields, to what Kubicek called the Houses of Ill Repute, primarily the highly speculative operations of J.B. Robinson, Barney Barnato and George Farrar. Minor groups were also looked at, amongst them George Albu, Goertz & Company, and the Abe Bailey interests. The 'crucial distinctions' that emerged from this detailed inspection of the various controlling groups were 'the different strategies employed by the controllers to profit from the claims and the shares they held in the mines, and … the various mechanisms and sources they used to raise capital'. 'Some were development oriented', concluded Kubicek. 'Others … combined a development function with very extensive speculative operations … [and] still others were pure and simple speculators with actual gold production playing little part in their financial plans'. These various business strategies in turn had 'three important effects upon the sources and volume of the capital which flowed into the gold mines'. In the first place, they stopped the gold mining industry 'from developing its full potential as a steady provider of substantial dividends … [because] far too many of the controllers stressed market operations rather than gold production'. Secondly, these practices caused developers and speculators alike 'to engage in self-defeating competition for capital'. The third consequence was 'extremely important'. Because the mining groups had 'so mismanaged its capitalization', major French and

29 Kubicek, "Randlords in 1895," 102.

30 Kubicek, *Economic Imperialism in Theory and Practice*, 18.

German banks were discouraged from 'taking a firm grip on the mines' capital structure'.[31]

This latter outcome was Kubicek's key finding. Covering a longer period than the 1890s alone, the book's stated ambitions were encapsulated in its main title, *Economic Imperialism in Theory and Practice*, and not so much in the sub-title, *The Case of South African Gold Mining Finance 1886–1914*. Its objective was an examination of the Witwatersrand gold mining industry's financial history in order to test 'various economic theories advanced to explain the great expansion of Europe in the three decades before 1914'.[32] And with bank capital shying away from concentrated direct investment in the Rand, there was little of comfort for 'adherents of the Hilferding-Lenin notion of "monopoly finance capital"' driving capitalist imperialism.[33] While Kubicek also had much of interest to say about the internationalisation of capital, few of his conclusions recommended themselves to prominent reviewers. Marks and van Helten, for example, disagreed with the book's treatment of the period after the South African War up until 1914, and found particular fault with its analysis of the relationship between the mining industry and the Kruger state before that time. For Marks, this was a direct consequence of Kubicek's 'focus on finance rather than local production'.[34]

More open to the potential value of an investigation of the gold mining industry's capital formation and structure, Van Helten nonetheless regretted what he saw as a lost opportunity. To suggest that 'South African developments should be seen basically as a function of clashing priorities and the inability of any one or combination of these forces (of Afrikaner nationalism, British imperialism and international capitalism) to achieve supremacy' was to direct 'the debate on imperialism and the gold mining industry down a cul-de-sac'. The relationship between mining and imperialism was more complex than this, declared Van Helten. 'Future research should incorporate not only the role of the Rand as a gold producer in the pre-1914 international economy, the centralization of relations of production in the mining industry, the crucial role of French and German banks in mining investment, but also the question of state-mining capital articulation in the Transvaal and in Britain'.[35]

31 Ibid., 195, 197–99.

32 Ibid., 3.

33 Ibid., 199, 201–2.

34 Shula Marks, "Scrambling for Southern Africa," *Journal of African History* 23 (1982): 109.

35 Jean-Jacques Van Helten, "Review Article. Mining and Imperialism," *Journal of Southern African Studies* 6, no. 2 (1980): 235.

While not every reviewer shared Marks and Van Helten's preoccupation with the relationship between the mining industry and the state at the point of production,[36] it did mean that the first of Kubicek's three important effects noted above, specifically that the business strategies pursued by the Randlords blocked the industry 'from developing its full potential as a steady provider of substantial dividends ... [because] far too many of the controllers stressed market operations rather than gold production',[37] was completely overlooked. Content with identifying the scale of financial speculation, Kubicek himself did not elaborate on its wider significance beyond establishing its pervasiveness during much of the 1890s. Neither at the time nor subsequently was any attempt made to gauge the impact of speculation on the gold mining industry's profitability.

Speculation also disfigured the development of gold mining in what became Southern Rhodesia. Although the Rand and Rhodesian mining markets were closely tied together during the 1890s, the two of them constituting what the City called the 'Kaffir Circus', financial speculation and market making in the latter region have received even less scholarly attention. Such accounts as there are, have tended to focus on the capital needs and share dealing activities of Cecil Rhodes' chartered British South Africa Company, and not on the mining market as a whole. The first of these was Robert Shenton's study of the Chartered Company's financial and political history between 1889 and 1898. Remarkably, it remains the only account to have traced the movement of Chartered share prices over the entire course of that crucial opening decade.[38] Some 20 years later, Paul Maylam, Arthur Keppel-Jones, and Robert Rotberg examined aspects of the British South Africa Company's finances, albeit in the context of broader studies; respectively, the early history of the Bechuanaland Protectorate,[39] the colonial conquest of Zimbabwe,[40] and a biography of Rhodes.[41] Between them, they looked at the Chartered Company's complicated capital arrangements and linkages, the results of 'dubious manouvering

36 J. Butler, review of *Economic Imperialism in Theory and Practice,* by Robert Kubicek, *Africana Journal* 10 (1979): 275–77.

37 Kubicek, *Economic Imperialism in Theory and Practice*, 197.

38 Robert Shenton, "The Chartered Company, 1889–1898. A Financial and Political History of the British South Africa Company" (PhD diss., Harvard University, 1961), 100.

39 Paul Maylam, *Rhodes, the Tswana, and the British: Colonialism, Collaboration, and Conflict in the Bechuanaland Protectorate, 1885–1899* (Westport: Greenwood Press, 1980).

40 Arthur Keppel-Jones, *Rhodes and Rhodesia. The White Conquest of Zimbabwe 1884–1902* (Pietermaritzburg: University of Natal Press, 1983).

41 Robert Rotberg, *The Founder. Cecil Rhodes and the Pursuit of Power* (New York: Oxford University Press, 1988).

and machination', in Maylam's phrase,[42] as well as the financial pressures which some contemporaries believed had precipitated war against the Ndebele in 1893, not an interpretation that either Keppel-Jones or Rotberg found persuasive.[43]

By contrast, an entire chapter was devoted to the Company's speculative operations and their wider ramifications in John Galbraith's history of its early years when the patchiness of the gold deposits was obscured by glowing reports and promises of rich rewards: 'This dependence on illusion rather than reality attracted to Mashonaland syndicates which specialised in paper rather than gold'. 'All the companies were greatly over-capitalised', he continued. 'Promoters allotted the largest proportion of the shares to themselves, and the chartered company received up to half of the vendor's scrip ... [The] preoccupation on stock exchange transactions rather than on mining was abetted by the [BSA] company policy which imposed no requirement of serious development'. There were also reports in the financial press of the 'influence of outside pools [of speculators] in close touch with the company's management in pushing up the price of shares'. A number of Chartered Company directors, Galbraith believed, 'were not averse to such dealings provided that they were kept secret'. Similar themes were subsequently taken up by the present writer.[44]

42 Maylam, *Rhodes, the Tswana, and the British*, 58.

43 Keppel-Jones, *Rhodes and Rhodesia*, 289–94, 308–11; and Rotberg, *The Founder*, 437–38.

44 John Galbraith, *Crown and Charter. The Early Years of the British South Africa Company* (Berkley: University of California Press, 1974), 260, 282, 269; and Ian Phimister, "Speculation and Exploitation: The Southern Rhodesian Mining Industry in the Company Era," *Zambezia* 30 (2003): 178–89; Ian Phimister, "Late Nineteenth Century Globalisation: London and Lomagundi Perspectives on Mining Speculation in Southern Africa, 1894–1904," *Journal of Global History* 10, no. 1 (2015): 27–52; Ian Phimister, "Markets, Mines, and Magnates: Finance and the Coming of War in South Africa, 1894–1899," *Africa* 2, no. 2 (2020): 5–22; and Ian Phimister, "Lendy, Lobengula, and London: The 1893 Anglo-Ndebele War Revisited," *Global Nineteenth-Century Studies* 2, no. 2 (2023): 101–41.

CHAPTER 3

Boom, 1894–1895

In the second half of the 1890s, Britain experienced a rapid phase of company promotion, largely driven by low interest rates, which caused investors to shy away from low-yielding Consols (interest-bearing government bonds), in favour of more risky ventures which offered a better return.[1] Money was cheap and could be borrowed for speculative purposes. Against this backdrop a second and far bigger boom in South African gold mining shares erupted. Unlike the first Rand boom of 1888–9 which had mainly turned on South African capital floated on the Johannesburg Stock Exchange,[2] this one began as British and ended as international, although most investment was mobilised by and through the City of London. The earlier boom had taken off once fears that the gold deposits were shallow had been disproved. When gold was found at depths of 500 feet and more, this led to shares zooming upwards.[3] By the end of 1886 there were already some 90 companies in existence; this number increased to 270 in 1887; and to almost 500 by the end of 1889.[4] These shares, as one observer noted, 'were generally quoted at small amounts, usually at less than one pound each … [and] every facility was furnished to persons of small resources to gratify their gambling proclivities. Large amounts of stock were absorbed by the public, and under the stimulus of heavy speculation premiums on shares rose to an unreasonable height, ranging from 50 to 5000 per cent'.[5]

---

1 Searle, *Corruption in British Politics*, 34. See also, R. Michie, "Options, Concessions, Syndicates, and the Provision of Venture Capital, 1880–1913," *Business History* 23, no. 2 (1981): 149–150; Peter J. Cain and Antony G. Hopkins, *British Imperialism 1688–2000. Second Edition* (Harlow: Longman, 2001), 172–73; and M. Edelstein, "Foreign investment and accumulation, 1860–1914," in *The Economic History of Britain since 1700. Second Edition. Volume 2: 1860–1939*, eds Rode Floud and Donald McCloskey (Cambridge: Cambridge University Press, 1997), 186.

2 See especially, Mariusz Lukasiewicz, "From Diamonds to Gold: The Making of the Johannesburg Stock Exchange, 1880–1890," *Journal of Southern African Studies* 43, no. 4 (2017): 715–32.

3 Harry Klein, *The Story of the Johannesburg Stock Exchange 1887–1947* (Johannesburg: Committee of the Johannesburg Stock Exchange 1948), 31. What immediately follows is a much expanded and revised version of section one of Phimister, "Frenzied Finance."

4 Kubicek, *Economic Imperialism in Theory and Practice*, 43. For slightly smaller numbers, see Klein, *Johannesburg Stock Exchange*, 30.

5 William Jett Lauck, *The Causes of the Panic of 1893* (Boston: Houghton, Mifflin and company, 1907), 44.

 | DOI:10.1163/9789004690790_004

As it became clear, however, that the handful of mines actually producing gold, in fact less than 50 out of nearly 500 firms, were most of them mismanaged and unable to successfully treat pyritic ore encountered at depth, the share market crashed. Prices fell after May 1890, hitting bottom in December of the same year. Scarred by the Baring crisis, British investors tended to avoid Rand ventures, but with the introduction and rapid spread of the MacArthur-Forrest cyanide extraction process in 1891, working mines recovered a much larger proportion of their gold, and this gradually restored market confidence.[6] Never one to mince words, Lord Randolph Churchill reported from Johannesburg in July 1891 that 'recent bad times and the insensibility of the London Money Market have had an admirable effect upon the directors and managers of the gold mines here'. 'They have been compelled', he continued, 'by force of circumstances to divert their attention from the floatation of new companies and from the pushing up of shares to absurd premiums by making fallacious returns of [ore] crushings, and by other dodges familiar to the promoter. They are now concentrating their efforts on the development of their mines … and on economical administration. Many companies have been reconstructed … [Their capital] has been ruthlessly cut down … and although this reduction undoubtedly represents a heavy loss in the past, it probably precedes a profitable future'.[7]

Just how spectacularly profitable a future few could have predicted in 1891. But when fortune returned a few years later, it was once again propelled by renewed speculation rather than expanding production. Not that the steadily increasing output of gold was not hugely impressive. By 1893, the gold mines of the Witwatersrand were already responsible for one fifth of the world's production. Between the start of 1894 and the end of 1895, the Witwatersrand's output of gold steadily expanded from £6,963,100 to £7,840,779, while dividends declared went up from £1,527,284 to £2,046,852.[8] By far the most spectacular increases within this period, however, were registered by share prices; that is, by speculation not production. In the twelve months from January to December 1894, Rand and Rhodesian gold mining shares jumped from £19,752,615 to £55,351,537, that is, by two and three-quarter times. Dividends distributed in 1893 amounted to about £1,019,000; in 1894 to roughly £1,500,000. An increase

6 Frederick Hatch, and John Chalmers, *The Gold Mines of the Rand. Being a Description of the Mining Industry of Witwatersrand South African Republic* (London: Macmillan 1895), 3.

7 Lord Randolph Churchill, *Men, Mines and Animals in South Africa* (London: Sampson Low, Marston & Company 1893), 59–60.

8 "The Rand to Date." *South African Mining Journal*, September 25, 1909.

of only £480,000 in dividends had become a capital appreciation of roughly £35,600,000.[9]

From July 1894 onwards, Rand mining shares attracted more and more attention. An early harbinger of the fortunes being made by insiders was the purchase in August 1894 by Charles Rudd, joint managing director of Consolidated Gold Fields, of 'a town house at Hyde Park Gardens, a handsome residence which belonged to the late Lord Petre'.[10] A single day's trading in October witnessed at least a million pounds' worth of business done, when 'most of the leading South African merchants, including Messrs. Julius Wernher, Alfred Beit, and B.I. Barnato were to be seen in Throgmorton Street, which has not displayed such evidences of tense excitement for the last eighteen months'.[11] During November and December 1894, speculation in South African gold shares was the over-riding feature of the Stock Exchange, reported one trade journal. 'The amount of business transacted was enormous, and probably exceeded all previous records'.[12] The mining market 'may now compare with any branch of the Stock Exchange in the hugeness of the individual operators in it', reported *The Critic*. 'The English Rothschilds ... are identifying themselves much more closely than hitherto with Transvaal shares. Baron Ferdinand de Rothschild is going out to Johannesburg by the "Dunottar Castle" on December 1st'.[13]

'Purchases are now being made on an enormous scale on behalf of French capitalists, while a mammoth New York firm is reported to be heavily buying Rand stock', confided the same periodical a few weeks later. 'Dealers have been deserting "Yankee rails" and other departments of finance for the "Kaffir Market", which now numbers some 700 operators, and is therefore the largest in the House'.[14] Other journals agreed. 'During the past week business in the Mining market has been transacted on a tremendous scale', the *African Review* reported at the beginning of December 1894. 'Many of the brokers' offices have been open all night, and in nearly every case additional assistance has had to be obtained, tremendous wages having been paid to clerks acquainted with stock exchange business temporarily engaged'.[15] Three weeks later, the same journal noted how extremely broad the market had become. 'An immense quantity of scrip formerly held by the leading houses and dealers has now been taken up in parcels of tens and hundreds, by bona fide investors, not only in this Country

9 Paul Emden, *The Randlords* (London: Hodder and Stoughton Limited, 1935), 352.
10 *The Critic*, August 3, 1894.
11 *The African Review*, October 6, 1894.
12 "London Mining Market in 1894." *The Mineral Industry* 3, 1894, 659.
13 *The Critic,* December 7, 1894.
14 Ibid., December 28, 1894.
15 *The African Review*, December 1, 1894.

but throughout the markets of Europe, and even in the United States and still more distant portions of the world. This it is that makes the present boom unlike all its predecessors'.[16] Commenting over the course of several issues on the 'feverish condition of the "Kaffir Circus"', *The Economist* described 'an excited crowd of dealers and brokers block[ing] the way in Throgmorton Street long after the "House" [Stock Exchange] had closed, bidding … on Christmas Eve … for shares for the new account'.[17] 'The prevailing condition has closely approached pandemonium', noted another journal, 'and it has frequently happened that orders have been unable to be fulfilled, simply on account of the deafening noise in the "House"'.[18]

By April 1895, the market was still rising rapidly,[19] causing John Hays Hammond, Consolidated Gold Fields' overweening chief mining engineer and Rhodes *confidant*, to write privately to Baron Ferdinand Rothschild in Paris, advising him to buy 'some Simmer & Jack, also some Nigel Deeps and Central Nigel Deeps. These properties are undoubtedly very cheap at present prices, and I think within a year will see considerable appreciation. … The Gold Fields have been branching out rather extensively, and I think you would do well … to participate in the new enterprises brought out under our Company'.[20] 'There is at present no slackening in the wild revels of English and Continental speculators for shares in Transvaal gold mines', wrote the *Critic*'s City correspondent. 'On the contrary, the danger lies in the recklessness with which the public is plunging in all the rubbish available… The advance of Chartereds to [£]4½ is another indication of the speculative tone of the market'.[21]

In part, the boom rested on the knowledge that the Rand was turning out to be the greatest gold-producing field in the world,[22] but that near-certainty was not the only reason for frenzied buying. A short-lived break in the market in May notwithstanding,[23] the boom went merrily on. Its unprecedented scale was widely appreciated by contemporaries. 'Within the recollection of the oldest member of the Stock Exchange', conceded *The Economist* in August 1895, 'there has been no speculative movement at all comparable, in point either of duration or of volume, to the existing "Kaffir Boom", which has gone

16 Ibid., December 29, 1894.

17 *The Economist*, December 1, 1894; and ibid., December 29, 1894.

18 *The African Review*, December 29, 1894.

19 *The Economist*, April 27, 1895.

20 Bodleian Library, Micro. Afr. 368–370, Hays Hammond Papers, Folio 77, J. Hammond to Baron Ferdinand Rothschild, May 20, 1895.

21 *The Critic*, May 24, 1895.

22 *The Economist*, July 13, 1895.

23 Ibid., May 18, 1895.

on practically without interruption for fully twelve months, and shows as little sign of abatement as ever'.[24] Rand mining companies with a nominal capitalisation of about £16,000,000, the magazine noted, were now quoted at nearly £86,000,000, an appreciation since March 1894 not far short of £60,000,000.[25] Increasingly apparent was the fact that 'of late … the speculation for the rise in Rand Gold shares … has been much less active in the dividend-paying companies than in those which have not yet reached that stage, such as Buffelsdoorn, East Rand, Modderfontein, and Randfontein. This is certainly a curious phase of the "boom", which rather seems to suggest that in the opinion of speculators it is an advantage rather than the reverse that market valuations should be based entirely upon prospective results, and not upon actual distribution of profits'.[26]

Just before the market broke two months later, one of London's leading journals, *The Nineteenth Century*, carried an article on 'The Gold-Mining Madness in the City'. It too acknowledged that the speculative rise in Southern African mining shares 'has by degrees assumed dimensions which place it foremost among the economic features of the moment, and also among the topics of the day'. 'There can scarcely be a person in the United Kingdom who is not aware of its existence', the journal claimed:

> Everybody speaks of it, or hears others discuss it; everybody presumed to have some means is the recipient of at least five or six mining prospectuses a week. … In clubs and trains, in drawing rooms and boudoirs, people are discussing "Rands" and "Modders"; even trades-men and old ladies have taken to studying the Mining Manual, the rules of the Stock Exchange, and the highways and byways of stockbroking. Frequent instances are quoted of persons who have made many thousands by "judicious operations", and there are very few people who do not try to reach the same desirable end along the same apparently easy way.

'In short', *The Nineteenth Century* concluded, 'we are in the midst of one of those eras of feverish speculative activity which, as all students of finance and economics know, are constantly alternating with periods of stagnation and depression'.[27]

---

24 Ibid., August 17, 1895.

25 Ibid.

26 Ibid.

27 S.F. Van Oss, "The Gold-Mining Madness in the City," *The Nineteenth Century* 38, no. 224 (October 1895): 537–38.

The mania for gold mining shares not only spread to the furthest fringes of the Rand, but also infected other goldfields. Large amounts of capital flowed into Western Australian and Southern Rhodesian ventures, although seemingly not at the expense of Rand shares which continued to rise.[28] Particularly noticeable was the 'very active promotion of companies for exploiting Rhodesia, as the territories of the British South Africa Company have come to be called', reported *The Economist*. 'Several parties of mining experts and speculators have been exploring the country for some time, representatives of the Consolidated Gold Fields of South Africa being among the foremost. Discoveries of gold are reported daily, and the mining experts are said to be most enthusiastic'.[29] Reported in January 1895 as 'moving up rapidly',[30] Chartered shares which had been trading at £1 3/4 each in April 1894, reached £4 5/8 each a year later, a rise in total market value of £5,250,000.[31] The previous November, Cecil Rhodes, the driving force behind the Company, as well as joint managing director of Consolidated Gold Fields, Life Governor of the De Beers diamond mining cartel, and Premier of the Cape Colony, had gone to London to do everything he could to whip up market enthusiasm for the region's gold mining prospects. Privileged insiders had their own sources of information. 'We understand that our cousin Natty gave a grand dinner to pay honour to Mr. Rhodes', wrote Baron Gustave Rothschild from Paris. 'In vino veritas, I dare say that some good tumblers of 1874 Hiedzig might have made him speak and your letters tomorrow should bring us interesting news as to the gold mines'.[32]

Ordinary investors had to make do with the belief that Rhodes would make 'a "bullish" speech' at the BSA Company's annual general meeting in January 1895.[33] An estimated two thousand people crammed themselves into the Cannon Street Hotel's largest hall, 'all waiting with ill-concealed anxiety for the arrival of the man who has been described, and not without justice, as the greatest imperialist of his day and generation', simpered the *African Review*.[34]

28 John McCarty, "British Investment in Overseas Mining, 1880–1914" (PhD diss., University of Cambridge, 1961), 86.

29 *The Economist*, September 29, 1894.

30 *The Critic*, January 25, 1895.

31 *The Economist*, August 17, 1895.

32 R[othschild] A[rchives], 8/41 Baron Gustave, Paris, to his cousins, London, 21 November 1894.

33 *The Economist*, December 29 1894.

34 "The Annual Meeting. Mr. Rhodes in the City." *The African Review*, January 19, 1895. See also, Sir Lewis Michell, *The Life and Times of the Right Honourable Cecil John Rhodes 1853–1902*, II (London: Mitchell Kennerley, 1910), 130–31; and especially *The South African Trade*

FIGURE 1
Cecil Rhodes, 1890
SOURCE: *ROY MACNAB, GOLD THEIR TOUCHSTONE. GOLD FIELDS OF SOUTH AFRICA, 1887–1987: A CENTURY STORY*, (JOHANNESBURG: J. BALL, 1987), P. 5.

They were not disappointed. Greeted with 'enthusiastic cheering and waving of hats', Rhodes was described as having made 'an extremely strong and unassailable case for the Company'.[35] To sustained applause and cheers, Rhodes congratulated shareholders on possessing 'a very large piece of the world' which was theirs to enjoy since the overthrow of the Ndebele polity just over a year earlier. 'Our people ... saw very clearly that unless they tried issues with the Matabeli they would have to leave the country. ... They did it for the sake of right and property'. Further cheering and a burst of laughter followed his

Journal and Shipping Gazette, February 1895: 'The meeting was remarkable if not unique. The great hall of the Cannon-street Hotel has been the scene of many city gatherings of great interest to which the public flocked in large numbers, but we cannot recall an instance in which the eagerness of people to gain admittance reached a dangerous pitch and where as many had to go away as were accommodated. The enthusiasm of those who thought themselves happy in being able to be present was also extraordinary, and even Mr. Rhodes, cynic as he is in such matters, must have experienced a thrill at the hurricane of cheers with which he was greeted'.

35 "Rhodes in the City." *The African Review*, January 19, 1895.

declaration that now 'the Matabeli difficulty has disappeared. They have incorporated themselves with us'.[36]

Shareholders heard what they wanted to hear. A report by Hammond in November 1894 on the territory's gold mining prospects had made it clear that its general geology was quite different from the Witwatersrand. Unlike the banket formation characteristic of the Rand, such gold as Rhodesia possessed was found in quartz reefs similar to those in other goldfields around the world. While they were 'true fissure veins', this did not necessarily 'imply the occurrence of pay shoots or bodies of commercial value in their veins'.[37] But on Rhodes' telling, this finding became a virtue rather than a vice. 'There has been a suggestion made that the reefs are not true fissure reefs', he claimed. 'If you will look at this report, you will find ... [Hammond] says that "a most careful and exhaustive examination was made to determine the character of the veins as affecting the persistency or permanency of the ore deposits. The evidence is most conclusive that the auriferous veins ... belong generally to the class of ore deposits known as true fissure veins"'. As no-one had ever argued to the contrary, Rhodes was throwing dust in the eyes of the Chartered Company's shareholders. Left with the impression that the 'whole country is mineralised', whatever that was supposed to convey, but taking it to mean it was rich in gold, his mesmerised audience cheered him repeatedly.[38]

Rhodes went on to confide that:

> We must always remember in connection with mining that it is very speculative, as I told a friend of mine the other day – they are always bothering me about mines – and I said to one of my friends – a French financier – I will give you advice at last. He was delighted – (Laughter) – and asked what I would advise. I said, either buy French Rentes or Consols. (Laughter). Then he went away annoyed. (Renewed laughter). What, however, I desire to put to you is that when you go into a mining venture you go into a speculative venture; but as a proposition with a capital of £2,000,000, dealing with a country almost as big as Europe, which is mineralised, and with that subscribed capital for its development – and as regards its administration the revenue paying for the expenditure – it is a fair business-like proposition. (Cheers). When you consider this comparatively – and that is the great secret in life – it represents in capital perhaps one Randt mine.

---

36 Ibid.

37 John Hays Hammond, *The Autobiography of John Hays Hammond. Volume 1* (New York: Farrar & Rinehart, 1935), 277.

38 "Rhodes in the City." *The African Review*, January 19, 1895.

Hanging on to his every word, Rhodes' attentive listeners gave him a standing ovation.[39]

Shareholders were also reassured to hear that no increase in the Company's capital was envisaged. 'What [future] expenditure can there be?', Rhodes asked rhetorically. 'There can be no more wars. There are no more people to make wars'. After the laughter and cheering that followed those remarks had subsided, he explained that as 'we are now practically almost paying our way … I hope … that we shall keep to our capital of £2,000,000, and I cannot see in the future any reason which will cause us to increase it. If the country is a failure, the capital had better not be increased; if it is a success, further capital will not be wanted'.[40] Rhodes' point was underscored by the Company's restless, irrepressible Administrator, Leander Starr Jameson. His utterly garbled remarks scarcely registered with shareholders only too pleased to be addressed by the man who a little over a year earlier had defeated Lobengula of the Ndebele, and conquered Matabeleland for the Company. 'I will merely point out to you that, as Mr. Rhodes says, our capital is £2,000,000, that in one of the companies the other day, supposing we were to take our share of scrip, that that alone would pay 5 per cent. on our whole capital', Jameson bafflingly observed, 'and I leave you to calculate for yourselves what kind of a dividend you may have in the immediate future'.[41]

Less than six months later, in July 1895, the Company issued 500,000 £1 shares at £3 10s. each, *pro rata* to existing shareholders. As Chartered shares then had a market value of £5 each, the underwriting arrangements in which Consolidated Goldfields, Wernher, Beit & Company, and Hirsch & Company, the latter's preferred London agency, 'guaranteed the issue at 5% commission was widely condemned as a "job", but the issue was nonetheless successful'.[42] 'Out of this money', as A.J. Wilson of the *Investors' Review* subsequently discovered, '£500,000 of 6 per cent. debenture stock issued in 1894 at par was paid off at [a premium of] 110, to the great profit of the holders thereof, together with the outstanding 6 per cent. debentures whose authorised total was £250,000 and which was issued to pay interest the Company had no cash to meet'.[43]

39 *British South Africa Company, 4th Annual Meeting*, January 18, 1895, 11.

40 "Rhodes in the City." *The African Review*, January 19, 1895. For Rhodes' speech in full, see Vindex, *Cecil Rhodes. His Political Life and Speeches 1881–1900* (London: Chapman and Hall, 1900), 417–42.

41 "Rhodes in the City." *The African Review*, January 19, 1895.

42 McCarty, "British Investment in Overseas Mining," 107. See also, *The Economist*, July, 6 1895.

43 Alexander Wilson, *An Empire in Pawn* (London: T. Fisher Unwin, 1909), 248–49.

FIGURE 2 The Duke of Fife addressing the British South Africa Company annual general meeting, January 1895
SOURCE: *THE AFRICAN REVIEW*, JANUARY 19, 1895.

In much the same period, British South Africa Company shares were 'run up on the market to a price that enabled those who had large masses of them to realise [sell them] at fabulous profits. They rose above £8 for the £1 share and were considered cheap at £6'. 'Underwriting profits were also made by the inner ring', Wilson added. The Chartered Company's solicitors admitted that the contractors for the July share issue had 'netted £87,500 by way of underwriting commission'. Several Chartered directors benefitted from that 'little purse'.[44] They were well aware that the underwriters' offer and the present state of the market 'gives us a means of obtaining a sufficient sum of money to pay off our debts and leave us with a handsome balance in hand'.[45]

This was only the tip of the iceberg. A rent-seeking operation, intended to be a vast holding concern, 'profiting always from successful enterprises, losing

44 Ibid., 249.

45 Bodleian Library, Cawston Papers, s77–96, Grey to Cawston, 25 June 1895; as cited in Shenton, "Chartered Company," 78.

nothing but paper from the failures',[46] the Chartered Company had no intention of becoming directly involved in mining itself; under its mining regulations fifty per cent of the vendor's scrip of any company floated within its jurisdiction was reserved for the British South Africa Company. It is 'an enormous thing', exulted Rhodes to his London Board, 'as it practically means ... we shall get half the minerals of the country'.[47]

At first, the going was slow. Early in 1894, in the immediate aftermath of the Anglo-Ndebele War, all that the Chartered Company's directors could record by way of new investment was 'a sum of over half a million subscribed in cash by independent Companies'.[48] The situation a year later was very different, as a booming and undiscriminating mining market carried Rhodesian mining and development shares to ever greater heights. By then it was 'not only raining, but simply pouring with new Rhodesian companies'.[49] In the first nine months of 1895 alone, 84 Rhodesian companies with a total registered capital of £13,000,000 were floated in London. More than half the companies were over-capitalised at between £200,000 and £250,000 each, of which £75,000 – £100,000 in shares went to the promoters and the same number to the Chartered Company, leaving on average only 50,000 shares at £1 to be issued for working capital.[50] The same phenomenon caught the eye of a bank official in Bulawayo. 'In a list before me the total issued capital of companies recently formed to operate in Rhodesia totals the large sum of £5,500,000', he reported. 'Up to now the capital brought into this territory through the medium of this Branch alone since 1st January 1895 has been just over £500,000'.[51]

The disproportionately small provision made for working capital reflected the fact that a premium was placed on company promoters' fees and speculative gains, not gold production. Accordingly, development was 'gravely performed by cable and telegraph, and not by sweat and tears'.[52] As even the novelist Olive Schreiner's *Trooper Peter Halkett in Mashonaland* understood,

46 J. Flint, *Cecil Rhodes* (Toronto: Little, Brown, 1974), 132.

47 N[ational] [Archives of] [Zimbabwe], L[ondon] O[ffice] 8/3/1, C. Rhodes to Duke of Abercorn, 31 March 1890.

48 "Directors' Reports and Accounts for the year ending 31 March 1894", *British South Africa Company*, 31.

49 *The African Review*, August 3, 1895.

50 McCarty, "British Investment in Overseas Mining," 106. See also, "Directors' Reports and Accounts for the year ending 31 March 1895," *British South Africa Company*, 9.

51 Standard Bank Archives, INSP 1/1/17, Inspection Report on Bulawayo Branch at 15 November 1895.

52 *Rhodesia Herald*, March 16, 1894.

'It's the shares that you sell, not the shares that you keep, that make money'.[53] Looking back a decade or so later, the authoritative *Mining Journal* was in no doubt that the 'primary objective of many of those controlling the earlier Rhodesian mining and exploration companies was not so much the production of gold at a profit, but the manipulation and off-loading of as large a quantity of scrip as possible on the public. Rhodesian mining finance has in very many instances in the past been little short of scandalous'.[54] For Henry Hess, the crusading and caustic editor of Johannesburg's *African Critic*, and latterly the London-based *Critic*, it was a case of 'trading upon the unknown, this traffic in fairy tales, this capitalisation of dreams'. 'The motto which ought to be inscribed in letters of gold over the Chartered Company's offices in St. Swithin's Lane is, "No one knows what is there!"'[55]

For the most part, commented *The Economist*, Rhodesian companies

> have very little to show in the way of accomplished facts. They have made certain arrangements with the Chartered Company, usually unspecified, and directly [after] they have got themselves floated they have set to work to form subsidiary companies, and these again have in many cases gone through the same process, upon a kind of ad infinitum scale, until it has become well-nigh impossible for those interested to know how matters stand. In this way capital is being steadily piled up, while the actual work of development is proceeding very slowly. In other words, there is much more exploitation than exploration, and the real work of proving Rhodesia and establishing it upon a commercial basis is being postponed. Indeed, if the present system of piling unproductive capital is continued, it will require the discovery of a series of Rands to make the capitalisation effective.[56]

Be that as it may, the City's valuation of the British South Africa Company nonetheless stood at over £18,000,000 in August 1895, compared to under

53 Olive Schreiner, *Trooper Peter Halket of Mashonaland* (London: T. Fisher Unwin, 1897), 33–34. See especially, Laura Chrisman, *Rereading the Imperial Romance. British Imperialism and South African Resistance in Haggard, Schreiner, and Plaatje* (Oxford: Clarendon Press, 2000), 120–42.

54 *Mining Journal*, May 16, 1908.

55 *African Critic*, October 5, 1895.

56 *The Economist*, August 17, 1895.

£4,000,000 one year previously.[57] Speculators, not investors, controlled Rhodesia, concluded one historian.[58]

The inner circle of the British South Africa Company and its friends grasped every opportunity to make the market work for them. 'North Shebas ... have been made the subject of a successful "rig" by the astute Mr Abe Bailey and his father-in-law, Mr John Paddon', disclosed *The Critic*. 'Inspired paragraphs have been published as from the mine manager, without any name, stating that the mine is looking very promising. Now the unfortunate thing is that no-one here seems to know who the mine manager is, what his opinion is worth, what the capital of the company is, or even whereabouts the mine is situated'.[59] A less blatant but much more ambitious operation concerned the Bechuanaland Exploration Company, a firm whose modest name belied the regional scope and scale of its operations. Formed in 1888 with a nominal capital of £150,000, and a board of directors comprising Lord Gifford, George Cawston, and Major

57 Ibid. See particularly, "Rhodesia – Its Past and Future," *African Critic*, February 1, 1896,: 'I have been at some pains to ascertain ... what was the exact amount of capital invested by the English public in Rhodesian companies in 1895. Eliminating such private syndicates and other concerns of which no data were available, and basing my calculations solely upon the official statistics given in the various prospectuses of companies that have been actually floated, I find that the total sum provided, or to be provided, by the public, when all the calls have been paid, amounts in the aggregate to £14,367,350! This huge sum is not a mere estimate, ... it is the nominal capital of the combined companies that appealed to the public for subscriptions. In all probability, therefore, if the registrations at Somerset House and the private flotations had been included, it would be found that the total share capital of all Rhodesian companies floated last year would amount to considerably more than twenty millions sterling. If to this we add another ten millions to cover the flotations during the inclusive period between the occupation of Mashonaland down to the end of 1894 (which sum would also include the capital of local syndicates for those years as well as for 1895), it will be safe to compute that the total capital invested in Rhodesia today, excluding that of the British South Africa Company and the Beira Railway, does not fall short of thirty millions sterling. Even assuming that the ten millions I have put down as having been invested in Rhodesia during the first four years of its existence should prove a too liberal estimate, and that we deduct it by one-half, it will be admitted, I think, that sufficient capital and to spare has been generously provided to determine the question of its future as a payable gold-producing country. To further particularise, exactly 112 companies have an aggregate capital of 16 millions sterling, and probably another 112 companies exist, the capital of which cannot be estimated, as absolutely no data are available ... so far as Rhodesian mining is concerned, little can be said that is in its favour ... [but] it did not stop the company-monger from filching over £14,000,000 sterling from the pockets of the public for wholly unproved properties'.

58 Shenton, "Chartered Company," 53.

59 *The Critic*, March 1, 1895.

F.I. Ricarde-Seaver, the London representative of the Caisse des Mines of Paris who had originally bought the concession and sold it on to the Bechuanaland Exploration Company, its original focus was on a mining concession in Khama's country north of the British Bechuanaland protectorate. Amongst the company's influential backers drawn from Paris and the City of London were Baron Henry de Rothschild and Henry Oppenheim. The Bechuanaland Exploration Company's subsequent attempts to win mining rights in Matabeleland first brought it into competition and then close cooperation with the Rhodes-Rudd initiative of much the same period. Key interests were merged in the Central Search Association, later the United Concessions Company, and with Gifford and Cawston on the board of the British South Africa Company from the start, it was a relationship that hugely expanded the range of the Bechuanaland Exploration Company's mining and other operations.[60] It also whetted the company's appetite for what *The Economist* had come to recognise as 'South African Financial Methods'.[61]

'We have this week a striking illustration of the methods of finance which it has become the fashion to resort to by some of those who conduct the affairs of South African mining and other undertakings', reported *The Economist* in July 1895.

> At the instance of 'a powerful and influential Anglo-French group represented by the Banque Commerciale et Industrielle of Paris', the directors of the Bechuanaland Exploration Company propose to double the capital of the company, which at present amounts to £200,000, in £1 shares; 100,000 of the new shares being offered to the existing shareholders at 30s[hillings] per share, in the proportion of one share for every two now held by them, and it is provided that 'in the event of the whole of this issue not being taken up by the shareholders, the Anglo-French group guarantee to take the balance at the same price. In consideration of this guarantee and the influential support of this powerful combination, both here and on the Continent, they stipulate to have the call of the remaining 100,000 shares up to December 31st next at 35s per share'.[62]

60 Charles Goldmann, *South African Mines; Their Position, Results, & Developments: Together with an Account of Diamond, Land, Finance, and Kindred Concerns* II, (London: E. Wilson & co, 1895–6), 138–139. See especially, Galbraith, *Crown and Charter*, 53–86; and Maylam, *Rhodes, the Tswana, and the British. Colonialism, Collaboration, and Conflict in the Bechuanaland Protectorate, 1885–1899* (Westport, Connecticut, 1980), 49–58.

61 *The Economist*, July 6, 1895.

62 Ibid.

Essentially, this 'powerful and influential group' was awarding itself a share option worth £125,000, and probably very much more. The price of Bechuanaland Exploring shares was then about £3, and at that level, existing shareholders would naturally apply for their full allotment of 30s shares, which they could immediately sell for double the price. As this would eliminate the need for any guarantee, unidentified interests were being given the right of 'calling' shares without having to subscribe 'a single penny'. It was an 'absurd proposition', readers were warned, 'in which shareholders will assuredly be worsted if they are idiotic enough to sanction it'. In the event, that was precisely what the shareholders did. Apart from the handful who sold off their entire holdings, most of them confirmed the journal's suspicion that they were 'greater fools than we take them to be'.[63]

By this advanced stage of the boom, fools were in plentiful supply. On the Rand itself, it seemed that nothing could arrest the frenzy. Shares in Rand Mines Ltd which were 125 shillings in 1893, climbed to 460 shillings in 1894, and doubled again to 910 shillings by September 1895. Similarly, Simmer and Jack shares went from 60 shillings in 1893, to 280 shillings in 1894, and 560 shillings in 1895.[64] 'In several instances within the past few days South African mining, land and exploration shares have been dealt in at the highest prices ever recorded, and so far from any damping down of excitement ... it has broadened out, and become more feverish and more intense', marvelled *The Economist* in April 1895:

> And the peculiarity of the recent course of speculative activity is that it has been most energetic in land and exploration shares, upon which dividends have never yet been paid, and in deep-level shares, the values of which are of an entirely prospective and problematical character. Shares which, until the present "boom" set in, were absolutely unsaleable have lately been taken in hand by turns, and by judicious manipulation on the part of the insiders interested in them, have been pushed into prominence, with the result that eager bidding has taken place at pounds a piece for shares which less than a year ago would not have realized as many shillings.[65]

---

63 Ibid.

64 *Standard & Diggers' News*, September 24, 1895.

65 *The Economist*, April 27, 1895.

'We have reached the *reductio ad absurdum* of the "boom"', announced *The Critic* at the end of May 1895. 'This week the legitimate values have been utterly neglected … while there have been sensational advances in Potchefstrooms, Lisbon-Berlyns, Moodies and other more or less shady concerns'.[66]

'There are no signs of abatement in the activity which has characterized the "Kaffir Circus" for more than a twelvemonth past, practically without interruption', wrote *The Economist.* 'On the contrary, the area of the speculation is broadening out in all directions, and the settlement in mining shares which has taken place within the past few days was about as little like the usual condition of things in the Stock Exchange during the "dead season" as it is possible to conceive'. According to its own calculations, the total market valuation of capital involved in the Witwatersrand gold mining industry was a staggering £215,372,624, broken down into dividend paying mines, non-dividend paying mines, and land and exploration companies. Their respective issued capitals and current market valuations were £6,554,727 and £38,564,400; £27,729,954 and £113,229,016; and £15,872,679 and £63,579,178. So far as dividend paying mines were concerned, capital issued had been 'magnified' nearly 500 per cent on average, 'in some cases, such as City and Suburban, Ferreira, Langlaagte, Simmer and Jack, and Transvaal Gold being enormously above that percentage'.[67] Although it had proved impossible to trace in detail every single company and syndicate, a market valuation of over £215,000,000 for 'only a portion of the companies interested entirely, or nearly so, in the Transvaal gold-mining industry, shows to what a pitch the speculation in "Kaffir" shares has reached', the journal concluded.[68] 'We do not question the great extent and importance of the gold deposits of the Transvaal or of the actual mining industry which has been built up in that region', the *Engineering and Mining Journal* observed, 'but upon this foundation promoters and speculators have built up a gigantic structure so far out of proportion to the base upon which it rests that its ultimate collapse is inevitable'.[69]

Witwatersrand mining groups, large and small, threw themselves into the hugely lucrative business of making speculative profits on a gigantic scale. Deeply involved from start to finish were three Randlords, Barney Barnato, J.B. Robinson and George Farrar, whose reputations for market excesses were already legendary. No less compromised, however, were Wernher, Beit, and Consolidated Goldfields, whose financial probity was taken for granted by most investors if not by the entirety of the financial press. 'Barney Barnato's

66 *The Critic*, May 24, 1895.

67 *The Economist*, September 14, 1895.

68 Ibid.

69 *Engineering and Mining Journal*, October 26, 1895. See especially, McCarty, "British Investment in Overseas Mining," 88.

TABLE 1 Capitalisation of the witwatersrand gold mining industry: September 1895

Dividend-paying mining companies

Company	Issued capital £	Market valuation £	Dividends 1894 %	Dividends 1895 %
Chimes (New)	100,000	325,000	25	45
City and Suburban	83,000	2,295,000	50	75
Crown Reef	120,000	1,440,000	50	25
Durban Roodepoort	125,000	1,093,750	60	30
Ferreira	90,000	1,845,000	150	65
Geldenhuis Estate	200,00	1,387,500	30	30
Geldenhuis Main Reef	150,00	264,100	—	10
Glencairn	225,00	998,400	12 ½	15
Heriot (New)	88,750	976,250	40	90
Jubilee	50,000	537,500	120	60
Jumpers	100,000	875,000	55	25
Kleinfontein	185,000	1,087,000	12½	12½
Langlaagte Estate	470,000	3,172,000	45	25
May Consolidated	252,500	970,600	10	5⅞
Meyer and Charlton	85,000	627,000	55	25
Nigel	200,000	1,525,000	50	20
Orion	160,000	650,000	105	20
Primrose (New)	278,750	2,160,000	40	25
Robinson	2,750,000	6,118,750	10	6
Roodepoort United	150,000	1,181,250	20	25
Simmer and Jack	250,000	5,437,500	30	20
Stanhope	34,000	52,500	100	30
Transvaal Gold	260,000	2,502,000	10	10
Wemmer	55,000	619,000	—	100
Worcester	90,727	442,300	70	30
Total	**£6,554,727**	**£38,564,400**		

Non-dividend-paying mining companies

Company	Issued capital £	Market valuation £
Abbott's Consolidated	120,000	127,500
Afrikander	200,000	612,500

TABLE 1 Capitalisation of the witwatersrand gold mining industry: September 1895 (*cont.*)

Company	Issued capital £	Market valuation £
Agnes Block	87,507	39,250
Agnes Munro	98,000	116,400
Alexandra Estate	225,000	309,400
Angelo	175,000	1,050,000
Apex	1,050,000	2,000,000
Ariston	30,000	40,125
Aurora	65,000	150,300
Aurora West United	100,000	281,250
Balmoral Main Reef	58,570	219,000
Banket	200,000	82,500
Bantjes	83,000	622,500
Barrett	120,000	240,000
Ben Trovato	220,000	337,500
Big Golden Quarry	149,720	97,318
Black Reef Proprietary	1,251,000	328,125
Bonanza	200,000	525,000
Blinkpoort	38,000	47,500
Buffelsdoorn Estate	550,000	4,950,000
Buffelsdoorn Consolidated	225,000	703,125
Buffels Land and Mining	180,000	99,000
Cameron Block	100,000	40,000
Champ d'Or	128,851	451,000
Champ d'Or Deep	275,000	790,625
Chimes West	150,000	487,500
Cinderella	100,000	200,000
Clewer Estate	100,000	500,000
Coetzeestroom	35,000	63,000
Comet (New)	175,000	765,620
Croesus (New)	500,000	1,593,750
Crown Deep	250,000	3,625,000
Doornkop	250,000	137,500
Driefontein	175,000	634,375
Durban-Roodepoort Deep	290,000	2,030,000
Eastleigh	250,000	546,875
Eastleigh Deep	250,000	500,000
East Orion	270,000	275,000
East Rand Proprietary	650,000	5,288,500

TABLE 1 Capitalisation of the witwatersrand gold mining industry: September 1895 (*cont.*)

Company	Issued capital £	Market valuation £
East Rand Central	152,500	533,750
Geldenhuis Deep	265,000	2,848,750
Geldenhuis Southern	120,000	27,000
George and May	140,000	280,000
George Goch	100,000	375,000
Ginsberg (New)	160,000	340,000
Goldfields Deep	450,000	5,118,750
Graskop	125,000	281,250
Great Britain	170,000	945,625
Harmony Gold Preferential	300,000	127,500
Harmony Ordinary	300,000	67,500
Harmony Proprietary	1,000,000	1,050,000
Heidelberg Gold	450,000	731,250
Henry Nourse	100,000	775,000
Johannesburg Goldfields	250,000	78,125
Kimberley-Roodepoort	185,000	1,063,650
Klerksdorp Estates	200,000	520,000
Knight's	287,500	3,126,600
Lancaster	226,500	552,100
Langlaagte Block B	535,000	1,537,800
Langlaagte Deep	75,000	93,750
Langlaagte Royal	150,000	600,000
Langlaagte Star	200,000	675,000
Langlaagte United	150,000	450,000
Lisbon-Berlyn	127,621	676,400
Lower Roodepoort	150,000	52,500
Luipaards Vlei	350,000	560,000
Main Reef (New)	135,000	286,900
Marais Reef	275,000	82,500
Marie Rose	175,000	185,900
Metropolitan (New)	80,000	240,000
Midas Estate	100,000	300,000
Minerva	150,000	497,000
Modderfontein	225,000	3,487,500
Molyneux	37,500	108,000
Moodies	240,000	510,000
New Blue Sky	150,000	187,500

TABLE 1 Capitalisation of the witwatersrand gold mining industry: September 1895 (*cont.*)

Company	Issued capital £	Market valuation £
New Louis d'Or	100,000	16,250
New Rand	70,000	56,875
New Florida	105,000	328,125
New Gypsy	45,000	22,500
New Unified	130,000	105,625
Nigel Deep	495,000	2,185,625
North Randfontein	235,000	837,200
Nourse Deep	375,000	3,421,875
Orion Belt	225,000	323,400
Paarl Central	200,000	550,000
Pioneer	21,000	162,750
Princess Estate	142,000	621,250
Porges' Randfontein	500,000	1,625,000
President	65,000	162,500
Rand Central Ore	114,000	114,000
Randfontein	2,000,000	8,375,000
Rand Mines	332,708	12,892,435
Rand Southern	100,000	81,250
Rietfontein (New)	270,000	1,366,875
Rietfontein Deep	250,000	256,250
Rietknil	90,000	213,750
Robinson Deep	175,000	1,618,750
Roodepoort Deep	180,000	877,500
Roodepoort Heidelberg	90,000	191,250
Roodepoort New Main Reef	150,000	1,143,750
Rose Deep	300,000	2,250,000
Rosenblock	60,000	56,000
Rothery Block	100,000	106,250
Royal Sheba	50,000	75,000
St. Angelo	175,000	1,028,125
Salisbury (New)	70,500	380,550
Sheba	847,500	1,959,850
Silati	120,000	52,500
South Nigel	150,000	177,500
South West Rand	158,000	316,000
Southern Jumpers	750,000	103,125
Spes Bona (New)	120,000	360,000

TABLE 1 Capitalisation of the witwatersrand gold mining industry: September 1895 (*cont.*)

Company	Issued capital £	Market valuation £
Steyn Estate	125,000	296,875
Spitzkop	93,012	186,024
Sutherland Reef	220,000	143,000
Treasury	60,000	240,000
United Ivy Reefs	45,000	53,437
United Pioneer	75,000	84,375
Van Ryn (New)	160,000	1,600,000
Van Ryn North	116,091	261,205
Van Ryn West	120,000	645,000
Village Main Reef	177,000	1,504,500
Violet	150,000	207,562
Vogelstruis Estate	200,000	1,300,000
Vulcan	90,000	39,375
Western Nigel	250,000	562,500
West Kleinfontein	110,000	412,500
West Rand	240,000	765,000
West Roodepoort Deep	230,000	602,750
Wolhuter	130,000	1,430,000
Wolverand	57,771	54,169
York	90,000	102,500
Total	**£27,729,954**	**£113,229,046**

Land, exploration, finance etc. companies

Company	Issued capital £	Market valuation £
African Estates	240,000	855,000
Alexandra Estates	625,000	820,312
Anglo-French Exploration	350,000	2,143,750
Ballis Eersterling	235,000	188,000
Ballis Land	260,000	240,500
Barnato Bank	2,500,000	8,750,000
Barnato Consolidated	1,250,000	6,562,500
Consolidated Deep Levels	187,250	1,404,375
Consolidated Goldfields	625,000	10,546,875
Consolidated Preference	937,500	1,171,875

TABLE 1 Capitalisation of the witwatersrand gold mining industry: September 1895 (*cont.*)

Company	Issued capital £	Market valuation £
Consolidated Debentures	600,000	678,000
Henderson's Estates	250,000	1,250,000
Johannesburg Consolidated Inv.	800,000	5,050,000
Johannesburg Estates	200,000	300,000
London-Paris Corporation	500,000	2,000,000
Lydenburg Land	175,000	306,250
Lydenburg Mining Estate	300,000	2,775,000
New African	193,333	1,643,330
Oceana	326,000	1,304,000
Oceana Development	50,000	81,250
Oceana Development [same name]	50,000	78,125
Potchefstroom	389,750	803,860
Robinson Bank	3,000,000	7,875,000
South African Gold Trust	220,000	2,516,250
Transvaal and General Association	185,000	763,125
Transvaal Consolidated Land	485,131	1,455,393
Tvl. Estates and Development	389,300	778,600
Transvaal Goldfields	200,000	1,025,000
Transvaal Lands	79,915	79,995
Transvaal Lands [same name]	170,000	116,250
Transvaal Mortgage	99,500	16,583
Totals	**£15,872,679**	**£63,579,178**
Grand totals	**£50,157,360**	**£215,372,624**

SOURCE: THE ECONOMIST, SEPTEMBER 14 1895.

gaudy promotions and unstable temperament fostered the creation of highly speculative undertakings based mostly on marginal or undeveloped properties', one historian concluded. His Johannesburg Consolidated Investment group used these undertakings 'to flood the market with a vast quantity of watered stock'.[70] At the beginning of September 1895, the Barnato Bank Min-

70 Kubicek, *Economic Imperialism in Theory and Practice*, 122, 118.

ing and Estate Company was floated with the intention of taking the former's speculative operations to another level. No prospectus was issued and when pressed on the point, Barnato replied that this was something he had never done in the past and would not be doing now.[71] His insouciant answer was taken as proof of a sure bet. Explaining that the 'functions of the Company will be to act as financiers and stock-holders', the *Financial Times* assured its readers that 'with Mr Barnato as the moving spirit the institution will have every chance of getting into good things in South Africa … [We] must confess to a feeling of envy towards the successful applicants for shares at the issue price'.[72] In theory, 'a holding company for his various ventures, in ill-disguised reality a gambling machine', 'Barney's Bank' was initially capitalised at £3,250,000.[73]

This was more or less on the same scale as the Robinson South African Banking Company, also named for its proprietor, in this instance J.B (later Sir Joseph) Robinson, an independent and irascible operator as much disliked by contemporaries as Barnato was publicly feted.[74] Not that investors cared one way or another. Despite the fact that the South African Banking Company dealt almost exclusively in the shares of Robinson's own Randfontein Estates and its five subsidiary companies, all of whom 'operated in great secrecy', within a month of the Bank's launch, its shares had very nearly tripled in price.[75]

For *The Economist*, the provocation could scarcely have been greater, but in the same circumstances, the great majority of its peers were at best circumspect or at worst compromised. The explosive rise of London's 'new financial journalism' in the 1880s and 1890s, up from 32 financial papers in 1884 to 50 a decade later, was accompanied by widespread fraud. While the *Financial Times* and its rival, the *Financial News*, both claimed to provide 'good investment information, exposing bad companies and steering investors toward good ones', neither was beyond reproach, the latter's long-serving editor, Harry Marks, being notoriously open to bribes.[76] By the early twentieth cen-

71 *City Recorder*, August 31, 1895.

72 *Financial Times*, 28 August 1895.

73 David Kynaston, *The City of London. Volume II. Golden Years 1890–1914* (London: Chatto & Windus, 1995), 128.

74 Richard Lewinsohn, *Barney Barnato. From Whitechapel Clown to Diamond King* (London: E.P. Dutton & Co., Inc., 1937), 221–23.

75 Kubicek, *Economic Imperialism in Theory and Practice*, 129, 128. For more on Robinson, see Geoffrey Wheatcroft, *The Randlords* (London: Weidenfeld & Nicolson, 1985), 165–71; Jeremy Lawrence, *Buccaneer. A Biography of Sir Joseph Benjamin Robinson, first Baronet* (Cape Town: Gryphon Press, 2001); and Leo Weinthal (ed.), *Memories, Mines and Millions, Being the Life of Sir Joseph B. Robinson* (London: Simpkin Marshall Ltd, 1929).

76 George Robb, *White-Collar Crime in Modern England. Financial Fraud and Business Morality 1845–1929* (Cambridge: Cambridge University Press, 1992), 115–18; and Searle, *Corruption in British Politics*, 36–38. Amongst others in a voluminous literature, see also, Dilwyn

FIGURE 3
J.B. Robinson
SOURCE: PAUL EMDEN, *RANDLORDS* (LONDON: HODDER & STOUGHTON, 1935), BETWEEN PP.120–21.

tury, 'although the most thoughtful do not attach too much importance to the "Financial News" and "Financial Times", they are read every morning by nine-tenths of the Financial and Mining men, and thus go a long way to form City opinion'.[77] 'That the City has a large number of "reptile" journals, which will praise – and for that matter also condemn – anything as long as they are paid

Porter, "'A Trusted Guide of the Investing Public': Harry Marks and the Financial News 1884–1916," *Business History* 28, no. 1 (1986): 1–17; David Itzkowitz, "Fair Enterprise or Extravagant Speculation: Investment, Speculation, and Gambling in Victorian England," *Victorian Studies* 45, no. 1 (2002): 121–147; Ian Klaus, *Forging Capitalism. Rogues, Swindlers, Frauds, and the Rise of Modern Finance* (New Haven: Yale University Press, 2014), 168–203; and Martin Vander Weyer, *Fortune's Spear. The Story of The Blue-Blooded Rogue Behind the Most Notorious City Scandal of the 1920s* (London: Elliott & Thompson, 2011). For contemporary accounts, see especially, Alexander Wilson, *Practical Hints to Investors. And Some Words to Speculators* (London: Clement Wilson, 1897); [A Financial Journalist], "The Art of Blackmail," *Contemporary Review* 74, no. 392, August 1898, 196–205; S.F. Van Oss, "In Hooley Land," *Journal of Finance* V, no. 21 (January 1899): 1–20; Charles Duguid, *How to Read the Money Article* (London: Effingham Wilson, 1901); and H. Warren, *The Modern Bucket Shop* (London: Everett, n.d. [1906]), 185–201.

77 Mitchell Library, Sydney, Walter James Papers, ML MSS 412/1, volume 1, Letterbook 1904–1906, James to Premier of Western Australia [Henry Daglish], December 9, 1904.

for it', wrote the financial journalist S.F. Van Oss, 'is by this time well known to anyone who is not a tyro in finance'.[78] 'Nearly the entire Press of Great Britain and France has proved itself to be venal and corrupt in this matter of giving paid-for puffs [endorsements] in their columns', declared *The African Review*, itself not always immune from temptation. 'The shameless way in which the leading society papers and nearly the whole tribe of financial journals puff and boom the most notorious "wild-cats" [hopeless ventures] is really a matter of national disgrace'.[79]

Only A.J. Wilson's *Investors' Review* and *The Economist* were consistently honest.[80] So were Henry Hess' *The Critic* and *African Critic,* the latter banned in the Transvaal at Kruger's insistence in December 1896.[81] The well-known mining expert and author, J.H. Curle, himself a special correspondent for *The Economist,* had 'no hesitation in stating that the majority of financial papers frequently publish incorrect mining matter. These papers are subsidised by one or more of the big mining houses or groups, either by direct payment, or by periodical options on shares, or, most usually, by frequent and highly paid advertisements'.[82] Not even *The Economist* was above the general practice of inserting reports of shareholders' meetings sent in by company secretaries in the news columns, where it looked 'as if it had been prepared by a reporter sent to the meeting by the journal in which it appears'.[83] These reports were paid for by the company concerned. As T.A. Rickard, later editor of *Mining Magazine,* recalled, 'even such eminently respectable financial publications as the "Statist" and "Economist" – even the "Times" – follow this pernicious custom'.[84] It only subsequently emerged that Rickard himself was compromised by publishing news and editorials about Herbert Hoover, later president of the United States, but then well-known as an engineer and financier, in such a way that both his reputation and his mining promotions were tremendously enhanced. 'Constant "puffs" by what soon became the foremost mining publication in Europe were bound to give Hoover a following among the investing public'.[85]

---

78 S.F. van Oss, "The 'Limited Company' Craze," *The Nineteenth Century* 43, May 1898, 742.

79 *The African Review*, August 17, 1895.

80 Kynaston, *City of London,* 178–79.

81 Command Paper C8423, *Further Correspondence relating to Affairs in the South African Republic, April 1897* (London, 1897), Messrs. Guedalla & Cross to Colonial Office, 12 January 1897.

82 James Curle, *The Gold Mines of the World* (London: Waterlow and Sons, 1899), 5. For the 'faintest [of] question marks' over Curle himself, see Ruth Edwards, *The Pursuit of Reason. The Economist 1843–1993* (London: Hamish Hamilton, 1993), 446–448.

83 Thomas Rickard, *Retrospect. An Autobiography* (New York: Whittlesey House, 1937), 131.

84 Ibid.

85 Walter Liggett, *The Rise of Herbert Hoover* (New York: H.K. Fly Company, 1932), 151.

In the course of a long investigative report on speculative excess in mining markets, *The Economist* declared that an

> even more striking phase of the recent course of events in the South African market has been the wild gambling in the shares of companies of the Trust order. [These are] founded and dominated by one or other of the prominent South African millionaires, but as to the assets of which [,] the public have little, if any, means of informing themselves. None of them have been registered here, nor … have any prospectuses or schedules of holdings been issued. They are essentially 'blind pools' … [and] active bidding for the shares of these companies is based partly upon the names and far-famed wealth of Messrs. Barnato and Mr. J.B. Robinson, and partly upon rumours and conjectures of what they have put into the companies as a basis of operations. The shares handed over may be worth more than the nominal capital, or less. The point could only be settled by the disclosure of the holdings, and that is not forthcoming.[86]

It then proceeded to investigate each operation in turn.

The Johannesburg Consolidated Investment Company, floated with a capital of £650,000 to take over undefined interests from Barnato and his South African Trust and Finance Company, was reported as having made £1,000,000 in its first six months of existence, 'but how the profit was obtained and to what extent it has been realized has yet to be ascertained'.[87] All that the shareholders know,

> is that a dividend of 20 per cent. for the six months, or £130,000, has been declared, and that £400,000 is said to have been placed to reserve. And on the strength of these statements the shares have risen to nearly 6 ½, giving the company a market valuation of well over £4,250,000. Of the more recently introduced Barnato Consolidated Mines even less, if that be possible, is known. The company is believed to have a nominal capital of £1,250,000, and is supposed to have been formed to take over 1,500 claims in the Rand district and certain other interests held by Messrs Barnato; but where the claims are situated and what the interests represent 'depondent sayeth not'. And yet upon such a nebular hypothesis the shares have been run up to about 5, representing a market valuation of, say, £6,250,000.[88]

86 *The Economist*, August 17, 1895.

87 Ibid.

88 Ibid.

Just as irrationally exuberant were dealings in the shares of the Robinson South African Banking Company, where even before the market knew the size of its capital or the nominal value of the shares, 'the quotation had been rushed up to over [£]10. It has since transpired that the capital is £3,000,000 in £4 shares, and the company has attracted so much attention that the shares stand at [£]11, or £8,250,000 for the lot'. 'Prudence would suggest that before rushing into an undertaking standing in the market at £8,250,000', concluded *The Economist*, 'it would be well to ascertain what the capital represents'.[89] At the end of September 1895, the combined market value of these three companies, none of whom had issued prospectuses or lists of assets, was £20 million.[90]

There was seemingly nothing that overwrought investors in London, Paris and elsewhere would not snap up. 'When the "X Y Gold Mining shares" began to run short, there was still a sufficiency of "United New Consolidated XY Extension and Development Block D Proprietary Gold Mining shares"', explained one close study of the Randlords and their operations. 'Every claim, so long as it was situated "somewhere", became the substratum of a flotation, and if it was absolutely impossible, without going altogether too far, to call a venture a "gold mine", it was christened "Land Company" or "Exploration Company" or "Banking Company" ... Shares which up to then had been unsaleable were pushed into prominence and were sought after at pounds when a year before they had been offered at as many shillings without finding a buyer'.[91] At the height of the boom these were frequently companies of the 'no-prospectus' variety; 'that is to say the promoters dispensed with the formal issue of a prospectus, trusting to get rid of the shares they wished to sell through the instrumentality of dealers in the "House"'.[92] Although a prospectus was no guarantee of a mine's success, at least the 'publicity given to the statements made imposes upon the directors and officials named in it a certain measure of responsibility', thought *The Economist*. Otherwise, it was 'as difficult to find anybody upon whom to fix responsibility as to place the proverbial pinch of salt on a bird's tail'.[93]

Many of the 'thinly-disguised frauds among ... no – prospectus concerns' typically started life with the purchase or option to purchase of a property, 'not a difficult operation ... as there are always plenty of concessionaires about'. Then, no matter how remote the property actually was from the Witwatersrand itself, the name of a successful Rand mine was selected, suitably

89 Ibid.

90 McCarty, "British Investment in Overseas Mining," 87.

91 Emden, *Randlords*, 242–43. See especially Appendix A for the names of many of such companies floated in 1895.

92 *The Economist*, January 1, 1898.

93 Ibid.

qualified 'by prefixing, or adding, to the title "upper", "lower", "north", "south", "east", or "west"'. Finally, the promoting groups took the shares '*en bloc* as the purchase consideration for the property, and set to work to "make a market for them"'. A Stock Exchange dealer would be given shares outright, 'with the call [right to buy] of other shares at a fixed price for an agreed period'. 'Thus provided, he ... [would] naturally do his best to produce a semblance of active dealings, with the assistance of the "tape", and to create the impression that the shares are really in demand by the public'.[94]

As most promoting groups usually 'ran' or controlled one or more newspapers, shareholders were 'inundated with paragraphs pointing out that, for example, East Ferreira shares, fully-paid one-pounders, ... [were] being quietly picked up at 5s or 6s by well-informed operators; that the mine was yielding quartz assaying phenomenally and that the shares were sure to be worth pounds apiece before long'.[95] So long as the shares were being 'peddled out, and perhaps for a while afterwards', *The Economist* explained, reports about the property were 'of the usual glowing character; then generally follows less frequent news, a breakdown of the pumps or some other event explaining delay; reconstruction, if the shareholders are idiotic enough to assent to it, and the other stages preliminary to winding-up'. 'It is a discreditable business', with 'thousands upon thousands of utterly worthless shares ... palmed off upon the public'.[96]

George Farrar's East Rand Proprietary Mines was notoriously badly managed and starved of working capital, yet in the first nine months of 1895, ERPM shares advanced from just over £2 to nearly £13 each. Floated in 1893 with an initial capital of £650,000, ERPM subsequently acquired the East Rand Gold Mining Company. With the support of the Anglo-French Exploration Company, an earlier Farrar venture with London and Paris backing, ERPM came to control blocks of contiguous claims along a stretch of the main reef series nine miles east of Johannesburg. Six subsidiary mining companies were set up, initially with £90,000 working capital between them, to work the claims. These in turn were reconstructed until the point was reached in mid-1895 where their issued capital totaled £995,500, just over half of which was held by ERPM. These financial arrangements were entirely speculative and utterly inappropriate for mining development. Because ERPM subsidiaries were on land where the reefs were broken through a dyke intrusion very close to where they outcropped, they had not been as productive as the central Rand mines. 'To make the most of the reefs near the surface and develop their deep-levels', explained one historian, 'these mines, with a total area of almost 600 claims, needed far

94 Ibid.
95 Ibid.
96 Ibid.

FIGURE 4
George Farrar
SOURCE: LIONEL PHILLIPS, *SOME REMINISCENCES* (LONDON: HUTCHINSON & CO., 1924), BETWEEN PP. 170–171.

more working capital than was provided. At the same time, it became clear that Farrar and his associates had no intention of diverting profits from stock sales to make up the difference'.[97]

In Johannesburg, where 'men smoked like Sheffield and drank like Glasgow',[98] Farrar's personal eccentricities were as closely watched as the public company he kept. His 'extraordinary love of attending funerals' which obliged him to always keep 'a black mourning coat and silk hat in his office, never knowing when his instinct would call him', was equaled only by his unconscious habit of making a noise 'as if he were grooming a horse' when dusting and arranging the 'dozens of pairs of boots never worn for which he had been scrupulously measured … [and] kept in a glass-fronted cabinet'.[99] Farrar's closest associate was Carl Hanau, probably the Rand's most reckless speculator,[100] and much admired in certain circles as a man who always met his gambling debts, on

97 Kubicek, *Economic Imperialism in Theory and Practice*, 134–135. See also Emden, *Randlords*, 337. For details of the Anglo-French Exploration Company, see Charles Sydney Goldmann, *South African Mines; their Position, Results, & Developments: together with an account of Diamond, Land, Finance, and Kindred Concerns. Volume II. Miscellaneous Companies* (London: Effingham Wilson & Co., Royal Exchange, F. C., 1895–6), 137–38.

98 Louis Cohen, *Reminiscences of Johannesburg & London* (London: Robert Holden & Co. Ltd, 1924), 174.

99 Henry O'Kelly Webber, *The Grip of Gold. A Life Story of a Dominion* (London: Hutchinson, 1936), 89–90.

100 Kubicek, *Economic Imperialism in Theory and Practice*, 134.

occasion as much as £7000 dropped on a single card game.[101] 'A daring financier without experience of finance',[102] he dazzled credulous journalists in London and Paris with tales of 'pluck, perseverance, and pence'. At one time claiming credit for a merger that had 'enormously prolonged' the life of the original Simmer and Jack mining company', Hanau also insisted that a similar scheme had 'increased the term of ... [the Ferreira Mine's] existence fourfold at the cost of merely doubling its capital'. Ferreira shares, he accurately predicted, 'would touch £15, at which price they would continue to return good dividends'. Left unsaid was the manner in which the company was reconstructed. This had placed the larger part of its stock in the hands of Hanau and his backers.[103] For a while vice-president of the Chamber of Mines and later chairman of the Johannesburg Stock Exchange, Hanau divided his energies between supporting Johannesburg's fledgling Wanderer's Club, enjoying the company of prostitutes and promoting ventures of an increasingly dubious nature.[104]

FIGURE 5 Carl Hanau, 1893
SOURCE: BRITISH LIBRARY MECHANICAL CURATOR COLLECTION, DIGITAL STORE 10096.G.12.

---

101 Cohen, *Reminiscences*, 113.

102 Emden, *Randlords*, 213–14.

103 *The African Review*, October 6, 1894. See especially *The Economist*, April 28, 1894, and November 17, 1894.

104 John Lang, *Bullion Johannesburg. Men, Mines and the Challenges of Conflict* (Johannesburg: J. Ball, 1986), 42; Thelma Gutsche, *Old Gold. The History of the Wanderers Club* (Cape Town: Timmons, 1966), 27; Cohen, *Reminiscences*, 99–100; and Charles Don, *And Having Writ ... Memories and Impressions* (Johannesburg: Central News Agency, 1942), 65. For a sympathetic contemporary view of Hanau after the South African War, see "Mr Carl Hanau. The Pioneer of Deep Levels, the East Rand and the Coronation Syndicate." *The Rialto*, December 3, 1902. See also Alan Cartwright, *The Gold Miners* (Cape Town: Purnell and Sons, 1962), 151–154; and Eric Rosenthal, *Shovel and Sieve* (Cape Town: Howard Timmins N.D. [1959]), 57–62.

These were the two men who in 1892 gave their surnames, Hanau and Farrar, to what became the H.F. Syndicate, set up with a nominal capital of £70,000 for the purpose of reconstructing mining companies and acquiring claims. Much less widely known was that the Syndicate was heavily backed by Wernher, Beit & Company. 'The H.F. Syndicate practically means Eckstein and Co., of Johannesburg', disclosed *The Economist*, 'which in its turn is the local branch of the firm of Wernher, Beit and Co.'.[105] Nor was Wernher, Beit & Company a sleeping partner in the arrangement; quite the contrary, it was determined to have the leading role from the outset. Writing to Julius Wernher in August 1892 about H.F. Syndicate policy, Eckstein's Johannesburg manager and senior partner, Lionel Phillips, insisted that control should be in their hands. 'I am not at all in favour of the Syndicate holding the shares accruing from the various reconstructions, or of making a big pool', he confided. 'Hanau is very anxious to work with us, so if he likes to pool with us well and good, but we must have the manipulation'.[106]

Over the next four to five years, the Eckstein and H.F. Syndicate boards of directors combined their talents to make millions of pounds through market manipulation and company promotion. In 1893, the Syndicate sold its assets to Farrar's newly-floated ERPM, four directors of the Syndicate sitting as members of the latter's six-man board. As vendor, the Syndicate took up 420,000 £1 shares at par of ERPM's original capital of £650,000. At the same time, it reserved to itself the right to participate to the extent of 25 per cent in future distributions or increases in capital of the parent company and its subsidiaries, once £650,000 had been paid back to ERPM shareholders.[107] For its part, ERPM's board, or, 'the H.F. Syndicate, for the terms are really interchangeable', was empowered to issue whatever debentures, that is, interest-bearing shares, it pleased; and could raise its capital 20,000 shares at a time without having to seek shareholder approval. 'Seeing how very substantially the H.F. people were paid for their property', observed *The Economist*, 'the right reserved by them in forming the company was a piece of generosity, to themselves, which has a suggestion of burlesque in it'.[108]

105 *The Economist*, November 7, 1896. See also, *The Critic*, April 7, 1893, and Alan Cartwright, *The Corner House. The Early History of Johannesburg* (Cape Town: Purnell, 1965), 118–19.

106 Hermann Eckstein Papers, HE 151, Phillips to Wernher, 29 October 1892, in Maryna Fraser and Alan Jeeves (eds), *All That Glittered. Selected Correspondence of Lionel Phillips 1890–1924* (Cape Town: Oxford University Press, 1977), 63.

107 *The Economist*, November 7, 1896; and Kubicek, *Economic Imperialism in Theory and Practice*, 134.

108 *The Economist*, November 7, 1896.

Later increases in the capital of the subsidiary companies subsequently spun off from ERPM, 'more "gambling counters" for the group and its allies', said *The Economist*, were believed to have netted the H.F. Syndicate over £800,000.[109] When one such scheme seeking 'to put a very large amount of money into the pockets of the group of financiers who have already made a real "pile" from their association with the East Rand undertaking', was frustrated by the inquorate character of a meeting called in Johannesburg, it was promptly replaced by another designed to tighten further the grip of 'the dominating clique ... upon the properties, ... [so as to] more effectively work them for their own purposes'. 'The directors of the East Rand Company are large holders of H.F. Syndicate shares, and as such their aim is to subordinate the interests of the Proprietary Company to those of the Syndicate, by hook or by crook', *The Economist* concluded. 'So long as trust deeds permit the men in possession to look upon absent shareholders as merely negligible quantities and to regard properties in which they may have a comparatively small interest as their own preserves, British shareholders may well be excused for placing their capital in other directions'.[110]

But protest as *The Economist* might against 'this kind of thing ... which is causing feelings of alarm and disgust among the *bona fide* holders of South African shares',[111] hardly anyone was listening. In 1895 British and other European shareholders remained fixated on the 'Kaffir Boom'. Indeed, the biggest speculative profits were realised not by Barnato, Robinson and Farrar, but by Consolidated Goldfields, and by Wernher, Beit and Company operating on its own account or through proxies. After reaching agreement in November 1894 to purchase jointly certain deep-level properties,[112] the two mining houses frequently cooperated to great mutual benefit. Given advance notice of the balance sheet due to be presented at a Goldfields annual general meeting, Wernher, Beit & Company advised its Johannesburg Office of its intention to purchase a 'moderate amount' of its upcoming share issue. 'It is in our interest that Goldfields should obtain the funds required for the working out of their plans, and we have directly and indirectly as a rule benefitted by them'.[113]

Consolidated Goldfields' direct and indirect market operations were gigantic. Described in Charles Goldmann's authoritative contemporary account

109 Ibid.

110 Ibid., December 19, 1896. See also *The Economist*, January 2, 1897.

111 *The Economist*, November 7, 1896.

112 Mendelsohn, "Blainey and the Jameson Raid," 168.

113 B[arloworld] A[rchives] H[ermann] E[ckstein Papers] 60, London Letters, Wernher, Beit, London, to Eckstein & Company, Johannesburg, November 3, 1894.

of Southern African mining, exploration and finance companies as 'mainly a huge share trust company',[114] and by *TheAfrican Review* as 'one of the largest mining trusts in existence',[115] the volume of shares released by Goldfields staggered belief. Between 1893 and 1895, c.350,000 were disposed of. Some were shares in outcrop properties sold against deep-level propositions. 'It is advisable to realise our interests in outcrop Companies standing at high capitalisations', confided one Goldfields director, 'with a view to securing interests in Deep Levels standing at lower capitalisations'.[116] To take only one example, by June 1895 a deal had been struck with Percy Tarbutt, one of the first mining engineers to have grasped the extraordinary potential of deep-level operations to buy 100,00 Nigel Central, 30,000 Nigel Deep and 25,000 Sub Nigel shares for £300,000.[117] At the same time, Goldfields had learnt to tread carefully between raising funds through market manipulation and doing anything that might tarnish the good name of its deep-level prospects. When Hammond suggested a bear operation prior to the temporary closure of one mine's crushing mills, Goldfields' joint managing director, Charles Rudd, was incensed. 'You must clearly understand that nothing in the nature of what you suggest in that cable can possibly be carried out by this Company', he wrote to its resident director in Johannesburg. 'Any large sales preceding the shutting down of the mill would do enormous harm to our Company, and absolutely preclude the possibility of meeting Shareholders on a fair platform later on, or asking for any increases of capital. … the Company's prestige must be put far before any consideration of actual profit'.[118]

Rudd was anyway more concerned to retain control in London than he was opposed to share market operations. Within weeks of his brusque dismissal of Hammond's suggestion, Rudd was party to a self-aggrandising issue of new shares. Without obtaining the agreement of Consolidated Goldfields shareholders to an issue of 625,000 preference shares, the Company's directors

114 Charles Goldmann, *South African Mines; Their Position, Results, & Developments: Together with an Account of Diamond, Land, Finance, and Kindred Concerns* I (London: E. Wilson & Company, 1896), 141.

115 *The African Review*, October 20, 1894.

116 C[ory] L[ibrary], Gold Fields Collection, MS 16087, H.E.M. Davies, London, to Capt. F. Rhodes, Johannesburg, November 20, 1894.

117 CL, Gold Fields Collection, MS 14999, London cable to Johannesburg, June 17, 1895. For Tarbutt, see Ian Phimister and Jeremy Mouat, "Mining, Engineers and Risk Management: British Overseas Investment, 1894–1914," *South African Historical Journal* 49, no. 1 (2003): 1–26; and obituaries in *The African Review*, June 4, 1904, and *The Critic*, June 4, 1904.

118 CL, Gold Fields Collection, MS 16087, C. Rudd, London, to F. Rhodes, Johannesburg, November 16, 1894. See also, Robert Kubicek, "The Randlords in 1895: A Reassessment," *Journal of British Studies* 11, no. 2 (1972): 93.

'placed' half of the issue amongst themselves and their 'friends'. 'This system of forestalling shareholders', thought *The Economist*, 'is utterly reprehensible'.[119] But it was Hammond whom Rudd was determined to stop, not a 'reprehensible system'. 'It would be ridiculous for us in London to instruct Hammond in regard to shaft sinking, and I contend it is equally ridiculous for a Consulting Engineer upon the Rand to take a market view and judge what stocks should or not be sold'.[120]

For his part, Hammond, while no friend of the 'great number of absolutely rotten concerns' threatening to discredit the Witwatersrand gold mining industry as a whole,[121] had always insisted that share ('stock') options should underpin his highly paid Goldfields remuneration.[122] Consequently, he was outraged to discover in October 1895 that Rudd and H.E.M. Davies in the company's London head office had 'cut down participation promised [to] me personally very materially'. 'My contract with [the] Company is based on [an] assurance of fair participation at bedrock price', he reminded Frank Rhodes in October 1895. 'I shall insist on obtaining my full rights or tender my resignation to the Company'.[123] 'Rudd and Davies I think are too small minded', wrote Hammond a week later, 'to realise that this has been an extraordinary year for money making, and that any man connected with the Gold Fields could have made much more money acting independently of them'.[124]

This was not how it appeared to others, however. Goldfields' 'stock-jobbing operations are upon an enormous scale', declared *The Economist*, 'and it is notorious that where the company itself speculates, some of those who are intimately connected with it have their speculations also'.[125] Over much the same period, its Rhodesian shareholdings registered significant gains. Obliged by Rhodes to come to the rescue of his near-bankrupt British South Africa Company, Goldfields' original grudging investment first quadrupled and then doubled again in value as the former's inner circle manipulated ownership of the

119 *The Economist*, December 1, 1894. See also, *The Critic*, December 14, 1894: 'Through … this new plan … the managers' future gains will increase considerably, and the remaining ordinary shares will have much better chances of seeing frequent market fluctuations, to the shrewd wirepullers' ultimate benefit'.

120 CL MS 16807, Rudd to F. Rhodes, November 16, 1894.

121 Bodleian Library, Hays Hammond Papers, Micro. AFR. 368, Private Letter Books, January 1895–October 1897, folio 434, Hammond to C.W. Truslow, New York, December 2, 1895.

122 Van Onselen, *Cowboy Capitalist*, 49.

123 Bodleian Library, Hays Hammond Papers, Micro. AFR. 368, Private Letter Books, January 1895-October 1897, folio 341, cable, Hammond, Johannesburg, to Captain F. Rhodes, Cape Town, October 14, 1895.

124 Ibid., folio 360, Hammond to Captain F. Rhodes, October 21, 1895.

125 *The Economist*, May 19, 1894.

mining concession on which the entire chartered adventure ostensibly rested to reward themselves and their City friends.[126] 'A corporation like the Consolidated Gold Fields of South Africa, during a time of "boom", is not widely distinguishable … from a sublimated City "bucket-shop"', thought Edmund Garret of the *Cape Times*.[127]

At the beginning of November 1895, Consolidated Goldfields announced a profit of £ 2,161,778, one that was 'certainly larger than any I ever anticipated when we founded this company', declared Goldfields' chairman, 'and larger than any ever realised by any limited liability company in the City of London'. The board of directors recommended a dividend for the year of 125 per cent on ordinary shares and the transfer of £200,000 to the reserve fund, leaving a balance of £1,145,742 to be carried forward.[128] 'The main source of the company's income has been the profits on the sale of shares', *The Economist* reported. Consolidated Gold Fields 'has had quite exceptional opportunities, and has used them to the fullest extent, of making enormous profits by share-dealing transactions'.[129]

FIGURE 6
Hermann Eckstein
SOURCE: JAMES BENJAMIN TAYLOR, *A PIONEER LOOKS BACK* (LONDON: HUTCHINSON & CO, 1939), BETWEEN PP. 112–113.

126 "Ramifications of the Chartered Company." *The Economist*, November 18, 1893; and *The Times*, November 21, 1893.
127 Edward Cook, *Edmund Garrett. A Memoir* (London: E. Arnold, 1909), 239.
128 Alan Cartwright, *Gold Paved the Way. The Story of the Gold Fields Group of Companies* (London: Macmillan, 1967), 83.
129 *The Economist*, November 2, 1895.

Like Consolidated Goldfields, Wernher, Beit & Company's growing preoccupation with spreading the risk associated with deep-level mining and raising the enormous sum of capital required for its development went hand in hand with large-scale market making and speculation over an extended period. In 1892, just as the Witwatersrand was beginning to recover from the collapse of the first boom in gold mining shares, Lionel Phillips, later senior partner in Ecksteins, had attempted to make a case for putting production before speculation. 'Which do you think the most profitable way of dealing with good properties?', he asked Beit. 'To make shares and sell them, or to work the mines? ... I think in such a continuous [gold-bearing] formation and regular yielding deposit as this, and with an article which does not fluctuate in value, *large* fortunes are to be made rather by working than by selling shares'. 'With the experience we have now gained', he went on, 'we know that 100 [crushing] stamps are practicable ... one might reckon on supplying 250 stamps from a good-sized property. One can put down boreholes to prove the reef at the South [Reef] boundaries if one wants to insure oneself before incurring great capital outlay'. 'It seems to me', Phillips concluded, 'the market may pay the value, or more than the value, for indifferent properties, but in *first rate* ventures more can be made by working. ... [It] seems to me where one has an A1 property (actual value of which in the case of the Rand is almost demonstrable) the biggest fortunes will accrue rather to workers than sellers. I should like your and Mr. Wernher's views on this'.[130]

In reality, it was never a case of either one or the other. Wernher, Beit & Company showcased the prospects of 'first rate ventures' to boost the share prices of 'indifferent properties'. Stock values were pushed up artificially and worthless shares unloaded.[131] Sometimes this was done openly; at other times, more discrete methods were employed. Working closely with N.M. Rothschild and Sons, Wernher, Beit & Company were 'the prime movers behind the Porges-Kann share syndicate, formed to stir the market and indulge in private speculations'. The syndicate operated with a capital of £500,000, and 'speculated heavily on the London Stock Exchange in Transvaal Consolidated Land Company, Randfontein, Rand Mines and New Heriot equities'.[132] On still other occasions, Wernher, Beit & Company operated with or through the Eastern

130 HE 151, Phillips to Beit, September 10, 1892, in Fraser and Jeeves, *All That Glittered*, 60.

131 Kubicek, *Economic Imperialism in Theory and Practice*, 66–67.

132 Van Helten, "British and European Economic Investment in the Transvaal," 123. The Paris Bourse was 'personally conducted by the Rothschilds in this matter, their wealthy and influential following giving an appearance of general interest to what was hitherto limited to a small clique'; see *The Critic*, November 23, 1894.

FIGURE 7 Lionel Phillips
SOURCE: THELMA GUTSCHE, *NO ORDINARY WOMAN – THE LIFE AND TIMES OF FLORENCE PHILLIPS*, (CAPE TOWN: H. TIMMINS, 1966).

Investment Company of Sir Edgar Vincent, of whom it was alleged he had amassed a personal fortune by abusing his position as Director to play fast and loose with the Ottoman Imperial Bank's investment portfolio.[133]

By far the most important of Wernher, Beit & Company's stock exchange business, however, was channeled through a firm of London brokers, Lionel Hirsch & Company. 'On the Paris market Wernher Beit & Co.s' operations were very clever; they never acted personally, entered into no kind of business relations with the great speculators there, and accordingly were beyond the range of any subsequent attacks', one account concluded. 'They used the London firm of outside brokers L. Hirsch & Co. who in the years of the mining

133 R. Davenport-Hines and Jean-Jacques Van Helten, "Edgar Vincent, Viscount D'Abernon, and the Eastern Investment Company in London, Constantinople and Johannesburg," in *Speculators and Patriots. Essays in Business History*, ed. R. Davenport-Hines (London: Frank Cass & Co. Ltd., 1986), 41. See also, Christopher Clay, "The Imperial Ottoman Bank in the Later Nineteenth Century: A Multinational 'National' Bank?," in *Banks as Multinationals*, ed. Geoffrey Jones (London: Routledge, 1990), 152; and Paul Auchterlonie, "A Turk of the West: Sir Edgar Vincent's Career in Egypt and the Ottoman Empire," *British Journal of Middle Eastern Studies* 27, no. 1 (2000): 64–65.

FIGURE 8
Julius Wernher
SOURCE: WIKIMEDIA COMMONS: HTTPS://COMMONS.WIKIMEDIA.ORG/WIKI/IMAGE:JULIUS_WERNHER00.JPG?USELANG=IT#FILE (LAST ACCESSED 17 MAY 2024).

development acquired extraordinary importance; amongst its partners were Alfred Beit's brother, subsequently Sir Otto Beit, … and Ludwig Neumann, the brother of [Randlord] Sir Sigismund Neumann'.[134] Regarded as a 'most useful "shunter" of shares even by such eminent firms as Messrs. Wernher, Beit and Co', Hirsch also placed shares in Germany, reputedly making 'as much as £5,000 in a single week in commissions alone, sufficient proof of his influence amongst small speculators and investors in his native land'.[135]

Because of the opaque manner in which it operated, it is extremely difficult if not impossible at this distance in time to establish with any precision the scale of Wernher, Beit and Company's operations. For example, even where the movement of Beit and Wernher's personal holdings in the British South Africa Company could be traced as a result of public disclosure in 1889 and subsequent journalistic investigation, the number of shares actually purchased or sold was almost certainly under-counted. This was because the Company having been incorporated by Charter rather than under the Joint Stock Companies acts was not required to file returns with the Registrar of Companies.

134 Emden, *Randlords*, 351.
135 "The Messrs. Hirsch and the Kaffir Market," *The Rialto*, September 17, 1902.

Nor were the names of shareholders and the extent of their transactions revealed.[136] Beit apparently reduced his personal holding of BSA Company shares from 122,376 in July 1895 to a mere 7,496 by March 1896, yet according to one account at the time, 'the figures relating to … Mr. Beit are ridiculously inadequate; for the Beit Syndicate, Beit and Rhodes (this firm sold 209,491 shares), Beit and Cawston, Rhodes and Beit, Rhodes, Rudd, and Beit, Goldfields of South Africa, etc., etc., "off-loaded" during the same period on the same vast uncompromising scale'.[137]

The original source for these figures was Henry Labouchere, Liberal Member of Parliament for Northampton and editor of *Truth.* A long-standing critic of Rhodes and the Chartered Company, Labouchere's opinions were frequently derided by contemporaries and have more often than not been dismissed by historians.[138] But on this occasion, the figures themselves, however indicative, were not challenged; nor was his further discovery that in the same period 'of shares held jointly … [Beit and Rhodes] sold 220,891 from a holding of 221,400'. Nor did they register transfers when they occurred.[139] Regarded as one of the shrewdest operators on the London Stock Exchange, Beit was credited in 1895 by *Mining World* with having amassed a fortune of £10,000,000 through 'taking good things and sticking to them, or by purchasing for his partner to sell'. Julius Wernher was worth £7,000,000, obtained 'by selling things bought by his Partner Beit'.[140] Wernher's private grumble about Beit's 'wild' behavior in the share market sat uneasily with his earlier admission that the company had unloaded 'rubbish' onto mining markets by manipulating share values. These might be practices 'not worthy of a great firm', but they did not stop him from taking full advantage of them.[141]

---

136 Shenton, "Chartered Company," 21.

137 Edward Rose, *The Truth About the Transvaal. A Record of Facts based upon Twelve Years' Residence in the Country* (London: E.B. Rose, 1902), 113.

138 For example, Jeffrey Butler, *The Liberal Party and the Jameson* Raid (Oxford: Clarendon, 1968), 177. But see, Eleanor Mabin, "'Truth' and the British South Africa Company. The Development of a Radical's Opposition to the Development of Capitalist Imperialism in a Southern African Context" (MA diss., Simon Fraser University, 1982).

139 R. Hind, *Henry Labouchere and the Empire 1880–1905* (London: Athlone Press, 1972), 25–26.

140 Galbraith, *Crown and Charter*, 284.

141 Wernher to G. Rouliot, December 29, 1895, as cited in Mendelsohn, "Blainey and the Jameson Raid," 170; and Wernher to Rouliot, November 15, 1895; ibid. to Phillips, December 5, 1895, both as cited in Kubicek, "Randlords in 1895," 97; where Wernher is described as 'the man primarily responsible for shaping the firm's investment policy, profit taking and capital issues'. See also, Raleigh Trevelyan, *Grand Dukes and Diamonds. The Wernhers of Luton Hoo* (London: Faber & Faber, 1991).

Much of the capital chasing Southern African mining shares originated in or through London. But it was soon joined by Paris, Berlin, St Petersburg, Vienna and Constantinople. Of these latter, the Paris bourse was by far the most important. While German banks were closely associated with several smaller Rand Houses, such as the Dresdener Bank with the Albu and Goertz companies, major French banks like the Banque Francaise de l'Afrique du Sud in Paris enjoyed institutionalised links with Wernher, Beit & Company.[142] Initial contacts with European banks and speculators had been made through the diamond merchant, Julius Porges, who before returning to London's Hatton Garden from Kimberley, had formed a partnership with Eckstein and Company to manage his Witwatersrand operations.[143] Having previously introduced diamond shares in Vienna, Berlin, Hamburg and Amsterdam, Porges and Company enjoyed 'great influence among Banking Houses on the Continent ... with a large number of investors willing to support any flotation made by the firm'.[144] Porges then moved to France where he worked closely with his cousin, Rudolphe Kann, a banker whose house, filled with 'fine pictures and tapestry', was much envied,[145] and other Paris financiers. Kann and Porges between them managed a syndicate in which Wernher, Beit & Company was heavily involved, having 'at its disposal several hundred thousand marketable shares with a book value in excess of £700,000.[146] 'When Beit realised that it would be necessary to obtain the support of international financiers and bankers in order to raise all the capital required for the gold-mining industry' recalled one contemporary, 'he decided to broaden the market by giving participations to the Rothschilds of Germany, Austria, and France. Through Rudolph Kahn of

142 Richardson and Van Helten, "The Gold Mining Industry in the Transvaal," 22. See also, Kubicek, *Economic Imperialism in Theory and Practice*, 178–82.

143 Jean-Jacques Van Helten, "La France et l'Or des Boers: Some Aspects of French Investment in South Africa between 1890 and 1914," *African Affairs* 84, no. 335 (1985): 250.

144 James Taylor, *Recollections of the Discovery of Gold on the Witwatersrand* (Cape Town: unpublished 1936), 7–8. See also his, *A Pioneer Looks Back* (London: Hutchinson & Co., 1939).

145 Lionel Phillips, *Some Reminiscences* (London: Hutchinson & Co., 1925), 133. See especially, *The Rialto*, February 15, 1905: 'The death of Rudolphe Kahn (sic), which has just taken place in Paris, is much to be regretted, and he will be greatly missed by a wide circle of friends, not only in the French capital, but on this side of the Channel. In the early days of the Rand he was closely associated with J.B. Robinson and Jules Porges, and subsequently he became an intimate friend of Cecil Rhodes. His house in Paris contains pictures and art treasures of great value, and his social entertainments were always in the best of taste. He was a kindly man, with a large heart, and did much good with his wealth, which was considerably over one million sterling'.

146 Kubicek, *Economic Imperialism*, 179.

Paris he secured the support of many banking houses: in fact, all those houses which had made money out of diamond shares became eager to participate in gold shares'.[147]

In October 1894, Ecksteins was informed by Wernher, Beit and Company in London that a new company had been formed by 'an influential French group headed by Messrs. Goudchaux of Paris who are intimately connected with Credit Lyonnais'. 'The Company will have its head office in London, so that it should be worked under English laws', Ecksteins was told, 'but the moving spirit will be Mr Albert Kahn ... who seems to us to be a very clear headed man, and who has thoroughly grasped the value of deep-level properties. We think the rise which is now taking place in Rand Mine and other Deep Level shares is principally owing to his buying and that of his friends'.[148] This followed the establishment two months previously of the Syndicat Sud-Africain by Wernher, Beit & Company and the investment bank, Banque de Paris et des Pays-Bas.[149] Even to the editorial staff of the Kruger-supporting *Standard & Diggers News* in far-off Johannesburg, it was clear that 'capital has ceased to be circumscribed by arbitrary distinction such as frontier boundaries; that the kings of capital are not so much French, German, or English as cosmopolitan, and have almost lost their international significance'.[150]

A standard ploy was to buy selected Rand mining shares through Paris and Berlin agents in the hope that English speculators would be inspired by seemingly spontaneous continental confidence.[151] It was a practice so common that *The Rialto* could not resist mocking in its spoof *Cyclopaedia of Stock Exchange Mining and Financial Terms*: 'Paris selling: "Orders sent to Paris by the London magnates, and duly executed on the London Stock Exchange by brokers reputed to do a 'large Continental business'"'.[152] The reverse occurred just as often. Persuaded by signs that the boom had reached the point where the price of just about every available share had shot up, *The Critic* attributed the movement not only to the 'advent of an important section of continental speculators into the kaffir circus', but also to the fact that big mining houses had put a 'helping hand to the wheel'. 'The Continental Bourses, and the Paris one

147 Taylor, *A Pioneer Looks Back*, 109–10.

148 BA, HE 60, London Letters, Wernher, Beit, London, to Eckstein & Company, Johannesburg, October 27, 1894.

149 Lukasiewicz, "Gold, Finance and Speculation," 239.

150 John Buttery and A. Key, *Why Kruger Made War or Behind the Boer Scenes* (London: Heinsmann, 1900), 27.

151 McCarty, "British Investment in Overseas Mining," 268.

152 "The Rialto Cyclopaedia of Stock Exchange Mining and Financial Terms." *The Rialto*, October 28, 1903.

especially, have been personally conducted by the Rothschilds, their wealthy and influential following giving an appearance of general interest to what was hitherto limited to a small clique'. Wernher, Beit & Company, the paper continued, have been able to promote gambling 'to an almost unlimited extent by the judicious *contango*-facilities given to the market, the capital necessary being always obtainable in times of plethora to firms of high standing below even Bank of England rates'.[153]

One such operation was conducted by the Compagnie Francaise de Mines d'Or de L'Afrique du Sud, originally the Compagnie Francaise de Mines d'Or & d'Exploration, whose backers included prominent Parisian bankers, as well as Hamilton Smith, a leading American mining engineer employed by the Rothschilds, and Farrar's Anglo-French Exploration Company. It not only 'absorbed or marketed a lot of unpromising watered stock',[154] but also worked closely with the London office of Wernher, Beit & Company. In April 1895, the Cie. Francaise de Mines d'Or successfully made a market for Durban Roodeport Deep shares. It did so by liaising with Wernher, Beit & Company in order to calibrate the number and agreed price of shares daily released to French brokers. Too few shares 'would bring very likely a rise which would go much more quick and high than you and us wish for the sound development of the market', while too many might not reach the desired price.[155]

Writing to Wernher towards the end of the month, Hamilton Smith alerted him to the fact that Durban Roodeport Deeps would be introduced to the market the following day at the agreed fixed price of £4 a share, 'just enough, I think, has been whispered about the mine to make the issue a success'. But, he emphasised, 'it will be important to have some trading done in the shares tomorrow in London, so please put orders in the hands of your traders to buy two thousand shares @ eighty-five shillings for a/c of the Cie Franc-Mines d'Or. Also instruct your brokers so that the shares will be quoted on the [Exchange Telegraph Company] tape and also in the newspapers on Wednesday morning. My French friends think this last is very important, so please see that it is done'.[156] Everything went according to plan, and within 48 hours Wernher

153 *The Critic*, November 23, 1894.

154 Kubicek, *Economic Imperialism in Theory and Practice*, 180–81; and Lukasiewicz, "Gold, Finance and Speculation," 240. See also, Robert Turrell and Jean-Jacques Van Helten, "The Rothschilds, the Exploration Company and Mining Finance," *Business History* 28, no. 2 (1986): 188–89.

155 BA, W[Ernher] B[eit], 19C, Private Letters, General, January-December 1895, Compagnie Francaise de Mines d'Or & d'Exploration, Paris, to Wernher, Beit, London, March 28, 1895.

156 Ibid., Hamilton Smith, Compagnie Francaise de Mines d'Or & d'Exploration, to Wernher, April 22, 1895.

received the good news that the market was 'excellent'. 'The people are very glad to have seen the regular rise to-day from 125 to 130 [francs] – shares are quoted; large business has been done, for account and for settlement. We feel confident you will have now the French market as well disposed as possible for Durban Roodeport Deep level shares'.[157]

The Robinson group was similarly able to conduct 'an enormous business' in Paris through a financial consortium in which the Societe Generale was prominently represented. Indeed, the latter backed Robinson's Bank with £1.5 million in cash.[158] 'A very large proportion of the [capital] amount was taken by French investors', claimed Robinson's authorised biography, 'and French directors were elected to the board of the Company'.[159] Barnato too had a large following in Paris. Discretely held in shape by 'light-fitting stays' and invariably wearing white silk socks,[160] he stayed either at the Hotel Bristol or the Hotel Continental, where he would 'dispose of parcels of his shares to the Haute-Banque and the "Coulisse"', the first 'to receive his tips … [being] the merry ladies he visited'.[161] Much bigger speculative offerings in Barnato-controlled companies were placed through the Imperial Ottoman Bank, itself dominated by French interests. Together with officials from the Comptoir d'Escompte and the Vienna-based Landesbank, the Ottoman Bank helped float Barnato's Bank, Mining and Estates Company. 'Its shares reached £3 10s. in September 1895 amidst hectic trading … [and] according to … Kahn (sic), … the Ottoman Bank co-operated with Barnato throughout the whole affair operating as bulls on the coulisse with stock valued at more than £1 million'.[162]

'The Rand financiers should certainly remember the French speculator in their prayers', *The Critic* declared. 'His faith in certain instances seems to be more than heavenly, while in a great many more he has that quality which is worth even more for the market manipulators – ignorance'.[163] Struck by the 'strong tone' in Rand mining shares because of 'vigorous' buying primarily from France and Germany, the same journal drew attention in December 1894 to the entry into the market of 'the *Credit Lyonnais*, which is the largest private banking institution in France, with a capital of £8,000,000'. 'It has now taken up

157 Ibid., Compagnie Francaise de Mines d'Or & d'Exploration, to Wernher, Beit, April 24, 1895.

158 Kubicek, *Economic Imperialism in Theory and Practice*, 129.

159 Weinthal, *Memories, Mines and Millions*, 137.

160 *The Critic*, July 10, 1896; and "The Richest Man in the World. South Africa's Gold King." *New Zealand Herald*, December 28, 1895.

161 Emden, *Randlords*, 139. See also, Lukasiewicz, "Gold, Finance and Speculation," 247–48.

162 Davenport-Hines and Van Helten, "Edgar Vincent, Viscount D'Abernon," 42.

163 *The Critic*, November 30, 1894.

Transvaal mines', the paper noted, 'and is rapidly dispossessing the *Banque de Paris et des Pays-Bas* of its leading control of the market'.[164] Four months later, the continued rise in share prices was attributed to 'the eager disposition of continental operators to buy anything and everything South African'. 'So long as French and German speculators are "on the feed", and are able and willing to hold their purchases intact', *The Economist* concluded, 'so long will the "boom" last. When buying from the Continent ceases and selling is attempted, it will be a question of *sauve qui peut*; but there is no prospect of an early collapse'.[165]

'The most fashionable features of late have been huge "pools" formed by groups of Anglo-French investors, revealed *The African Review*. 'Many of these pools are controlled by the strongest financiers, and are handled by leading firms of brokers. The shares are syndicated at a "starting price" which usually varies from par to 100 per cent premium. They are then peddled out by the medium of the Stock Exchange, and by the assistance of puffs which are inserted (and paid for either in hard cash or in options on the shares) in the financial and other papers'.[166] In August 1895, the Société Générale was reported as having 'taken £500,000 of the capital [of the Robinson bank] at par, and to have bought from Mr Robinson £500,000 of the remainder for £1,000,000'. 'The combination of Mr Robinson and the Société Générale may be a most advantageous one for the shareholders, and the fact that Randfontein shares are being eagerly bought in Paris ... seems to indicate the activity of the partnerships', observed *The Economist*, 'but prudence would suggest that before rushing into an undertaking standing in the market at £8,250,000, it would be well to ascertain what the capital represents'.[167]

Sections of Britain's financial press habitually attributed volatile market movements in Paris to the excitable and reckless temperament of French investors.[168] Commenting in the dog days of the South African War, *The Rialto* thought that

> Whenever French ... buying takes place on the London Stock Exchange it is to our mind a sure sign of weakness, so far as the future is concerned. Our Continental friends are so irrational that whatever they do they do hastily. They become, in the first place, greedy to buy, which inflates prices

164 Ibid., December 7, 1894.
165 *The Economist*, April 27, 1895.
166 *The African Review*, August 17, 1895.
167 *The Economist*, August 17, 1895.
168 To take only two examples, *The African Review*, March 23, 1895; and *The Critic*, January 4, 1895.

> unnecessarily, and then they become anxious to sell, which depresses prices necessarily.[169]

The reality, however, was initially rather more prosaic. Consolidated Goldfields established an agency in Paris at the Banque Internationale de Paris and issued bearer shares printed in French;[170] Rand mining companies published their annual reports in French as well as English;[171] and speculators could consult any number of journals, books and guides written specifically for them, some of them, it was believed, discreetly subsidised by Wernher, Beit and Company, and by Gold Fields.[172] Above all, gold mining shares attracted attention because the Paris discount rate was the lowest in the world at the time, 'never rising above 4 per cent and domestic securities only averaged an annual return of around 3.5 per cent. Foreign securities on the other hand showed an average return of 4.2 per cent per annum ... [and] in the case of South African securities, they *promised* even higher returns, windfall profits and a chance to dabble in share speculation on a very large scale'.[173] London financial columnists informed their readers that in France '6 per cent, plus redemption of capital, is looked upon as a perfectly satisfactory mining investment'.[174]

Only much later were French shareholders swept up in an orgy of speculation. Towards the end of April 1895, it was reported that as the boom grew more speculative, accounts in Paris were being opened in 'second-rate and dubious shares', not least of which were Rhodesian.[175] 'We are officially informed', *The Statist* declared, 'that a large block of fully-paid United Rhodesia shares, belonging to the Zambesia Exploring Company has been placed in Paris, at a substantial premium. These are share warrants to bearer, and are printed in English, French, and German. The influential group which has this business on hand has an extensive connection throughout Germany'.[176] 'These days gold mines are the main subject of conversation, everybody seems in a feverish ardour about the matter, from people at the bottom to those on top

169 *The Rialto*, March 5, 1902.

170 *The African Review*, October 20, 1894.

171 Such as *Rand Mines Limited, Annual Reports, 1894, 1896–1900* (London: W.W. Sprague, 1895, 1897, 1898, 1900, 1901).

172 Amongst others, the weekly *Revue Sud-Africaine*, and Louis De Launay, *Les Mines D'Or du Transvaal* (Paris: Librairie polytechnique, Baudry et cie, 1896). See especially, "Kaffirs in Paris. Mr Henri Dupont 'puts up the shutters'." *The Rialto*, August 16, 1905.

173 Van Helten, "La France et l'Or des Boers," 251.

174 *The African Review*, March 23, 1895.

175 *The Critic*, April 26, 1895.

176 *The Statist*, September 21, 1895.

of the ladder', wrote Baron Alphonse Rothschild from Paris to his cousins in London. 'Today the ardour turned on East Rand and Rand mines and a fantastic rise of these shares can be anticipated'.[177] By September, French investors were thought to have taken up very nearly £100,000,000 worth of South African mining shares.[178] 'How well I remember, typifying this boom year, that big crowd on the steps of the Paris Bourse', recalled *The Economist's* mining correspondent, J.H. Curle. 'Above the roar, stentorian voices shouted "Mossamedes! Mossamedes a soixante quinze!" Here were shares of a district [in Portuguese West Africa (Angola)] a thousand miles from the Rand, where no gold existed, and I knew then that the French investor was doomed. If not he, why not others?'.[179]

The first signs of trouble came in mid-September 1895, with *The Economist* reporting that the 'greatest difficulty was experienced in adjusting the [mining share] account and though rumours that "carrying over" facilities would be curtailed led to the closing of a good many transactions, the stiff rates generally charged in the mining market, while money was so cheap and abundant in other departments, showed that, in the opinion of the "House" much of the speculation is in very weak hands'. 'There can be no doubt', the journal believed, 'that many shrewd operators have recently been taking their profits, passing on their holdings to outside gamblers, who are not alarmed at the level of prices'.[180] 'The market has been rather irregular and there has been a good deal of forced selling and with the exception of … East Rands, Anglo Farrars and Robinson [shares] … all prices have declined from 5 to 20 percent', Wernher informed Ecksteins in Johannesburg. 'Whether this is the beginning of a serious reaction is very difficult to say, we are rather of [the] dispossession that the market will again recover'.[181]

What appeared to have been a momentary market wobble passed and shares, particularly in Paris, resumed their upwards trajectory. Now, for the first time, Brussels was drawn directly into the buying frenzy. Shares of the Belgian Mining Trust of South Africa, an offspring of Consolidated Gold Fields,

177 RA, RAL T16, translations, 1892–1896, 3/65 Baron Alphonse, Paris, to his cousins, London, September 18, 1895.

178 Hubert Meredith, *The Drama of Money Making* (London: Sampson Low, Marston, & Company, n.d [1931]), 188.

179 James H. Curle, *The Shadow Show* (London: Methuen & Co Ltd., 1912), 54. For frustrated hopes of gold in the Cassinga mines of south-central Angola, see William Gervase Clarence-Smith, *Slaves, Peasants and Capitalists in Southern Angola, 1840–1926* (Cambridge: Cambridge University Press, 1979), 17–18.

180 *The Economist*, September 14, 1895.

181 BA, HE 60, Wernher, Beit, London, to Ecksteins, Johannesburg, September 14, 1895.

would shortly be quoted on the Paris and London markets, reported the *Independance Belge*. 'This is the first South African enterprise dealt in largely on the Brussels Bourse, and the shares have been in very active demand of late at rising prices'.[182] Associated from first to last with Baron Robert Oppenheim, the Trust was 'a concern of a purely speculative character', finally collapsing in November 1902 when it failed to meet its obligations.[183] In London, too, market mania showed little sign of abating, for all that conniving company promoters and 'bogus' mining ventures were standard fare in plays and musicals. By the time Sir Augustus Harris' Drury Lane spectacular, 'Cheer, Boys, Cheer', in which English pluck overcomes swindles and treachery in South Africa, opened in the last week of September 1895,[184] 'The Company Promoter' sung by Charles Collette had long enjoyed music hall success, not least because of its catchy chorus line, 'Though every mine is all "moonshine", from diamonds to tin; Still the money, money, money, comes a-rolling in'.[185]

The mining market respite was short-lived, however. At the beginning of October, 'massive sales in Paris led to prices slumping in London … [and] over the next week the relapse in prices continued more or less unabated'.[186] Compared to most press coverage, reports in *The Economist* were positively restrained. 'For some time past cautious operators, warned by the difficulty experienced in "carrying over" shares, have been clearing out', it noted. 'More recently the support so long given to the market here by French purchases has not only ceased but has been followed by considerable realisations from Paris and from other continental centres'.[187] By contrast, *The Statist* did not mince its words; 'the position of the London Mining department, especially that section known as the Kaffir Circus, may be summed up in one word, namely, liquidation. The selling has been on a most gigantic scale'.[188]

---

182 *Independance Belge*, as cited in *The Statist*, September 7, 1895.

183 "Brussels and the Kaffir Fall." *The African World*, November 29, 1902. See also, Goldmann, *South African Mines* II, 139–40.

184 "South Africa at Drury Lane. Sir A. Harris's Latest Spectacle. The Rand on a London Stage. Wilson's Last Stand," *The African Review*, September 21, 1895.

185 Bernard Ince, "Natural-Born Showman: The Stage Career of Charles Collette, Actor & Comedian," *Theatre Notebook* 63, no. 1 (2009): 1–25. For the 'virulence and depth' of the anti-City backlash that followed the collapse of the boom, see especially, Ranald Michie, *Guilty Money: The City of London in Victorian and Edwardian Culture, 1815–1914* (London: Pickering & Chatto, 2009), 133–40, where Headon Hill's *Guilty Gold. A Romance of Financial Fraud and City Crime* (London: C. Arthur Pearson, 1896) is discussed.

186 Kynaston, *City of London*, 129–30.

187 *The Economist*, October 12, 1895.

188 *The Statist*, October 19, 1895.

This was not initially how it appeared to the biggest mining house of them all. Unperturbed by what it thought was an overdue correction, Wernher, Beit and Company at first looked to buy shares cheaply on a falling market. 'The market had a wholesome shaking, and ... will remain a little unsettled until lower prices bring support', its London Office reassured Johannesburg in the middle of October. 'Of course, it will take time to re-establish the old cheerfulness. We have done [fishing?] to see what the market would do and found that deserving shares could at all times be dealt with at lower rates'.[189]

FIGURE 9 The company promoter
SOURCE: G.C. ANEWICK AND V. DAVIS, *THE COMPANY PROMOTER*, MUSIC SHEETS (LONDON: PATEY & WILLIS, N.D.).

189 BA, HE 60, Wernher, Beit, London, to Ecksteins, Johannesburg, October 12, 1895.

Over the next few weeks, the tone of the correspondence was largely unchanged. Although the 'Kaffir Circus' experienced 'violent fluctuations' and the decline in prices had begun 'to take alarming proportions', Wernher, Beit & Company continued to buy on the fall.[190] As 'a little resolution quickly frightens the bears',[191] the 'offering of good shares was at no times great, and they are by no means easy to buy at quotations'.[192] At the beginning of November, Wernher, Beit & Company was still buying good quality shares, if anything 'a little more freely when stock was offered, for account of our Syndicates',[193] but as the month progressed, so the news became progressively worse. 'The market is in a very bad condition, verging on a panic', Ecksteins was advised on the 8th.[194] A fortnight later the situation had deteriorated still further. A terse London letter conveyed the news that 'the market has been awfully bad, and prices have again fallen considerably … Several large operators in Paris have been liquidated'.[195]

Any surviving animal spirits in the Southern African mining market were severely tested in late November 1895 when Lionel Phillips of Ecksteins, speaking to a Johannesburg audience in his capacity as President of the Chamber of Mines, appeared to throw down the gauntlet to the Boer authorities in Pretoria.[196] 'All we want in this country is purity of administration and an equitable share and voice in its affairs', declared Phillips. 'I hope that wiser counsels may prevail, and that the Government of this country may be induced to see that the present policy will not do. Nothing is further from my heart than a desire to see an upheaval which would be disastrous from every point of view, and which would probably end in … bloodshed. But I should say this, that it is a mistake to imagine that this much-maligned community … will consent indefinitely to remain subordinate to the minority in this country'.[197] Leading articles dealing with the speech 'bore the heading "The writing on the wall" and "Mene, Tekel"; which is to say that the writing on the wall was interpreted by Daniel to mean that God, having weighed Belshazzar and his kingdom, found them wanting and would destroy them'.[198]

190 Ibid., October 19, 1895.
191 Ibid.
192 Ibid., October 25, 1895.
193 Ibid., November 1, 1895.
194 Ibid., November 8, 1895.
195 Ibid., November 22, 1895.
196 Carl Jeppe, *The Kaleidoscopic Transvaal* (London: Chapman 1906), 188.
197 Emden, *Randlords*, 198.
198 Ibid.

What was left of the erstwhile boom was then snuffed out by the fiasco of the Jameson Raid at the end of December 1895, a failed attempt by a mixed bag of financiers and filibusters to overthrow the Kruger government and replace it by a regime more amenable to their direction.[199] After an ignominious surrender to sharp-shooting Boers by raiders 'who appear[ed] to have had all the fight knocked out of them by a day's starvation',[200] not even Barney Barnato's appearance outside the Stock Exchange 'in the largest of fur-lined overcoats ... [where he] was immediately surrounded by a crowd of adulators ... succeed[ed] in galvanizing any sort of life into the market'.[201] 'The gloom in the mining market grows deeper', lamented *The Critic*, 'and the *habitues* of the Kaffir Circus, from being the liveliest members of the Throgmorton Street crowd, are now the most subdued'.[202]

Contemporaries attributed the collapse of the so-called 'Kaffir Boom' to the increasing reluctance and eventual refusal of London banks to accept Paris bills of purchase. 'The cause of the fall is, of course, perfectly plain', *The Critic* insisted. 'In the first instance, it was due to the action of the banks in refusing to support customers whose purchases were, they believed, heavier than their resources. The ball being set rolling in this way ... it was [then] perceived by "bears" that a favourable opportunity was available for depressing prices and buying in again, and they set vigorously to work with that object'.[203] 'A large proportion of the purchases have been made through the financial establishments of the French capital', explained *The Economist*, 'which have made large profits by advancing money at 8 to 10 per cent. and over, and by getting their "finance bills" discounted here at the current rates. But with a disinclination on the part of the London market to take these bills, there has concurrently been a desire in Paris to realise securities'.[204]

The Statist similarly thought that it was 'the refusal of the London banks to take such bills drawn upon the London branches of Continental banks' that had caused prices to fall.[205] Paris bankers had been advancing funds to clients 'in the form of three-month bills on London to tempt them into the "kaffir" market, ... [which] bills were then offered for discount in the City through the

199 See especially, Van Onselen, *The Cowboy Capitalist*, passim.

200 E. Fairfield to J. Chamberlain, 5 January 1896, as cited in Ethel Drus, "A Report on the Papers of Joseph Chamberlain relating to the Jameson Raid and the Inquiry," *Bulletin of the Institute of Historical Research* 25 (1952): 42.

201 *The Critic*, January 24, 1896.

202 Ibid., February 28, 1896.

203 Ibid., November 15, 1895.

204 *The Economist*, October 12, 1895.

205 *The Statist*, October 12, 1895.

banks and discount houses'.[206] However, 'the practice ran into disfavour in the City as bill brokers and discount houses discovered that the discount rate on foreign paper was rather low while the legality of paper, the drawer and acceptor of which resided abroad, was in doubt'.[207] Because the City then restricted its discounting operations of foreign bills, this obliged those same banks 'to call in money from the market, thereby also compelling borrowers to sell their … South African gold mining shares at any price'.[208] More broadly, this blow by London banks was particularly hard to absorb 'as it coincided with a large-scale remittance of French capital to Russia as part of a recent loan'.[209] The result was that the 'malaise on the Paris mining market quickly spread to London and later Johannesburg, where "kaffir" prices plummeted and the share bubble burst in spectacular fashion'.[210] No reckless gamble went unpunished. In Constantinople, the Ottoman Bank had to 'declare a month's moratorium on cash payments'.[211]

But had the mining share market bubble burst of its own accord, or had it been deliberately pricked? At first, *The Economist* merely voiced suspicion before backing off. 'It has been freely suggested that the "slump" has been greatly encouraged, if not actually engineered, by some of the big operators, who welcome in it an opportunity of purchasing sound, dividend-paying shares at "knock-out" prices', it recorded.

> That this influence, and the further influence of "bear" selling has not been entirely absent from the market is evident; but it is extremely doubtful whether the former influence has been at work to any considerable extent, for the leading insiders, while anxious enough to get rid of those weak speculators who so often give them trouble by selling at the wrong time, are aware that in forcing out undesirable operators it would be easy enough to bring the whole business to the ground like a house of

---

206 Jean-Jacques Van Helten, "Mining, share manias and speculation: British investments in overseas mining, 1880–1913," in *Capitalism in a Mature Economy: Financial Institutions, Capital Exports and British Industry, 1870–1939*, eds. Jean-Jacques Van Helten and Youssef Cassis (Aldershot: Edward Elgar Publishing, 1990), 172.

207 Ibid.

208 Ibid.

209 Ibid.

210 Ibid., 173.

211 Clay, "Imperial Ottoman Bank", 154. See also, André Autheman, *La Banque impériale ottomane* (Paris: Comité pour l'histoire économique et financière de la France, 1996), and Jonathan Conlin, *Mr Five Per Cent. The Many Lives of Calouste Gulbenkian. The World's Richest Man* (London: Profile Books, 2019), 48–50.

> cards. But the very possibility of a few wealthy and interested men being able to make the market or to break it should induce special caution on the part of the outside public.[212]

As the weeks passed, though, *The Economist's* tone changed. 'Another point which investors cannot afford to ignore is the direct and indirect control exercised by the leading financiers over the South African market', the paper warned at the end of October. 'The whole fabric of speculation is dependent upon a few capitalists ... [and] the fact that the business is practically at the mercy of inside cliques is not calculated to impress the public with its prospects of stability and permanence. The mining market is an essentially fickle institution at the best; it is, and must be in the nature of things, more or less under the control of those who possess inside information, and have the means of using it to their own advantage'.[213] Other journals sounded an equally sceptical note. What would happen, *The Statist* wondered, if investors generally 'got it into their heads ... that the leaders whom they have trusted have played with them, boomed the market until they got rid of their stocks, and then have broken the market to buy back cheaply?'[214]

The feeling that mining markets had been deliberately 'banged', that is, been subjected to a 'bear' attack early in October, hardened into conviction on the part of some commentators following the Jameson Raid at the end of December 1895. Prominent amongst those arguing that 'the rising in Johannesburg and the invitation to Jameson were all part of a concerted plot to depress the market', was A.J. Wilson, long-standing editor of *The Standard* and owner and publisher of *The Investor's Review*. Described by a contemporary scribe as 'the knight, without fear or reproach of City Editors',[215] Wilson was 'a financial editor of great integrity' who had passed up a fortune by not taking advantage of prior information that Disraeli's government 'intended to buy shares in the Suez Canal company'.[216] He was supported by Sir William Harcourt, Leader of the Liberal Opposition in the House of Commons. Addressing the House in May 1896, Harcourt described the Raid as 'a sordid and squalid picture of stockjobbing Imperialism ... The very lingo is the language of the company promoter, and you might think you were reading the prospectus of a set of croupiers [Laughter and Opposition cheers]. You read about a "flotation" that

212 *The Economist*, October 12, 1895.
213 Ibid., October 26, 1895.
214 *The Statist*, October 19, 1895.
215 James Milne, *A Window in Fleet Street* (London: John Murray, 1931), 35–36.
216 Edwards, *Pursuit of Reason*, 404.

is the word for an armed insurrection; a flotation of the "new company", the "shareholders' meeting", [and so on]'.[217]

None of this commended itself to *The Fortnightly Review*. Defending Rhodes at length in June 1896, 'Imperialist', who many at the time suspected was the editor himself, the Reverend John Verschoyle,[218] strongly objected to the 'suspicion ... sedulously fostered by the pro-Boer organs in the press that the big financiers not only intended to seize the revenues of the Rand and so rehabilitate the Chartered Company, but that they actually sold huge "bears" of the shares of the mines with the knowledge that the rising they were pushing on would, when it came, cause a collapse of prices'. Many people were inclined to believe this version of events because they had been expecting 'a recovery [in share prices] and were hit by this unexpected fall [following the Raid's failure]'. This in turn led them to make the 'extraordinary jump from the cypher telegrams, because, I suppose, they are couched in the terms of mining codes, to the conclusion that this was a mere financial conspiracy'. This attitude seemed to 'Imperialist' to be 'absolutely unjustified and irrational'.[219]

'If it were indeed true that Mr. Beit or his firm had speculated heavily for a fall which they were assisting to bring about by the aid and encouragement they gave to the Reform party in Johannesburg', the article continued, 'then no words would be strong enough for their condemnation' 'But ... [has] this grave charge ... any basis of fact whatsoever?'. 'Imperialist' thought not. Wernher, Beit & Company, he declared, 'might have made millions by floating untried companies, [yet] it was a matter of common knowledge in Johannesburg that they did nothing of the kind. The credit of their name, as the first firm on the Rand, the most careful to test a property before taking it up, was maintained with scrupulous care; while other capitalists were hurrying out untried properties and sweeping in the profits'. But this was not evidence, 'Imperialist' acknowledged, 'so I can only say, let them [Wernher, Beit & Company] be challenged to permit an audit [of their books], by absolutely first-class auditors, of their transactions ... and let the public know the result'. 'All this talk of a financial plot, a stock-jobbing speculation', he concluded, 'is very wide of the mark'.[220]

217 Sir William Harcourt, May 8, 1896, in 40 *House of Commons, Parliamentary Debates, (4th series)*, col. 889.

218 See especially, Esther Rhoads Houghton, "John Verschoyle and the 'Fortnightly Review.'" *Victorian Periodicals Newsletter* 1, no. 3 (1968): 17–21.

219 "Imperialist", "The Plain Truth about Mr. Rhodes and the Transvaal", *Fortnightly Review* 354, June 1, 1896, 852–53.

220 Ibid., 853.

Something of an innocent abroad when it came to the Southern African mining market, 'Imperialist's intervention seems not to have shifted public opinion. It remained divided, especially after Henry Labouchere joined the fray. Admired for his wit, but disliked in his capacity as editor of *Truth*, a newspaper seen variously as fearless or muck-raking, and dismissed by many of his peers as obsessed with the alleged iniquities of Cecil Rhodes and the Chartered Company, Labouchere struggled to be taken seriously in the Commons. In January 1896, *Truth* had already claimed that 'recent disclosures point distinctly to A WIDESPREAD FINANCIAL CONSPIRACY which had been in progress for some time, both in London and South Africa',[221] and in February Labouchere had unsuccessfully called for a 'much wider inquiry into the [British South Africa] Company's financial and political history than that for which the Government was prepared'.[222] Now his opening remarks were jeered by both sides of the House. Laughter and cheers followed his insistence that for 'the last two or three years exceedingly shady financiers had carried on a gambling establishment [in Rhodesia] with the Union Jack flying over it … this Chartered company was one of the most disgraceful and scandalous companies that ever existed'.[223]

Undeterred by the mockery, Labouchere persisted. Tying the Jameson Raid to the Chartered Company's declining fortunes north of the Limpopo River, he argued that 'when those gentlemen found there was no gold to be had in Matabeleland, and that the prices of the shares they still held must be kept up, they resolved that something must be done. They cast their eyes on the Transvaal'. When that particular sally was also greeted with laughter, he proceeded to ask how Rhodes gained by the conspiracy. 'There was no gold in Mashonaland, but there was a great deal in many parts of the Transvaal, and the object of the conspiracy was to … [get] hold of those parts where there was gold and annex them to the Chartered land. … The Chartered Company's shares would have gone up enormously and Mr. Rhodes and his confederates would have reaped a large profit'.

Certain that an official investigation would prove that Beit and Rhodes' confidential agent, later secretary of the British South Africa Company, Rutherfoord

221 *Truth*, January 16, 1896.

222 Hind, *Henry Labouchere and the Empire*, 24. See also, Herbert Sidebotham, revised by H. Matthew, "Labouchere, Henry Du Pré (1831–1912), Journalist and Politician," *Oxford Dictionary of National Biography*, 2004.

223 Hesketh Pearson, *Labby. The Life and Character of Henry Labouchere* (London: Harper & Brothers, 1936), 276.

FIGURE 10
Henry Labouchere
SOURCE: NATIONAL PORTRAIT GALLERY, LONDON, ELLIOTT & FRY EXHIBITION PRINTS, 1863–1930.

Harris, 'and several other gentlemen of that kidney met together in the City', Labouchere claimed that the London conspirators determined that,

> although they might eventually gain by laying hold of this portion of the Transvaal, undoubtedly the first effect of a raid there would be … a heavy fall in all the shares of the South African market. They therefore confederated together and employed a gentleman to sell for them – what was called in the City an enormous "bear" in these securities, in order that they might gain. But there was a little coldness among these gentlemen themselves because although they had all agreed to sell on a joint account, it was found that the worthy Dr. Rutherfoord Harris had anticipated them and quietly effected a little sale of 10,000 shares for himself before the fall. Why, there was not even honour among thieves!.[224]

Despite or because of these sentiments, Labouchere was appointed by the Colonial Secretary, Joseph Chamberlain, to the Parliamentary Select

224 H. Labouchere, May 8, 1896, in *House of Commons, Parliamentary Debates* 40 (4th series), col. 895. See also, *Truth*, May 7, 1896.

Committee on British South Africa. This was done over the objections of *The Times* to Labouchere's perceived anti- British South Africa Company bias, but was welcomed by other Rhodes supporters for precisely the same reason. 'The fact of Labby being on the Committee may do good', conceded Albert Grey, 'particularly if he devotes his energies to showing up the financial swindles wh[ich]. he alleges'.[225] 'Labouchere, who was a greedy man, always alleged that Rhodes planned the Jameson Raid for money-making purposes', recalled Lloyd George some twenty years after the event. 'I did not and do not believe that for a moment. Rhodes had gone beyond money. He wanted power for himself and England. But Labby would never believe it. He was always harping on the value of shares'.[226] Established to report on the Jameson Raid and the British South Africa Company's sphere of operations, the Committee sat between February and July 1897, and for all his efforts, Labouchere found himself stymied at every turn. In large measure this was due to the determination of what Sir Graham Bower called 'a packed and dishonest body' to work within the narrowest possible political remit in order to exonerate Chamberlain of complicity.[227] This object could only be achieved by not provoking Rhodes into fully disclosing who knew what and when. But it also turned on Labouchere's failure to persuade other members of the committee to examine the Company's financial dealings.

Nor was Labouchere able to land a telling blow on any of the key witnesses. Rhodes, Beit and Harris all brushed his efforts aside. Repeated attacks in *Truth* tried to bounce leading figures associated with the Chartered Company into starting legal proceedings 'in the course of which … [Labouchere] might secure evidence not otherwise obtainable'.[228] In June 1896 Labouchere went so far as to claim that 'the men who planned the Jameson raid also broke the market a few months before this unfortunate and mischievous enterprise was undertaken. We are also fully aware that these men had effected heavy "bear" sales after getting out of the bulk of their own holdings; and we know that the political grievances of the Uitlanders were only a pretence for the famous "flotation" enterprise, which ended so disastrously for British interests, and for the mining industry in the Transvaal'.[229]

225 Grey to Chamberlain, December 10, 1896, as cited in Butler, *Liberal Party*, 114.

226 Lord Riddell, *More Pages From My Diary 1908–1914* (London: Country Life, 1934), 144. *Conversation*, April 27, 1913.

227 Deryck Schreuder and Jeffrey Butler (eds), *Sir Graham Bower's Secret History of the Jameson Raid and the South African Crisis, 1895–1902* (Cape Town: Van Riebeeck Society, 2002), 124.

228 Hind, *Henry Labouchere and the Empire*, 24.

229 *Truth*, June 11, 1896.

Despite this provocation, however, Labouchere's intended victims ignored him. Indeed, the newspaper attacks backfired when Harris and Beit demanded in Committee that Labouchere either prove the allegations subsequently made under the protection of Parliamentary privilege or withdraw them.[230] Believing that he could rely on the testimony of 'a number of stockbrokers', Labouchere was initially confident that the charges would stick. Writing in a Belgian paper, *Gaulois*, Labouchere claimed that 'investigation has proved that the prime movers in this conspiracy were persons who had already fleeced the investing public by the promotion of companies almost all of which are over capitalised, and many of which are absolutely rotten, and that the alleged grievances of the "Uitlanders" in the Transvaal were only a pretext to enable these marauders still further to rob the investing public'. And when Harris, whom the famous *Times* correspondent, G.E. Morrison, thought 'a somewhat vulgar bounder',[231] under oath objected to these remarks, Labouchere thought that he had been given an opening at last to pursue the broader question of company speculation and fraud. 'Perfectly [so]', he informed the Select Committee. 'That has been my contention all along; and if we are prepared to go into the question of these sub-companies which have been brought out by these gentlemen, I shall be prepared to prove it with pleasure. I ask for nothing better'.[232]

Instead, Labouchere found himself censured for commenting on the case while the Select Committee was still sitting. Despite persistent rumours in the City that Harris had 'sold a very heavy bear of all Kaffir stocks, and consequently reaped a rich harvest, thanks to the panic which ensued [after the Jameson Raid]',[233] Labouchere's Stock Exchange informant refused to testify. In a letter read out in Committee, Labouchere unreservedly withdrew the allegation made against Harris. He insisted, however, that he would not have made so 'definite and specific a charge without being himself convinced that he had evidence to substantiate it'.

230 Hind, *Henry Labouchere and the Empire*, 24–25.

231 Diary of George Ernest Morrison, as cited in Davenport-Hines and Van Helten, "Edgar Vincent, Viscount D'Abernon," 54. See also, Robert Blake, *A History of Rhodesia* (London: Methuen, 1977), 57: '[Rutherfoord Harris] A born gas-bag, he talked incessantly and too much. He was unstable, impetuous, and anything but straight-forward. His part in the Jameson Raid was very shady'.

232 May 21, 1897, Evidence of Mr. Rutherfoord Harris, Second Report from the Select Committee on British South Africa; together with the Proceedings of the Committee, and Minutes of Evidence (London, House of Commons, July 13, 1897).

233 "Dr Rutherfoord Harris. What is he doing in Japan?." *The Rialto*, December 29, 1904.

FIGURE 11
Rutherfoord Harris
SOURCE: HUGH MARSHALL HOLE, *THE JAMESON RAID* (LONDON: PHILIP ALLAN, 1930), BETWEEN PP. 8–9.

I was given by a gentleman of high position and large business experience', he continued, '... the statement, together with the evidence on which it was based. I closely scrutinized this evidence, and carefully discussed the matter with my informant, and I came to the conclusion that the evidence was ample. I asked him whether I could make the statement public, and he said that I could. I therefore did so, believing that, if denied, it would be substantiated by the witness that he named. I find, however, that he objects to coming forward himself as a witness or to my calling the persons whose names he mentioned, because, on consideration, he is of opinion that he might be blamed for disclosing to me what he might be held to have learnt himself in confidence. ... There was unquestionably heavy selling of South African securities before the raid. But, beyond this statement in regard to the syndicate, I have no sort of evidence that Mr. Harris was a party to these sales.[234]

234 May 25, 1897, letter from Labouchere to William Jackson, Committee Chairman, Second Report from the Select Committee on British South Africa.

In the same letter, Labouchere conceded that he had never heard Beit's name mentioned in connection with the syndicate.[235]

Beit's own appearance before the Select Committee three days later was decidedly anticlimactic. Rhodes and Phillips had earlier emerged unscathed from questions about share market manipulation. Pressed by Labouchere about the extent of his Chartered holdings, Rhodes' answers had been vague in the extreme. Asked 'if the raid had succeeded, would it, in your opinion, have increased the value of the shares of the Chartered Company?', Rhodes, not surprisingly, answered: 'No, I do not think so'. He dealt equally brusquely with the next and last question. 'Then, that was not one of your objects in promoting the revolution?' 'Certainly not'.[236] 'Everyone paid the most extravagant deference to Rhodes', remembered Frank Harris, 'a deference which often called forth from him expressions of amused contempt'.[237] Invited by his own legal representative to state his opinion 'as to whether this insurrection was … really promoted and occasioned by the sordid schemes of financiers?', Phillips too had no difficulty in replying, 'Well, there was no sordid scheme whatsoever'.[238]

Although nervous about confronting Labouchere, author of the scurrilous column 'Moses Moss of Johannesburg to Benjamin Boss, London', published in *Truth*,[239] Beit prevailed on the day with a little help from his friends. Asked by the Committee chairman, William Lawies Jackson, 'if his action was prompted by monetary considerations', Beit vehemently denied it, admitting to only two small Chartered Company share transactions in the second half of 1895.[240] When Labouchere attempted to question Beit about Rand Mines Ltd and share market profits, he was stopped by the Committee chairman because he was 're-opening the case which you have, yourself, by letter withdrawn', this despite Beit having referred to the same charges when demanding that they be withdrawn.[241] A thoroughly misleading answer by Beit to a pointed question about the attitude of the mining industry towards the respective mining laws of the

235 Ibid. For Hess' exposure of Labouchere's own stock-jobbing transactions, see *Supplement to The African Critic*, October 2, 1897.

236 February 23, 1897, Evidence of Right Hon. C.J. Rhodes, *Second Report from the Select Committee on British South Africa*. See especially, Felix Gross, *Rhodes of Africa* (London: Cassel, 1956), 348–49, and "Mr Rhodes on Rand Taxation." *The Economist*, March 6, 1897.

237 Frank Harris, *Frank Harris. His Life and Adventures. An Autobiography* (London: Richards Press 1947), 499.

238 May 4, 1897, Evidence of Mr. Lionel Phillips, Second Report from the Select Committee on British South Africa.

239 Emden, *Randlords*, 165.

240 May 28 1897, Evidence of Mr. Alfred Beit, Second Report from the Select Committee on British South Africa.

241 Ibid.

Transvaal and the British South Africa Company was accepted at face value by Harcourt. 'I am sorry to say these are matters I know little about', he said, 'and I do not desire to know more; but I will take your opinion, which of course will have great weight with the people of Johannesburg, that they would willingly adopt the Chartered Company's mining regulations in place of those which are now in force in the Transvaal'.[242] Recalled the next day, Beit read out a prepared statement. 'Mr. Labouchere has charged me with breaking the market; with effecting bear sales before the raid, and generally with having been a party to the planning it for market purposes, using the Uitlanders' grievances as a pretence. I declare again upon oath that these charges are absolutely false'.[243] Secure in the knowledge that a significant part of Wernher, Beit & Company's share market transactions were untraceable, Beit 'offered to give the Committee access to the books of my firm to verify my statement. Mr. Labouchere has not asked me a single question in relation to these charges, nor has he, to my knowledge, offered one atom of evidence in support of his allegations'.[244]

Without support from other members of the Select Committee, Labouchere's only recourse was to propose an alternative draft to the one put forward by the Committee chairman. At the very least, Labouchere wanted the final report to reflect the fact that the Committee's self-imposed limitations had precluded from investigation the possibility that the Jameson Raid had been underpinned by stock exchange speculation. 'This can only be discovered by an investigation of the allotment, and the transfer books of the Company, which must show what these allotments were, and at what periods these sales, if any took place', he argued. 'Into this branch of the inquiry your Committee have not yet entered; indeed, it decided that so long as the raid alone was under investigation no questions might be asked the directors of the Company as to the mode in which they acquired their shares, or as to their dealings in them, except during the six months preceding the raid. It cannot, therefore, at present express an opinion in regard to this matter'.[245]

The still bigger question, thought Labouchere, was 'the exact object sought to be gained by the Chartered Company and those financially connected with it, if the plan had succeeded ... As directors, [Beit and Rhodes] ... can hardly be supposed not to have perceived that, in using its forces to invade the Transvaal,

242 Ibid.

243 June 1, 1897, Beit re-called and further examined, *Second Report from the Select Committee on British South Africa*.

244 Ibid. See also, George Seymour Fort, *Alfred Beit. A Study of the Man and his Work* (London: Ivor Nicholson & Watson 1932), 148–152.

245 Draft Report, proposed by Mr. Labouchere, *Second Report from the Select Committee on British South Africa*.

... [they] were incurring large monetary risks. It is difficult to imagine that they would have allowed these risks to be incurred without the expectation of prospective profit if their plan had succeeded ... The evidence as yet submitted to your Committee throws no light upon this matter'.[246] None of this was accepted. Labouchere's draft was turned down by ten votes to one, his own. Instead, the final report asserted that while 'suggestions have been made by questions to witnesses and otherwise that certain persons who were intimately connected with this matter ... embarked in the proceedings which culminated in the Raid from motives of self-interest of the meanest kind, in fact for stock-jobbing purposes', your Committee ... hold that the charge is entirely without foundation'.[247]

Neither the unedifying spectacle of Chamberlain dismissing 'absolutely these charges which affect ... [Rhodes'] personal honour' during a Commons debate on the Committee's findings,[248] nor the report itself commended themselves to discerning contemporaries. In the public mind, some of the conspirators would always be associated with shady, self-interested stock market deals. Chamberlain himself in private correspondence was under no illusions, describing Johannesburg's mining magnates as 'a lot of cowardly selfish blatant speculators who would sell their souls to have the power of rigging the market'.[249] For once, though, South African politicians had been ahead of the curve. As far back as December 1894, John X. Merriman, later prime minister of the Cape Colony, had asked a colleague what he thought of Labouchere 'on the genesis of the Chartered Co.? He is a horrid fellow but there is a damnable substratum of truth in much that he says'.[250] In an open letter to Rhodes published some ten months before the Jameson Raid, Henry Hess of *The Critic* had reminded the 'Dreamer of Empires and Creator of Territories, you forget in the pride of your might, in the power of your wealth and influence, that right is right and wrong no man's right. ... Charterland, an unpayable frost, so far, with nothing but deficiencies and increased debentures. ... The modern Napoleon!

246 Ibid.

247 Draft Report, proposed by the Chairman, *Second Report from the Select Committee on British South Africa.*

248 Chamberlain, 26 July, 1897, *House of Commons, Parliamentary Debates* 51 (4th Series), col. 1170.

249 Chamberlain to Selborne, April 5, 1896, as cited in Ronald Robinson, John Gallagher and Alice Denny, *Africa and the Victorians: The Official Mind of Imperialism* (London: Macmillan 1961), 432.

250 Merriman to J. Currey, December 15, 1894, in Phyllis Lewsen (ed.), *Selections from the Correspondence of John X. Merriman 1890–1898* (Cape Town: The Van Riebeek Society, 1963), 168.

FIGURE 12
Joseph Chamberlain
SOURCE: NATIONAL PORTRAIT GALLERY, LONDON, THE MARTIN PLAUT ALBUM: PHOTOGRAPHS OF PROMINENT PEOPLE AND EVENTS BY VARIOUS PHOTOGRAPHERS, 1880S-1911.

Let us hope there is no St. Helena in store for you in the future or – Robben Island. What a fate! To dream of Empires and to die on a rock or sand bank'![251]

If the prime minister of the day, Lord Salisbury, could not make up his mind whether Rhodes was "a charlatan or a patriot",[252] others were in no doubt. Refusing to see Rhodes as a patriot, Philip Stanhope, the Liberal Member of Parliament for Burnley, referred instead to 'what he might call a *fin de siècle* patriotism, which had its nursery on the Stock Exchange'.[253] When he was Chancellor of the Exchequer, Sir Michael Hicks-Beach would not do business with Rhodes. 'I have seen enough of the men who control the [B.S.A.] Company and their methods, from Mr. Rhodes downwards, to mistrust them utterly'.[254]

Rhodes, Mark Twain marveled, 'raids and robs and slays and enslaves the Matabele and gets worlds of Charter-Christian applause for it. He has beguiled

251 "Open Letter. To the Right Hon. Cecil John Rhodes." *The Critic*, March 1, 1895.

252 Henry Paulet, Marquess of Winchester, *Statesmen, Financiers and Felons* (Abbeville: Imprimerie F. Paillart 1935), 169.

253 P. Stanhope, July 26, 1897, *House of Commons, Parliamentary Debates* 51 (4th Series), col. 1098.

254 Hicks-Beach to Chamberlain, April 18, 1899, as cited in James Garvin, *The Life of Joseph Chamberlain. Volume Three 1895–1900. Empire and World Policy* (London: Macmillan, 1934), 386.

England into buying Charter waste-paper for Bank of England notes, ton for ton, and the ravished still burn incense to him as the Eventual God of Plenty. … I admire him, I frankly confess it; and when his time comes, I shall buy a piece of the rope for a keepsake'.[255]

'Now that the report of the South African Committee has been issued', pronounced *The Economist,* 'it must be confessed that the conclusion of the Committee's proceedings, like the proceedings themselves, are extremely unsatisfactory. The report cannot be said to deal adequately with facts put in evidence, and it shrinks from driving home to their logical and inevitable conclusions many of the most important findings'. Even admitting for the sake of argument that 'Mr. Rhodes' services may be set-off against his injuries to the Empire, such a defense cannot shelter his associates. No one can pretend that Mr. Beit and his brother capitalists engaged in the "Jameson plan" in order to further the interests of the British Empire. They, at any rate, engaged in the conspiracy in order that their own private interests might be advanced'. 'The fact … that the ineptitude, prolixity, and timidity of the South African Committee has been marked with disgust by the public cannot be denied'.[256] As *The Fortnightly Review* declared some years later, and after Verschoyle had relinquished the editorship, 'every Englishman in his heart was ashamed of that enterprise, with its nauseating flavor of stock-jobbery'.[257]

Beit never quite managed to cast off the lingering suspicion that he had master-minded the collapse of the share market. In June 1896, Chamberlain was informed of a letter from Rhodes to Beit dated the previous August which 'merely related to their rigging the share market'. It had occasioned no comment because 'there was nothing political in the letter so far as I was shown it'.[258] Knowledge not only of looming trouble in Johannesburg but also of some kind of armed intervention was widespread in the City in the dying days of 1895. A week before Christmas, Rochfort Maguire, 'the only one to whom in 1895 Rhodes gave his full confidence',[259] told Edward Fairfield, an official in the Colonial Office, that 'South African values have now reached a (downward) point at which it is thought by the best authorities in the City that the news of a row can have no other than a favourable effect'.[260] When news reached

255 Mark Twain, *More Tramps Abroad* (London: Chatto & Windus, 1897), 483.

256 *The Economist*, July 17, 1897.

257 Diplomaticus, "The 'New Situation' in South Africa." *Fortnightly Review*, July 1, 1899.

258 University of Birmingham Library, Joseph Chamberlain Papers, Letters and Correspondence, Colonial Office, JC 10/1/89, Fairfield to Chamberlain, June 7, 1896.

259 Emden, *Randlords*, 311.

260 Fairfield to Chamberlain, December 19, 1895, as cited in Garvin, *Life of Joseph Chamberlain*, 73.

London some days later that Johannesburg was having second thoughts about an armed insurrection, elements in the City were among the first to hear it. 'I met Hawksley, the Company's solicitor, last night', reported Fairfield, 'who said that he and his friends were being much chaffed in the City about the "fizzle" of their revolution. He seemed to think that Rhodes ... might be driven into an attitude of frenzy and unreason, and order Dr. Jameson to "go in" from Gaberones [in the Bechuanaland Protectorate] with the Company's police and manipulate a revolution, but Maguire, who has just been here, says that this is absurd. The general opinion in the City is that Kruger will now make the necessary reforms'.[261]

Somewhere behind it all lurked Beit, or so his critics believed. According to the details of a conversation in December 1896 between W.P. Schreiner, formerly Attorney-General in Rhodes' Cape Colony Cabinet, and Percy FitzPatrick, then head of Eckstein's Intelligence Department, Schreiner had been advised by an informed source that Beit and Rhodes had indeed 'banged' the market in 1895. 'I have been told lately', confided Schreiner, 'on what I regard as excellent authority, that Rhodes, through and in co-operation with Beit, practically doubled his fortune by huge [speculative share] operations in all parts of the world, timed to mature with the Movement [the Jameson Raid]. Now, if Rhodes has made a couple of millions out of it, the thing has a very ugly look – gaming with men's lives and the fate of a country; and I should have to re-cast my whole estimate of the man. ... Mind you I did not know this at the time of the Enquiry [the Cape Government's Enquiry into the Jameson Raid]; and I am glad of it, because I could not have said what I did had I heard this of him'.[262]

Overall, concluded Schreiner, 'the evidence given me was such that – well, if I were a judge, I *wouldn't hang* [emphasis in the original] a man on it, but ...!'. Shrugging his shoulders and raising his eyebrows 'in an unmistakable way', as FitzPatrick recounted the meeting to Beit, Schreiner added that 'if at the [Select Committee] Inquiry Rhodes and Beit face that point and offer to produce such evidence as they can and, if they rebut any that is brought against them, I shall feel that is an immense load off my mind. Because, with the resources of modern detectives and the ability and vindictiveness of Labouchere (and

261 Fairfield to Chamberlain, December 28, 1895, as cited in Garvin, *Life of Joseph Chamberlain*, 81. For a different interpretation of these events to the one presented here, see Jean van der Poel, *The Jameson Raid*(Cape Town: Oxford University Press, 1951), 80–84.

262 U[niversity of] C[ape] T[own] Library, W.P. Schreiner Papers, BC 317, File 7(4)(i), extract of letter from Percy FitzPatrick to Alfred Beit, Cape Town, December 10, 1896.

FIGURE 13
Alfred Beit (in London, 1894)
SOURCE: L. PHILLIPS, *SOME REMINISCENCES* (LONDON: HUTCHINSON & CO., 1924), BETWEEN PP. 88–89.

another whom I forget), something should be elicited if there is anything to be elicited'.[263]

But if Beit had indeed been the conduit through whom 'huge operations' were channeled, any damning evidence was safely hidden in the books of Hirsch & Co. and other proxies employed by the firm of Wernher, Beit & Company. Had Labouchere actually gained access to the share registers he wanted to examine, it is unlikely that he would have found anything to implicate Beit or Rhodes. As he did several months later when appearing before the Select Committee, Beit vehemently denied any wrongdoing. In March 1897, he invited Schreiner to a meeting in order 'to have an opportunity of proving that you have been misinformed'.[264] Although Beit claimed to be 'in a position to convince you absolutely',[265] Schreiner refused to meet. At the same time, he

263 Q3 A/LC, FitzPatrick to Beit, December 10, 1896 in Andrew Duminy and William Guest (eds), *FitzPatrick. South African Politician. Selected Papers, 1888–1906* (Johannesburg: McGraw-Hill Book Company, 1976), 70. This appears to be the full version of the letter cited above.

264 UCT Library, Schreiner Papers, BC 317 File 7, 4(iii), Beit to Schreiner, March 9, 1897.

265 Ibid.

also turned down a further request from Beit that he raise the matter when giving evidence to the Select Committee, 'decline [ing] to be the medium for giving publicity to any information the accuracy of which I am not personally able to substantiate'.[266] A challenge from Labouchere to bring a court action against him so that he could justify his allegations that Rhodes and Beit were motivated by 'stockjobbing' considerations was not taken up.[267]

The suspicions that swirled around Beit, periodically resurfacing from the murky depths of the Stock Exchange and voiced in Parliament, 'Wernher, Beit & Company nothing more or less than a common gang of thieves and swindlers',[268] were all the greater because of what was known at the time about the mining market's control and structure. Well before the end of the so-called 'Kaffir boom', *The Economist* had warned its readers that 'the market for the shares and the management of the mines are entirely in the hands of groups, and that these groups wield an influence that places this mining market in a position very similar to that occupied by the American market during the worst stages of its history'. Control, the periodical explained,

> makes itself evident in every case, and asserts itself everywhere; and every one of the abuses that have brought disrepute upon so many speculative American stocks is repeated here, nay, often improved upon, since the comparatively small capital of most companies makes manipulation easy – makes doubtful practices almost suggest themselves. True, there are one or two groups who often exercise their power to their own credit, and for the good of the shareholders. But control is always shifting, and "interests" are changing, and they that are safe to-day may to-morrow be brought face to face with an amalgamation or a reconstruction due to a change of control. And, sad to record though it is, most groups use their power for their own purposes. Hence the frequent occurrence and recurrence of dishonest acquisitions, and last, not least, of those market manipulations and maneuvers which, though for the present they result in high prices, are sure to lead ultimately to that collapse which is an essential part of the game.[269]

---

266 Ibid., Schreiner to Beit, March 11, 1897.

267 Labouchere, July 26, 1897, *House of Commons, Parliamentary Debates* 51 (4th Series), col. 1157.

268 V. Markham, March 19, 1901, *House of Commons, Parliamentary Debates* 51 (4th Series), cols. 453–55. See especially, Sir Edward Clarke, *The Story of My Life* (London: J. Murray, 1918), 329–31.

269 *The Economist*, July 6, 1895.

For the present, concluded *The Economist*, the controlling groups 'use their power chiefly to inflate or support values – an easy task with such an artificial market. If we deduct the shares held by those in control, and the number held more or less firmly by investors, but a small number is left to constitute the "market", and by slightly reducing or increasing this number, prices may be moved at will in either direction'.[270]

What *The Economist* identified as the 'direct and indirect control exercised by the leading financiers over the South African market' largely turned on the way in which the gold mining industry's capital was structured.[271] At its very core were vendors' shares. These were the shares allotted at par, usually £1, to the promoters and their associates of a particular mining company. More often than not, vendors 'obtained special privileges through taking up founders shares which entitled them to a percentage of the profits. They would also contribute some working capital by taking up additional shares at par. The remainder … were then offered to the public at prices well and sometimes incredibly above par. They also released a trickle of their cheaply obtained shares when the market was on the rise; and they pooled their shares in syndicates to better manipulate it'.[272] The number of shares offered to investors, warned *The Economist*, was 'a mere fraction of the nominal capital', that is, the amount specified in any given company's memorandum of association, the vendors 'in most cases taking the bulk of the share capital'.[273] As Table 3.2 below reveals for leading deep-level mining companies in 1894, in every case the vendors took most of the issued capital.

'That, unfortunately, is not an exceptional state of things in mining ventures', noted *The Economist*, 'but the peculiarity about these deep-level companies is, that the promoters and vendors have been able, by the process known as "making a market" to dispose of very large proportions of their holdings'.[274] In some cases, the periodical continued, 'the market has been worked so successfully that very large profits have been made'.

> To take the most flagrant case, that of the Rand Mines (Limited). This company has for its directors Messrs. Julius Wernher, Alfred Beit, Max Michaelis, Lionel Phillips, Charles Rudd, Harry Mosenthal, and Sigismund Neumann, most of these gentlemen having a very close connection with several of the rand mines and with the Rhodes-Rudd series of

270 Ibid. For the most important Groups and the companies they controlled, see Appendix B.
271 Ibid., October 26, 1895.
272 Kubicek, "Finance Capital and South African Goldmining," 387.
273 *The Economist*, December 28, 1895.
274 Ibid., March 10, 1894.

TABLE 2 Deep-level companies 1894: Issued capital and purchase price

Company	Issued capital £	Purchase price £
Consolidated Deep Levels	187,250	155,000
East Rand Proprietary	570,000	420,000
Geldenhuis Deep	285,000	175,000
Henry Nourse Deep	125,000	108,000
May Deep-Level	146,000	100,000
Rand Mines	330,000	330,000
Rand Deep-Level	250,000	194,150

SOURCE: *THE ECONOMIST*, MARCH 10, 1894.

> companies. The shares were introduced on to the London market at £5, that is, at 400 per cent. premium, and this week they were at one time worked up to £8 ¾, representing a valuation of close upon three millions sterling for the property. Nor is this all. The vendors appear to have taken the whole of the issued capital as their purchase consideration, and for the two offshoots already floated, shares have been accepted as payment. The working capital is to be provided by an issue of debentures, and rumour has it that this issue is to be of no less than £1,000,000.[275]

'This is certainly a novel system of mining finance', snorted *The Economist*, 'and its novelty will scarcely appeal to prudent investors'.[276]

At the same time, leading mining groups were careful not to increase the issued capital of the profitable producing mines. Of the 27 companies which paid dividends in 1895, 22 had retained their original issued capital of less than £200,000 each. The significance of this was that the small capitalisation 'enabled the groups to control and manipulate the shares, and produce spectacular dividends of 50% to 200% p.a. on par values. These glittering dividends seduced thousands of newcomers to mining investment, unable or unwilling to think in terms of effective yield on market value, after amortisation'.[277] By contrast, the capital of so-called 'fringe' companies was repeatedly reconstructed,

275 Ibid.
276 Ibid.
277 McCarty, "British Investment in Overseas Mining," 87–88.

invariably to the advantage of insiders. In 1894 some 50 such companies were reconstructed 190 times, 'so that on an average every one of these Companies had reorganized its capital nearly four times'.[278] 'The conditions under which reconstructions, often entirely unnecessary, have been arranged', thought *The Economist,* 'can scarcely be too strenuously reprobated'.[279] These and other dubious financial practices were made all the easier because most mining companies were registered in Johannesburg and not London. 'This meant they were freed from the necessity of giving a reckoning to shareholders, but it also meant they failed to meet requirements to be dealt with on official exchanges. Few of the mining companies were given official quotations and little was done to provide for carry-overs and settlements. In the absence of formal mechanisms for selling shares, the Randlords developed their own techniques, the general effect of which was to make many of them speculators in their own right who made and unmade markets with impunity'.[280]

Writing for *The Nineteenth Century* on the very eve of the mining boom's collapse, S.F. Van Oss, an exceptionally well-connected City observer, quoted a leading financier as saying that 'among the many ways of making money on the Rand, four are pre-eminent: flotation, amalgamation, reconstruction, and liquidation'. Van Oss, however, thought otherwise. Like *The Economist's* special correspondent, he understood that 'to "make money" on the Rand you require control', of which the 'most important side ... consists of its relations to the Stock Exchange'.[281] Noting that 'smallness of [nominal] capital is a feature of almost every one of the South African companies', rarely exceeding £150,000, Van Oss estimated that as c. 50,000 shares were usually held 'more or less firmly by investors', leaving a market supply of only 20,000 shares, a pool of 80,000 £1 shares was more than sufficient. 'The small market supply renders manipulation easy', he explained.

> By gradually diminishing it, prices can easily be rushed up to a height far exceeding intrinsic merits; and those at all acquainted with Stock Exchanges will know that, under such conditions, it is quite feasible for a powerful group to maintain artificially a high level of prices while a process of "unloading" is going on. At present this is done on a vast scale. Huge profits must of course result from such manipulations; and their

278 Emden, *Randlords*, 352, 241.

279 *The Economist*, October 26, 1895.

280 Kubicek, "Randlords in 1895," 86–87. See especially, "Kaffir Capital and Control." *Financial Times*, September 21, 1898.

281 Van Oss, "The Gold-Mining Madness in the City," 544.

> worst side is that, in spite of the sale of shares on a large scale, control remains where it was before, so that, in theory, the manipulators when they have sold their holdings still have it in their power to take such steps as will enable them to repurchase cheaply the same shares they have sold dearly. … determined "bears" can send it [the market] down almost at will.[282]

'A *hausse*', Van Oss concluded, 'is a voracious animal; it must be fed by a constant stream of good news. A *baisse* derives support even from mere neutral conditions. But yonder in South Africa there are plenty of people who can conjure up a long string of disappointment and disaster to force on a debacle as soon as they think the time for it has come'.[283]

The combined effect of a highly leveraged capital structure and the restricted nature of mining markets where the best shares were mostly retained by groups or the syndicates they controlled,[284] was the creation of a speculative arena extremely sensitive to intervention and direction. But as the boom intensified during 1895, the ensuing flood of 'jobbers, speculators, promotors and brokers … onto the market … seriously limited the ability of the major mining finance houses like Consolidated Gold Fields, Wernher, Beit and Company, the General Mining and Finance Corporation and Barnato's Johannesburg Consolidated Investment Company to influence market behaviour'.[285] In June 1895, Wernher complained to Ecksteins in Johannesburg that the market had become 'so big and so cosmopolitan that it becomes more hopeless than ever to prophesy'.[286] The following month, Wernher, Beit & Company wound up the Porges- Kann syndicate which had been operating on its behalf and that of N.M. Rothschild and Sons on the London Stock Exchange.[287]

282 Ibid., 545.

283 Ibid., 546.

284 Kubicek, "Randlords in 1895," 88; and his, "Finance Capital," 388. See also, Fraser and Jeeves, *All That Glittered*, 6–7: 'At the time of a flotation, mining claims and other assets were valued by the developers and transferred to the new company in return for shares. This represented the vendor's interest and it frequently led to the overvaluing of assets and to the watering of stock. Large-scale insider trading was another major source of profit for the developers. In short, the capital of many mining companies was "leveraged" and subject to easy manipulation by the industry controllers'.

285 Van Helten, "Mining, share manias and speculation," 173.

286 Wernher to Eckstein & Co., June 15, 1895, as cited in Kubicek, *Economic Imperialism in Theory and Practice*, 67.

287 Van Helten, "British and European Economic Investment in the Transvaal: With Specific Reference to the Witwatersrand Gold Fields and District, 1886–1910". PhD diss. University of London, 1981, 123.

This act of 'remarkable foresight' seems not to have been replicated elsewhere, however.[288]

In August 1895, the London Rothschilds and their French cousins, working through Hirsch and Company, Wernher, Beit & Company's preferred market maker, were still active on the Paris Bourse.[289] As late as mid-September, they were confident that if there was a day's reaction in the market, it would immediately be followed by a rise: 'a fantastic rise of these [East Rand and Rand Mines] shares can be anticipated'.[290] When the share market crashed, it clearly left the Paris Rothschilds baffled. Writing to his London relatives some three weeks after the event, Baron Alphonse noted that 'our Stock Ex. could but go forth in conformity with the big leaders in the gold mine market, with Messrs Werner [sic] Beit and Barnato, [by] not throwing shares in portfolio on the market, only to be obliged thereafter to take these shares up again'. 'There is a problem for which my waning intellect so far has got no answer', he continued. 'If indeed the negotiable value of gold mine shares can be rated at 12 milliard fr[an]cs how can it be that the different markets have got unengaged capital for such an enormous amount, and likewise to absorb the colossal quantity. For my part it is certain that a great many of these shares as yet are in portfolio or taken on speculation, only time can say whether such a big lot could have been pocketed'.[291]

While the possibility that a market coup had pocketed 'such a big lot' cannot be ruled out, no single culprit was ever identified with any certainty. A letter drafted to Phillips from Wernher, incomplete but contained in Phillips' own correspondence, identified a 'Mr Robellaz, putting him under your protection'. This information had earlier been cabled to Phillips 'at the request of some Paris friends'. A partner in the firm of [Nizabaum?] Paccard and Company, who 'have a large interest and have been constant supporters and believers and have done much to make shares popular in Paris', Robellaz was accused by 'some people … of having given the alarm and caused the big fall'. Doubting that a single rogue trader was responsible, Wernher advised Phillips that he had 'told the Paris people that these rumours did not affect your mind (sic) and that if they sent an expert out to report, we would be the last to be annoyed

288 Ibid.

289 R. Turrell and Van Helten, "The Rothschilds, the Exploration Company and Mining Finance," *Business History* 28, no. 2 (1986): 192.

290 RA, 3/65, Baron Alphonse, Paris, to his cousins, London, September 18, 1895.

291 RA, 4/20, Baron Alphonse, Paris, to his cousins, London, October 24, 1895.

if he gave his [conscientious?] opinion good or bad on anything he examined himself'.[292] There is no evidence of any follow-up.

In fact, the sheer scale of the 'unengaged' capital required to pull off such a market coup made it more likely than not that many shares were still held in portfolio by the 'big leaders'. What had been called in by the banks was unsecured debt. 'Perhaps the most striking feature about the *debacle* in South African shares', commented *The Economist*, 'has been the complete explosion of the fiction that the long and almost unbroken advance in market values has been due to the purchases of steady, permanent investors on both sides of the Channel, people who intended to stick to their holdings and to bequeath them to a grateful posterity'. 'The events of the past few weeks have proved beyond dispute', the paper continued, 'that the vast majority of the dealings had been effected by speculators and financial institutions, and that even among outside investors a large proportion of their transactions had been carried through by means of borrowed money, while small French holders, who were regarded as the backbone of the market, have sold with the utmost freedom at the first signs of a set-back in prices'.[293] The large parcels of shares first flung on the Paris market were seemingly those of smaller financial institutions and fringe speculators forced to realise paper assets for cash, and not apparently those of one or two big 'bears'. Barney Barnato, for one, was caught by surprise; 'usually so quick of hearing, [he] seem [ed] this time to have lost his market instinct; he did not believe that a serious set-back was coming, and in his optimism he was one of the courageous ones – and probably the strongest of them all – who tried to stem the approaching avalanche, but unavailingly'.[294]

Feted early in November 1895 at an official Mansion House banquet for his efforts to shore up the market,[295] Barnato had no inkling that it would soon fall very much further. He had been deliberately excluded from preparations

292 BA, HE 144, draft Wernher Letters, Wernher, London, to Phillips, Johannesburg, December 13, 1895.

293 *The Economist*, November 9, 1895.

294 Emden, *Randlords*, 139–40. See also Lewinsohn, *Barney Barnato*, 224–26.

295 Kynaston, *City of London*, 130. Hugh Stutfield, "Investors and their Money," *The National Review* 25, December 1895, 510–11, saw it rather differently: 'Things have got to a pretty pass when a South African millionaire [Barnato] who recently floated off upon the public a gigantic Trust of the pig-in-a-poke order at a high premium, is honoured by an official Lord Mayor's banquet, and the lieutenancy of the City of London. The state of the English and European bourses, and the suicides of eighteen speculators in Paris and Lyons alone offer, as I write, a striking commentary upon the beneficent action of this saviour of the City and his brother financiers'.

for the insurrection in Johannesburg planned to culminate with Jameson's intervention, but as the appointed time drew nearer it became increasingly obvious that the town's white inhabitants, 'uitlanders' [foreigners] to the Boers, were hardly enthusiastic revolutionaries. 'The Johannesburger is only a politician in lean times; and these are fat ones', the editor of the *Cape Times* noted in the middle of 1895 after interviewing Kruger.[296] Even better placed to take the political temperature was another newspaper editor, Frederick Hamilton of the Johannesburg *Star*. Appointed by Rhodes on a whim, and privy to confidential conversations, Hamilton was nonetheless of a distinctly independent frame of mind. As he later recalled, the prospect which was opening out,

> … would have fired the minds of a more phlegmatic population than that of Johannesburg. It must be remembered that the men who were directing the mines, administering the business, operating the Stock market, etc., were for the most part between 30 and 40, and Johannesburg is 6,000 feet above sea level. In that sunlit exhilarating atmosphere optimism is easy, and there was plenty to stimulate optimism. Claims pegged out two years before, which seemed to offer only an outside chance, now found eager purchasers at thousands of pounds … Shares went from shillings to pounds, and prices multiplied ten, twenty and even fifty times. Hundreds of poor men became really wealthy, thousands believed that they had become so, and hardly a man or woman along the Reef was untouched by the tremendous transformation of those eight months. Interests in politics and prices had always been in an inverse relationship, and it is not surprising if in 1895 men forgot their political grievances and concentrated upon their growing fortunes.[297]

At the end of June 1895, Hamilton 'received an urgent invitation from Lionel Phillips to dine at his house with him and Dr. Jameson'. Over the meal he was informed about the planned insurrection: 'Jameson finished by asking my opinion of the plan, [and] … I pointed out that no more unsuitable moment than the present could have been chosen for such a movement. People had forgotten all about politics and would regard anyone who interfered with the market as a public enemy … Jameson and Phillips both replied. Long before the end of the year the boom would be over, and men would have had plenty

296 Cook, *Edmund Garrett*, 209.

297 Vincent Harlow, "Sir Frederic Hamilton's Narrative of Events Relative to the Jameson Raid," *English Historical Review* 72, no. 283 (1957): 289–90.

of time to brood over their grievances, financial as well as political, and their remedy'.[298]

The boom ended in October 1895 and almost completely collapsed five weeks later following Phillips' provocative speech when opening the Chamber of Mines' 'new palatial buildings' in Johannesburg.[299] If the first stock market fall was not deliberately engineered, the second one certainly was. For the senior partner in Ecksteins and confidant of Rhodes to 'ring the tocsin' meant that 'restless times were looming'.[300]

Listening to Phillips' every word was Jameson himself.[301] The following day, 'Dr Jim' left for Cape Town, where he was able to satisfy Rhodes that 'everything [was all] right'.[302] Already shaky because of the news that same month of the failure of the first deep-level mine, the Geldenhuis Deep, to produce at a profit,[303] the market went into free fall. Phillips' speech had been preceded, so it was rumoured, by heavy selling by most of the big mining houses. The Stock Exchange, Engels observed, was 'a place where the capitalists took away each other's accumulated capital'.[304]

Still on the outside looking in, Barnato was once again left to prop up the market, but this time even his resources could not prevent a crash: 'He himself made enormous losses; the figure of three millions sterling was mentioned'.[305] Convinced that he knew 'from what [mining] camp the sales came', Barnato 'felt that he had not been rightly dealt with', but in early 1896 he nonetheless rallied to the side of the imprisoned members of the erstwhile Reform Committee set up to manage Johannesburg's abortive rising.[306] There may have been small satisfaction in knowing that 'some of those "bears" [were] … now in

298 Ibid., 290.

299 Lang, *Bullion Johannesburg*, 93–94. See especially, Carl Jeppe, *The Kaleidoscopic Transvaal* (London: Chapman & Hall, 1906), 188; and Denys Rhoodie, *Conspirators in Conflict. A Study of the Johannesburg Reform Committee and its role in the conspiracy against the South African Republic* (Cape Town: Tafelberg-uitgewers, 1967), 41–43.

300 Lewinsohn, *Barney Barnato*, 227.

301 William Taylor, *African Treasures. Sixty Years among Diamonds and Gold* (London: J. Long, 1932), 210.

302 Ian Colvin, *The Life of Jameson, Volume II* (London: Edward Arnold and Co, 1922), 38.

303 Blainey, "Lost Causes," 361.

304 Karl Marx, *Capital. A Critique of Political Economy. Volume III* (ed. by Friedrich Engels) (London: Lawrence and Wishart, 1977), 908.

305 Emden, *Randlords*, 140.

306 Ibid.

FIGURE 14
Barney Barnato
SOURCE: RICHARD LEWINSOHN, *BARNEY BARNATO. FROM WHITECHAPEL CLOWN TO DIAMOND KING* (NEW YORK: E.P. DUTTON & CO., INC., 1938), FRONTISPIECE.

gaol, and their "bear" operations [were] ... not likely to turn out as profitable as they at one time expected'.[307]

307 William Regan, *Boer and Uitlander. The True History of the Late Events in South Africa* (London: Digby, Long, 1896), 115. See also, Gross, *Rhodes of Africa*, 360–61.

CHAPTER 4

Bust, 1896–1899

For a brief period after the Jameson Raid debacle, speculative opportunities on the Rand appeared to be few and far apart. The 'Kaffir Circus', markedly smaller after October's collapse, was a shadow of its former self in the first six months of 1896. Commenting on 'the exodus which has lately taken place from the South African to the Westralian market', *The Economist* described the Southern African mining market as being 'as lifeless as the "Yankee" market, and the Westralian centre has become by far the liveliest and the noisiest part of the "House"'.[1] In fact, while everything had moved on, very little had changed. If anything, the control exercised by the biggest mining houses was greater than before the market had been winnowed of its weaker elements. Maintaining its close association with Farrar, once the death sentence passed on him for his prominent role in the Reform Committee had been commuted by the Boer authorities in Pretoria, and with Hanau through the HF Syndicate and ERPM, Wernher, Beit & Company continued to play the share market.[2] It did so from offices barely a year old in Bishopsgate; 'very well calculated to illustrate the gorgeous undreamable wealth of South Africa', gushed *The Critic*. 'The fittings are *repousse* copper, the walls are paneled and the floors are elaborately parqueteried. There is pavannazzo marble and hand-painted tiles in Persian blue and beautiful friezes and exquisite ceilings. The whole is sumptuously furnished by Maple & Co., Ltd'.[3]

With the help of widespread press bribery and intimate links with a number of Paris *hautes banques,* the firm of Wernher, Beit & Company successfully steadied the nerves of French investors,[4] even as it resuscitated speculative favourites. Together with Sir Edgar Vincent's Eastern Investment Company, it made money on a falling market. Vincent, who had established himself the previous year as a not always successful financier and investor in Rand mining companies, and around whom 'the whiff of corruption ... floated through London *salons*', brought to the table ownership of *The Statist*.[5] Helpfully

1 *The Economist*, May 23, 1896.

2 Ibid., November 7, 1896.

3 *The Critic*, November 30, 1894.

4 Van Helten, "Mining, share manias and speculation," 174.

5 Davenport-Hines and Van Helten, "Edgar Vincent, Viscount D'Abernon, and the Eastern Investment Company," 45–46. See also, Norman Etherington, *Theories of Imperialism. War, Conquest and Capital* (London: Croom Helm, 1984), 48, 55.

 | DOI:10.1163/9789004690790_005

FIGURE 15 1, London Wall, Head Office of Wernher, Beit & Company
SOURCE: AS REPRODUCED IN MARYNA FRAZER AND ALAN JEEVES (EDS), *ALL THAT GLITTERED; SELECTED CORRESPONDENCE OF LIONEL PHILLIPS 1890–1924* (CAPE TOWN: OXFORD UNIVERSITY PRESS, 1977), BETWEEN PP. 144–45.

interviewed by his own journal, Vincent proclaimed his belief in the richness of the country and its possibilities of great development.[6] By means of complex market and arbitrage operations, the Eastern Investment Company, and Wernher, Beit & Company and their associated syndicates, 'acted as vendors and promoted developments such as Angelo Deep on the Eastern Rand, and speculated on the stock exchange. Such activities were highly profitable'.[7] Eastern Investment doubled its capitalisation from £500,000 in 1895 to £1,000,000 in 1896, and once again working with Wernher, Beit & Company, purchased 'good and fair stocks where there were no other buyers in the market'.[8] By June 1896, these judicious market operations had netted Eastern Investment £442,485 in profits.[9]

Profits of this magnitude prompted *The Statist* to see the bright side of things. Compared to the British South Africa Company Administration in Rhodesia, where 'the spread of the native insurrection to Mashonaland, and the delay in adopting decisive measures for the suppression of the Matabele … weighed upon the market throughout the week', Kruger's Government was firmly in the saddle, argued *The Statist*. 'A rising of the Natives [in the Transvaal]

6 *The Statist*, June 29, 1895.

7 Davenport-Hines and Van Helten, "Edgar Vincent, Viscount D'Abernon, and the Eastern Investment Company," 46.

8 Ibid.

9 Ibid., 47.

is very improbable: firstly, because they are unarmed; secondly, because they are thoroughly cowed; and thirdly, because the Boers are on the watch, and will act with a promptitude and a severity which British people never display … Politically and industrially, then, everything looks as promising as possible'.[10]

It seemed the right moment for Consolidated Gold Field's reconstituted board of directors to assure Kruger that it had 'neither countenanced, authorised, nor approved any of the proceedings in Johannesburg which can be regarded as inimical to the peace of the Republic'.[11] Denying any knowledge beforehand of the use of its offices by the Reform Committee, the Gold Fields board claimed that as soon as it knew that some £70,000 of Company funds had gone towards meeting the Committee's expenses, 'repayments of the sums so advanced was immediately demanded and obtained'. Having 'now made such changes in the personnel and in the system of administration of the Company's affairs as seem to them to afford the best guarantee against the recurrence of such events in the future', Gold Fields' directors felt satisfied that after this explanation, 'the friendly relations between the Government … and the Board … which existed prior to the events of January last will continue to exist for the benefit of the Transvaal Government and the Company's shareholders'.[12]

The Critic was characteristically rather less sanguine. The paper carried a series of gloomy articles during March and April. 'Everyone … around here agrees that Kruger is not coming to England, and that he has practically flung Mr Chamberlain's proposals back in the Colonial Secretary's face', it claimed. 'The more pessimistic frequenters of Throgmorton Street simply say, "I hope the war will come soon and be over quickly"'.[13] Nor did the same paper see any reason to change its view as the months passed. An editorial in July 1896 argued that while there were 'many conditions in the present aspects of the market which make for an upward movement of prices … they are all nullified by the vague distrust which exists as the objects and methods of Dr Leyds [the Transvaal State Secretary]. That distinguished statesman is at the moment the one great obstacle to a revival in the Kaffir Circus'.[14] Not everyone agreed. There was another, more straightforward explanation. 'The oppressive heat and the

10 *The Statist*, July 4, 1896.

11 Corey Library, Goldfields Collection, MS 160 90, Directors of Gold Fields [Lord Harris, W.M. Farmer], London, to Their Honour, the President and Government of the South African Republic, Pretoria, July 28, 1896.

12 Ibid.

13 *The Critic*, April 24, 1896.

14 Ibid., July 4, 1896.

attractions of Henley have more or less emptied the mining market during the week, and dealings have been on an even smaller scale than before'.[15]

Whatever the reasons, the mining market continued to decline. Earlier in the year, it had been weighed down by the constant stream of bad news from the territories administered by Rhodes' British South Africa Company. 'No doubt prices would have receded considerably', confided Wernher, 'if there did not exist a very large bear account in most of the leading South African stocks, but especially in Charter shares.[16] As Chartered Company shares were, 'for the moment, the predominating stock, and an enormous business is transacted in them daily, the whole of the market ... [was] influenced by them'.[17] Some six months later, the situation was still 'very bad'. There was 'a general indifference to our market', Ecksteins was told, 'principally through the bad results of the Geldenhuis Deep [crushing returns]. ... The public at large will of course only go by results, and they consider that the whole deep-level theory is disproved by the output and working expenses of this mine. Until they improved, there would be 'no support forthcoming, and especially the Paris people will continue to sell until they see again a steadily rising market'.[18]

'During the early part of the week utter despondency reigned in the market, and the bears had a fine opportunity. They made good use of it', reported *The African Review* in October 1896.

> The complete apathy of the public and the temporary cessation of the support usually given by the big houses helped to aggravate the situation and accelerated the downward course of prices ... To our mind the main cause of the continued flatness is mainly to be found in the condition of the Paris Bourse. As is well known, Paris was the chief factor in the boom of last year, and without French buying we should certainly not have seen the prices of twelve months ago. Now the London market not only misses the generous support from Paris but has to cope with the selling orders coming daily from that centre; and even if the sales are not important, they tell upon a market which is not in a very strong condition.[19]

By the end of the month, however, *The Economist* was so convinced that the severity of the fall pointed to market manipulation by bears that it devoted

15 *African Review*, July 11, 1896.
16 BA, HE 62, Wernher, Beit, London, to Ecksteins, Johannesburg, April 4, 1896.
17 Ibid., April 18, 1896.
18 Ibid., September 26, 1896.
19 *African Review*, October 3, 1896.

several columns to the issue. 'The Kaffir Circus has gone from bad to worse, and has, in fact, become utterly demoralised. Heavy selling has taken place, not only on Home account, but also from the Continent and from Johannesburg', it reported.[20] Acknowledging that shares taken over at the time of last year's crash were now being sold, and that others were being realised before prices fell further, the periodical insisted that other forces were at work. 'It is freely stated by men of position in the market, however, that neither of these causes would have produced anything like such persistently adverse results as those which have eventuated from day to day; and that the far more potent influence affecting South African shares is that one or two of the firms most closely identified with the Rand industry have for some time past been selling for the fall, not directly nor through the usual channels, but by a roundabout process, much of the selling having been, as we have said, from the Continent and from Johannesburg', it noted.[21]

All of this had been accompanied, *The Economist* declared, by a complete *volte face* on the part of 'some of the papers that are generally understood to be, directly or indirectly, in the pay of one or other of the South African [mining] firms'. 'Time was, and that not long ago', it continued,

> when, according to them, the outlook was without a cloud; now there is scarcely a ray of sunshine. What with the decline in the grade of ore, the poor results from the deep levels (only two of these mines having at present reached the productive stage), the enormously greater capital requirements of the deep-level "propositions" than had been anticipated, and the grinding oppression of the Boer Government, all this and much else has been served up again and again for the comfort of nervous shareholders, many of the most damaging statements having, by some means or another, found their way into continental journals which have not in the past taken any particular notice of South African mining matters.[22]

'This is all very curious', the paper concluded. 'Perhaps when the speculation for the fall has become sufficiently widespread – and it cannot be far off that now – a "bear squeeze" will be engineered also in a mysterious manner, and the adverse in the present position of the Rand industry, especially in connection

20 *The Economist*, October 31, 1896.
21 Ibid.
22 Ibid.

with the dynamite monopoly and the capital requirements of the deep-level ventures, will assume a less gloomy aspect. We must wait and see'.[23]

Although quite sure that 'the heavy fall in prices should be attributed to contemptible market manipulation', *The Economist* admitted that 'the object of such a "bear" raid is not very obvious, for it might be supposed that "bosses" really interested in the Rand goldfields would be only too anxious to support prices'.[24] Other Stock Exchange watchers were equally certain that they knew precisely who was behind the market making and why. Early in December 1896, Chamberlain was contacted by the Governor of Natal, Sir Walter Hely-Hutchinson. The letter contained information to the effect that a 'well-informed' Johannesburg correspondent believed that 'the slump in gold shares had been deliberately engineered by the representatives of Wernher, Beit, and company … in order to force the republican government to alter its policy towards the industry so that the cost of production might drop. "If labour keeps coming in, and mines keep closing down … and prices of food keep mounting up as rinderpest spreads … genuine discontent will be the result. My reading of recent market operations is that certain people, headed by the house of Eckstein have determined to try and get the reforms in another way, which they failed to get by their muddle-headed revolution last year"'.[25] This was not the first intimation of its kind to reach the Colonial Secretary, but beyond finding it 'interesting', he took no further action.[26] 'The share market has been exceedingly quiet for some considerable time back, and the brokers and jobbers are doing very little at present', a bank report noted in February 1897. 'The large financial houses do not appear to be lending the market much support'.[27]

With London engrossed by the deliberations of the Select Committee, 'the lying-in state at Westminster', as the Liberal politician, Arnold Morley, memorably termed it,[28] in the Transvaal everything now seemingly hinged on the findings of the Industrial Commission. Established by Kruger's Government in April 1897 'to enquire into the state of affairs generally of the mining industry of the Witwatersrand', it sat between April and June of that year.[29] As the share

23 Ibid.

24 Ibid.

25 Johannes Marais, *The Fall of Kruger's Republic* (Oxford: Clarendon Press, 1961), 137.

26 Ibid.

27 INSP 1/1/83, Standard Bank, Inspection Report on Johannesburg Branch as at 31st December 1896, commenced 31st December, completed 27th February 1897.

28 Van der Poel, *Jameson Raid*, 230.

29 Witwatersrand Chamber of Mines, *The Mining Industry. Evidence and Report of the Industrial Commission of Enquiry, with an Appendix* (Johannesburg: Times Print. and Pub. Works, 1897), v.

market showed no signs of revival, the build-up to the Commission's sitting and its every subsequent move was dissected by London's financial press. In February, *The Statist* had reminded its readers that 'last October we referred to the shrinkage of 43 per cent. in the value of the leading South African mining shares, as compared with the prices a year previously'. Since then, the paper disclosed, 'there has been another very heavy shrinkage, which in respect of 83 companies ... represents a decline in market value from £91,713,000 to £66,991,000 ... This shrinkage of £25,022,000 is equivalent to about 27 per cent. decline'.[30]

Reporting confidentially that same month, the Johannesburg Office of the Standard Bank drew the bleakest of pictures. 'The Share Market, apart from brief intervals of activity, has been mainly on the down grade during the whole [past] twelve months ... So long as the existing mis-management lasts, the Industry must languish. It is clear that the investing public are not disposed to find much additional capital for development under present conditions, and without this aid, none of the "Deep" Companies can reach the producing stage. ... We do not wish to take an unduly depressed view of the position, but our impression is that things will be worse before they are better'.[31] 'The situation here remains as bad as possible', Wernher, Beit & Company's London Office advised Ecksteins in Johannesburg, 'there is great uncertainty about the everlasting Eastern Question and a complete want of confidence in matters Transvaal, and a great many people get frightened out of their holdings, and the bears have a fine time'.[32]

London's financial press saw no reason to disagree. 'Utter stagnation is still the order of the day', *The Economist* reported at the beginning of March 1897. Angered by what it perceived to be the deliberately depressed, even rotten state of the South African mining share market, *The Economist* began by directing its wrath at the usual suspects. 'The two "professional saviours of the Rand", Robinson and Barnato, have each interviewed the President [Kruger] during the week', it thundered.

> The usual amount of talking has taken place, and with the usual result – precisely nothing. The fulsome laudations showered subsequently upon

30 *The Statist*, February 27, 1897.

31 G[eneral]M[anager's] O[ffice]3/2/1/2, February 10, 1897, in Aalan Mabin and Barbara Conradie (eds), *The Confidence of the Whole Country. Standard Bank Reports on Economic Conditions in Southern Africa 1865–1902* (Johannesburg: Standard Bank Investment Corp, 1987), 414.

32 Barlow World, HE 61, Wernher, Beit to Ecksteins, March 5, 1897.

> these two worthies by their subsidised papers have been disgusting. Barnato has stated that he intends to take back the two white marble lions which he last year presented to the President as a mark of his intense displeasure; but if he would condescend to explain why his Consolidated Investment Company, which is supposed to have a dividend equalisation fund of several hundred thousand pounds, is not to pay anything to shareholders for the last half-year it would be more to the point.[33]

The Economist subsequently turned its fire on the mining market as a whole. Contrasting the generally buoyant position of the Stock Exchange because of the return of 'extremely easy conditions in the money market', with the increasingly depressed state of the 'Kaffir Circus', the paper pointed out that 'with each attempt to unload in a market where buyers are mainly conspicuous by their absence ... any temporary recovery invariably brings a fresh flock of would-be sellers into the market, with the result that the depression becomes more acute'.[34] It claimed that recent selling orders had 'largely emanated from the Continent; but there is a shrewd suspicion in Stock Exchange circles that while the orders come from Paris and Berlin, the deliveries will be made by some of the "insiders" here, who find it advantageous to disguise their operations. But whatever the sources of supply, the demand for Rand shares has become steadily smaller, even though prices have now reached a level which would have been regarded as preposterously low eighteen months ago'.[35] Relatively speaking, *The Economist* added, 'the heaviest declines have taken place in the Barnato group of properties ... though actually the most serious shrinkages have occurred in the Wernher-Beit-Eckstein-Farrar group, notably in Rand Mines, East Rand, Modderfonteins, and in some of the Deep Level concerns. The Consolidated Gold Fields series have also given way enormously'.[36]

Convinced that the mining market was in the grip of a protracted 'bear' operation conducted by its biggest operators, *The Economist*, eventually joined by other periodicals and newspapers, was openly sceptical about the mining industry's insistence that all its woes could be laid at Kruger Government's doorstep. It was strongly suspected that the publication of gloomy reports about the state of the industry, coupled with the threatened closure of various mines, did not so much reflect reality, as they were designed 'to force the hands

33 *The Economist*, March 6, 1897.
34 Ibid., April 10, 1897.
35 Ibid.
36 Ibid.

of the Transvaal Government'.[37] Even *The Statist* was moved to quote the opinion of 'one of the greatest mining experts, and one whose knowledge of Transvaal mining is beyond question' to the effect that 'so far as the quality of the Rand reefs goes, there seems to be no change as work progresses; and the only modification of my opinion of the value of the mines comes from the practical difficulties met with, arising from a variety of causes, chiefly over-speculation. These difficulties delay the achievement of the economic results hoped for'.[38] 'There must be many hundreds and perhaps thousands of people who have dropped their money', *The Rialto* later mused, 'and who will refuse to have anything more to do with a market where the value of the industry is not allowed to exercise its effect unhampered, but is continually made subservient to the aims of the men who control it'.[39]

Just before witnesses gave evidence to the Commission, *The Economist* set out what it understood to be the case for and against the gold mining industry. The case *for* the mining industry could be summed as one of maladministration by the Kruger state. 'The Boer Volksraad and the Executive Council are composed entirely of uneducated men, whose native shrewdness does not compensate for an entire lack of knowledge about government, economics, and finance. As a result, the great wealth of the State is being grossly misapplied', *The Economist* declared. More than this, 'valuable concessions and monopolies, such as the railways, dynamite, cement and brick-making by machinery, have been from time to time handed over to favoured individuals', while the civil service was ' in the hands of generally incompetent and often flagrantly dishonest men, who do not attempt to administer the laws, and who have not the administrative knowledge to do so were they so inclined'. If that were not enough, 'especial hostility is always shown to Englishmen, subjects of the paramount power, and the Boer policy towards the mining industry, which is principally conducted by Englishmen, is notorious'.[40]

The case *against* the gold mines, however, was considerably more damning. Acknowledging that 'this matter has hardly ever been discussed in detail, but it is none the less real for all that', *The Economist* proceeded comprehensively to indict the mining industry and its leaders. Most importantly, 'the good mines have, in many instances, been over-capitalised. The poorer mines have been re-constructed over and over again, instead of being long ago shut down. Many utterly worthless mines have been floated'. Nor had company promoters

37 Ibid., August 7, 1897.
38 *The Statist*, April 24, 1897.
39 *The Rialto*, December 10, 1902.
40 *The Economist*, May 8, 1897.

supervised spending; instead, 'the responsibility was handed over to consulting engineers and dummy directors; the former have proved extravagant, and the latter have not had the knowledge, or the power, to put things right'. At the same time, 'engineers and directors have often sold machinery, stores, timber, coal, and every other necessary, in which they were financially interested, to the companies, to the exclusion of fair trade. This has been a widespread and crying abuse. Financial companies, controlled by capitalists, act in some cases towards the mines controlled by these same capitalists in the various capacities of engineers, buyers, bankers, secretaries, and even auditors'.[41]

Mines had been 'overloaded with [crushing] stamps, causing the grade of rock milled to fall without any material reduction in costs', while the salaries received by managers were far too large. 'Many of them are so rich, through speculating', *The Economist* claimed,

> ... that they have become careless. They lounge about the club and attend the races regularly. They live in handsome houses provided by the company, which perhaps is £50,000 in debt. Some of them are unscrupulous and 'cook' the tonnage, so as to make the output per ton and the cost per ton, satisfactory to their vanity. Some are incapable, and mismanage their mines. The directors are usually too ignorant of mining to find this out. Incompetent friends of managers and directors are frequently shoved into good billets. This class of man, usually just out from England, invariably dresses in a riding costume for underground work.[42]

'The truth of the whole matter is that the mines and their workings have simply been used as a lever for the share market', the periodical concluded. 'A general policy of drift and extreme laxity in finance and superintendence, caused by the rapid manner in which the people at head of affairs have made fortunes, is largely responsible for the present depressed and almost rotten condition of most of the mines'.[43]

In the middle of May, the mining market abruptly changed course. 'The primary cause of the altered state of the market for Rand shares has been undoubtedly what is termed a "bear squeeze"', explained *The Economist*. 'A few weeks ago, it is rumoured, an understanding was arrived at among the companies and firms identified with the "Kaffir" business that the market should be left to itself until the commencement of the sittings of the Volksraad enabled

---

41 Ibid.
42 Ibid.
43 Ibid.

them to form a judgement as to the probable course of the industry, and more particularly, as to whether the position in the Rand would be regarded favourably or unfavourably by investors'. Consequently, speculators 'who had been "short of stock" for months past discovered not only that further carrying over facilities would be refused, but that whatever floating supplies there were in the market would be absorbed. The "bears" at once saw that their innings was over, and there was a perfect scramble to "buy back" before the settlement. The squeezing process, coupled with the development of a fairly large account for the rise, even in a few days, have been chiefly instrumental in the recovery of prices'.[44]

The evidence presented on behalf of the mining industry, covertly 'doctored' by Percy FitzPatrick,[45] was so unashamedly partisan that it was greeted with incredulity by financial press correspondents. Advised by Wernher to 'continue to ride the economic horse',[46] FitzPatrick appearing for Ecksteins, and Charles Goldmann representing the Chamber of Mines, for example, both denied that speculation had been pervasive. Asked whether 'overcapitalisation was not the chief cause of the depression, as pointed out by Mr. Labouchere … recently', FitzPatrick brazenly suggested that the editor of *Truth*, acknowledged in the City for his financial expertise,[47] could only have come to such a conclusion by counting the same share multiple times. 'It was impossible to say, except [if] one knew every particular instance, whether a Goldfields share holds an interest in a claim or a share in the Rand Mines, which holds a Jumpers Deep share, which holds a Jupiter share … Mr. Labouchere has the same amount three or four times … [while] I only took the amount once'.[48] Attributing the 'shrinkage of capital' since 1895, by which he meant the value of Rand mining shares, almost entirely to Government policies, Goldmann also denied that the industry had brought its problems on itself. 'Bogus' company flotations had been 'exceptional'. 'I will admit that there have been flotations which … should never have come into existence, but they form a small percentage of the companies which have been honestly floated'.[49]

44 Ibid., May 15, 1897.

45 Stanley Trapido, "FitzPatrick, Sir (James) Percy (1862–1931), politician in South Africa and author," *Oxford Dictionary of National Biography*, 2004.

46 RM FIT L/B 1, FitzPatrick to Wernher, May 1, 1897, in Duminy and Guest, *FitzPatrick. South African Politician*, 99.

47 Hind, *Henry Labouchere and the Empire*, 35.

48 Mr. J.P. FitzPatrick's Evidence, April 28–28, 1897, *Mining Industry. Evidence and Report of the Industrial Commission of Enquiry*, 71.

49 Mr. C.S. Goldmann's Evidence, May, 5–6, 1897, *Mining Industry. Evidence and Report of the Industrial Commission of Enquiry*, 127–128. This interpretation of the mining industry's

Noting the adverse effect this policy of admitting no wrong was having on Commission members, *The Economist's* correspondent described how its 'members, who during the first day or two seemed in good humour, and who listened to the evidence with real interest, have got tired of hearing the same things over and over again, and their interest in the evidence has visibly waned. The witnesses one and all have shown a lack of detailed knowledge on most of the subjects discussed, which has also made an unfavourable impression'.[50] Similarly, the City column of *The Pall Mall Gazette* expressed irritation at the self-serving evidence of the mining industry's representatives. 'According to the tone of the inquiry, so far, it would appear that the company promoters, and after them the directors and engineers, on the Rand had made few mistakes, that they had floated mines with reasonable capitals, and that they had never wasted money subsequently in either equipment or management'. 'This, to put it mildly', the paper tartly observed, 'is hardly the case'.[51]

In the event, though, the members of the Commission proved themselves to be more open to persuasion, if not entirely gullible, than had been generally assumed. The problem of the high cost of production could not be 'solved by probing the past of some mines', the Report asserted. 'We know that there are some mines where the gold reefs only exist in the imagination of the promoters, and it can safely be submitted that these mines will not pay, even were coal and dynamite delivered free of charge at the mines … [but] neither does the question of over-speculation or over-capitalisation affect the case'. A company might be overcapitalised, argued the Report, 'but the cost of mining property [sic] is in no way affected thereby'.[52] *The Economist* begged to differ. 'In the preamble to the report of the Industrial Commission it is stated, if the published summary be accurate, that over-speculation and over-capitalisation have nothing to do with the present condition of affairs, which suggests that the Commissioners were in a very charitable frame of mind when they framed their report, for they might have been easily excused if they had attributed much of the disappointment experienced by shareholders in Rand mines to the constant manipulation to which so many of the companies have been subjected'.[53]

---

presentations differs from both that argued by Alan Jeeves, "Aftermath of Rebellion – The Randlords and Kruger's Republic after the Jameson Raid," *South African Historical Journal* 10, no. 1 (1978): 112; and Lang, *Bullion Johannesburg*, 106–109.

50 *The Economist*, May 29, 1897.

51 *The Pall Mall Gazette*, May 31, 1897.

52 Report of the Commission, *Mining Industry. Evidence and Report of the Industrial Commission of Enquiry*, 446.

53 *The Economist*, August 14, 1897.

With the publication in August 1897 of the Industrial Commission Report, London's financial press was jubilant. Welcoming the apparent 'change of disposition on the part of the Government' and pointing to the significant reduction in working costs already achieved by several mining companies, *The Statist* described the Rand as 'awakening like a giant refreshed'.[54] Glimpsing a recovery in the share market, *The African Review* thought that a renewed 'boom in Kaffirs' was imminent.[55] 'I have just been reading the Report of the Mining Commission', wrote Sir Alfred Milner, the High Commissioner of South Africa, 'and I must say I think it is a startler. It never occurred to me as at all probable, that the Commission would give a verdict which is practically one of "Proven" to all the main charges of the Mining Industry'.[56] By October, however, as it became known in the City that Kruger's Government would not accept all of the Industrial Commission's recommendations, the share market was once again 'dull and inert'.[57]

But market sentiment was extremely volatile. Although the Chamber of Mines annual report for 1897 expressed its huge disappointment at the Volksraad's rejection of all but the most 'insignificant reductions', it also placed on record 'a remarkable improvement' in the amount of gold recovered, up by more than a third over the previous year. 'This remarkable improvement is due to several causes: first, more companies have been producing during the year; secondly, great progress has been made in the methods of treatment; and thirdly, the grade of ore crushed has been somewhat raised'.[58] The surprising steadiness of the market since its recovery from the first shock of disappointment could readily be explained, confided one financial paper. 'We have constantly endeavoured to impress upon our readers that the permanent factors affecting the mining industry such as the savings in wages, more scientific and cheaper methods of working, the advent of the deep-level era etc, must not be lost sight of, and that, while concessions from the Government were urgently needed, yet it was possible to exaggerate the importance of them. Little as the Government seems disposed to do for the industry, the essential facts remain that many of the mines are doing very well'.[59]

The African Review was not alone in voicing this opinion. Similar sentiments were expressed over the next few months by *The Critic, The Statist* and

54 *The Statist*, August 28, 1897.

55 *The African Review*, August 14, 1897.

56 Sir Alfred Milner to Conyngham Greene, 12 August 1897, in C. Headlam (ed.), *The Milner Papers. South Africa 1897–1899* (London: Cassell & Company, 1931), 82.

57 *The Statist*, October 23, 1897.

58 "Mr. Rouliott (President) on Mining in 1897. "*The African Review*, February 19, 1898.

59 *The African Review*, October 23, 1897.

the *Financial Times*, as the market continued to improve on the back of new deep-level mines joining the ranks of producing and profitable mines. Writing from Johannesburg at the beginning of October 1897, J.H. Curle, *The Economist's* special correspondent, declared that the gold mining industry was now more soundly based than ever before. 'Much of this is due to the introduction of the very finest machinery, of which a considerable part is driven by electricity, while the price of fuel is as low as anyone can wish', he reported. A lot was also down to the fact that many mines had developed ore reserves to the point where 'a regular output can be relied upon with certainty, and, most of all, to the fact that consulting engineers, managers, and directors now perform their several duties in the interests of the companies they serve to a far greater degree than formerly. To complete the improvement, we have cheaper stores, a better standard of work, for the same pay, from the white employees, and a largely reduced standard of Kaffir pay, which is now in successful operation'. In these circumstances, 'without, therefore, even the prospect of further assistance from the Boer Government, the general position of the industry, although far from satisfactory, is better than it has ever been before'.[60]

The mining market nonetheless remained highly susceptible to professional manipulation. 'In its comparatively short history the market for South African mining shares has had its full measure of changes, periods of inflation and depression having alternated in more or less rapid succession', *The Economist* reflected. 'Hence much of the popularity of the "Kaffir Circus" among professional operators, for while the outside public may be doggedly speculating in one direction, in nine cases out of ten as "bulls", the insiders are constantly varying their operations, and frequently secure two or three profits in a day or so by "jobbing in and out", as the phrase goes, although the general trend of quotations may appear to be steadily upward or downward'.[61]

Yet for all its insularity, the market for Southern African gold mining shares was easily swayed by external events. In late October 1897, the market took 'a sharp turn for the worse', due primarily, *The African Review* believed, 'to the despair with which the attitude of the Government and Volksraad of the Transvaal on the reform question had come to be regarded'. But, the paper added, the slump was aggravated by other causes. These sent 'a wave of depression over all the markets and bourses. The fear of dearer money both in London and on the Continent disturbed the minds of speculators; the American market and the Paris Bourse were agitated by reports to the effect that the relations between the United States and Spain had entered on a critical phase over the

60 *The Economist*, October 9, 1897.

61 Ibid., August 7, 1897.

Cuban business; and Paris was, moreover, weakened by the dispute between the Parquet and the Coulisse, and the proposed new tax on Bourse transactions. The troubles on the Indian frontier and in West Africa also added somewhat to the prevailing feeling of uneasiness'.[62]

One month later, the storm clouds had disappeared. At Consolidated Goldfield's annual meeting in November 1897, the Chairman, H.E.M. Davies, 'spoke hopefully and confidently about the future of the Rand gold-mining industry, and he especially deprecated the feverish anxiety shown by the market with regard to the long-delayed Government reforms, as if the very existence of the industry depended upon them'. Forced by the Volksraad's rejection of the Industrial Commission's Report 'to rely upon their own resources', mines controlled by Goldfields were no longer characterised by 'extravagance and mismanagement'. Working costs had fallen substantially as a result. On the Simmer and Jack Mine, the average cost of production was now 20s 6d per ton, down from 29s 1d per ton in 1896. Davies concluded by asserting that reduced working costs afforded 'ample proof ... of the reasonableness of our contention, that while the industry was fully justified in asking of the Transvaal Government a less excessive burden of taxation and the rigid suppression of irregular levies upon the companies, much might have been done by the industry as a whole in the stoppage of leakages in expenditure and the adoption of more systematic and economic management, for although a portion of the 30 per cent saving in the case of the Simmer and Jack Company has doubtless arisen from improvements in the machinery and increased knowledge and experience of the mineral formation, it is certain that a great deal of it has been due to more careful and effective supervision'.[63]

This disingenuous admission of past mining incompetence and waste was seen not as grounds for criticism but rather of celebration and cause for the market to rise. Leading the way was the sympathetically-inclined *Statist*. 'There has for some days been a decidedly better tendency in the market for leading South African shares, and particularly for those of all deep-level undertakings and of companies largely interested in such propositions', *The Statist* wrote. 'It is now clearly proved that the industry is making progress. ... The producing outcrop companies are increasing their dividend distributions, and the deep-level companies are showing that they contain as rich ore as those of the outcrop companies, sometimes, indeed, richer. This is a striking contrast with the pessimistic utterances regarding deep levels heard at the beginning of the year'. 'But for the sentiment attached to the withholding of concessions

62 *The African Review*, October 30, 1897.

63 *The Economist*, November 20, 1897.

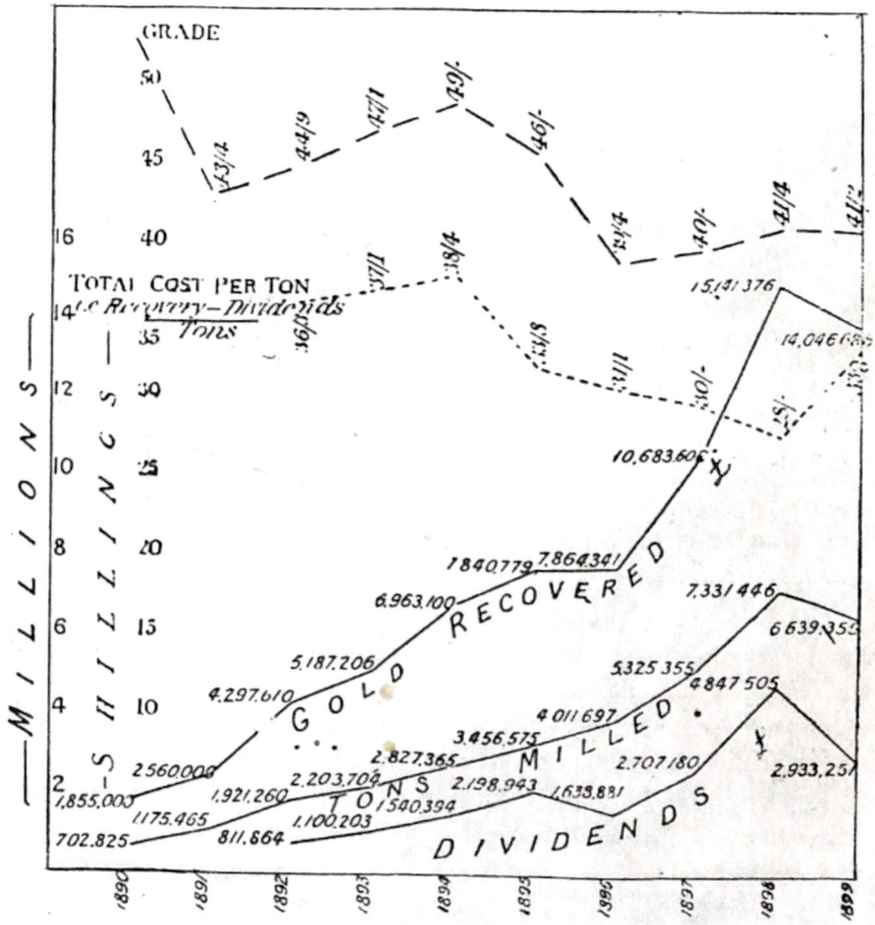

FIGURE 16 Witwatersrand Gold Mining: dividends, costs per ton, grade, 1890–1899
SOURCE: *MINING AND ENGINEERING WORLD* 36, MARCH 16, 1912.

by the Government, the change for the better that has gradually been going on for some while past would have been far more distinct ', the paper added. 'Too much importance is attached to the benefits the industry will derive from concessions, and too little is attached to the earnest efforts the companies have made to increase output, and to do their part of the work in the reduction of expenditure'.[64]

For once, *The Economist's* special correspondent and assembled mining experts did not dissent. Just before Christmas 1897, the magazine published

64 *The Statist*, December 18, 1897.

a lengthy special supplement devoted to the Rand's deep-level mines. Dealing with the subject under three headings, the supplement began by examining the theories originally held about deep levels, and the extent to which the original theories had been borne out by actual results. Lastly, it determined what it understood to be the facts of the situation. On all three counts, the Rand's deep levels scored highly. 'Most of the leading gold mining experts of the world have visited the Rand', explained the supplement, and 'their opinions … are unanimously in favour of the accepted theories; that is … of the continuation to great depths of the reef; of the reliability of its gold contents at any given depth; and of the sound nature of mining operations connected with its exploitation'. All this 'justified the sinking of large sums of money, and was, at an early date, confirmed by actual facts'.[65]

'It may indeed be accepted with perfect confidence', the paper continued, 'that, except in the very deep deep-levels, the working expenses will be no more than those of the outcrop mines. In the deeps there will be a rather higher cost for dynamite, owing to the harder nature of the ground; for labour, owing to the flatter reef necessitating more shoveling of the ore; and for coal, owing to the greater depth from which the ore has to be hoisted; but these are mere fractional increases, and are easily balanced by the economy effected by a finer equipment and a more compactly planned surface plant'. A few reservations aside, *The Economist's* overall verdict was highly favourable. 'We may sum up the position by stating that the theory of deep-levels has been amply borne out by results, and that the future, regarding these mines in the aggregate as sound, honestly managed mining ventures, is likely to be a particularly successful one'.[66]

The fact, however, that *The Economist* had qualified its otherwise positive assessment by concluding that large sums of capital would have to be found for the development of the second-row deep levels, elicited an almost immediate response from Consolidated Goldfields' chief mining engineer and erstwhile leading member of the Reform Committee, John Hays Hammond. 'This question of finance applies more seriously to the second row deep-levels', the periodical had observed. 'These mines require working capital of from £600,000 upwards, and no matter how good their prospects may be, it is at the present juncture almost beyond the resources even of the Consolidated Goldfield Limited to finance them. Some of these mines are, therefore, closed down, while

65 "Special Supplement: The Deep Level Mines of the Rand." *The Economist*, December 18, 1897.

66 Ibid.

only the presumably richest are being carried on'.[67] Hammond's reply denied that there was any such difficulty. At the same time, Hammond, who in 1895 had bitterly complained about Goldfield's failure to play the market more aggressively,[68] did his best to boost the company's shares.

Acknowledging that 'the discussion on the subject was generally admirable, and there can be no question as to the correctness of the summary', Hammond argued that 'the capital required … to open a second row deep-level mine … would not greatly exceed that for the development of the first row of deep-levels, since a large part of the machinery required would be identical in each case … The only additional expense in the case of the second row of deep-levels would be the additional cost of shaft-sinking, and of the heavier engines and boilers required. This extra expense should not exceed £800 per claim, where blocks of 250 claims are worked. The amortisation of this additional capitalisation would be covered by a very small extra expense per ton of ore mined'. 'I think I have shown that the disadvantages attending the development and exploitation of the second row of deep-levels, compared with those obtaining upon the first row, are not of much moment', his letter concluded. 'In view of the facts which I have presented, I think that I was justified in stating in my report of June 1897, to Consolidated Gold Fields, that, "judged by the present market values of the outcrop companies, the deep-level companies still possess a large margin for further appreciation". That the public entertained this view of the future of deep-level properties is attested by the rise in market values that has already taken place'.[69]

Reporting to Beit in early January 1898, FitzPatrick conveyed more good news. 'The output is just out and, as usual, has exceeded all expectations. I suppose we need expect but little sympathy from Government as long as this sort of thing continues. … There has really been a very great advance made in economies and work during the past year'. 'How much more could we not do if we had a real good Government', he mused.[70] It was a sentiment shared by Lionel Phillips. 'When we realise that a shilling saved means ultimately an extra 2½

67 Ibid.

68 Bodleian Library, Micro. Afr. 368–70, Hays Hammond Papers, folio 360, Hammond to Captain F. Rhodes, October 21, 1895: 'Rudd and Davies I think are too small minded to realise that this has been an extraordinary year for money making, and that any man connected with the Gold Fields could have made much more money acting independently of them'.

69 "Letter from John Hays Hammond, Consolidated Goldfields, 8 Old Jewry, London." *The Economist*, January 8, 1898.

70 Q2 A/LB XVIII, FitzPatrick to Beit, January 10, 1898, in Duminy and Guest, *FitzPatrick. South African Politician*, 140.

millions to a concern like the Rand Mines, then we appreciate the significance of good and economical management and good government', he wrote from London at the end of December 1897.[71] *The Statist*, too, was beside itself at the news that the £1,500,000 in dividends paid in 1896 had nearly doubled in 1897. This was chiefly due to 'more economical working and improved methods of extraction ... [resulting in] a considerable improvement in the tone of the market during the last few weeks'.[72]

Left to its own devices, the 'Kaffir Circus' could not sustain the rally. In mid-February 1898, the market suddenly underwent 'a complete and violent change'. The re-election of President Kruger, explained *The African Review*, 'produced at first no perceptible effect on prices ... [but] the summary dismissal of Chief Justice Kotze came this week as a rude shock to the investing public. It was taken to be an indication ... that reform was no part of President Kruger's programme, and that the mining industry had nothing to hope for from the governing authorities ... In these circumstances, the market ... became distinctly weak. For the last three days shares have been thrown on the market ... in alarm, and prices have seriously relapsed'.[73]

Approvingly citing evidence gathered by *The Investors Review* to the effect that 'in order to attract the public, accounts have been cooked, fictitious profits reported and the ore of the reefs carefully "picked" to produce abnormal returns', the *Financial Times* was convinced that, 'in order to breathe life into the market and improve the prospects of poorer mines, parent companies would once again embark on a process of reconstruction, so that the [share] holder, instead of finding the long-looked for recovery in the value of his interest, will simply get his depreciated shares reduced in number. There will be the usual exchange of two or three for one, with the usual provision of fresh working capital, which in due course will be exhausted in further fruitless work, and concurrently the new shares will gradually dwindle to the value of the present one'.[74]

The following month, after Chamberlain's affirmation of British suzerainty over the South African Republic, share prices weakened again. The market, declared *The Statist*, was in 'a very unsettled and nervous condition, not because of the intrinsic position of the industry, but in consequence of the

71 WB Cape Letters, Phillips to R. Schumacher, December 31, 1897, in Fraser and Jeeves, *All That Glittered*, 106.

72 *The Statist*, January 29, 1898.

73 *The African Review*, February 19, 1898.

74 *Financial Times*, March 2, 1898.

uncertainty as to the future of politics in the Transvaal'.[75] Other journals and newspapers agreed. 'It may be fairly said that the market is in a state of paralysis', concluded *The Critic*. 'Those speeches of Lord Salisbury and Mr Chamberlain have done much to bring about this unfortunate position … The failure of President Kruger to come up to … [reform] expectations has also disheartened the Kaffir Circus. No-one outside the Stock Exchange expected that he would … but the market with its usual optimism thought otherwise'.[76] Driving the point home, *The African Review* had earlier treated its readers to an updated version of Longfellow's 'The Village Blacksmith', now become 'The Kaffir Jobber'.

> Within the gloomy Stock Exchange
> The Kaffir jobber stands,
> whilst listless markets make the time drag slowly on his hands:
> few bargains can he find to book in "Chartereds", "Becks", or "Rands".
> His face is set with keen regret at days so idly spent,
> he curses that "Oom Paul" was re-elected President,
> he looks around and wonders if to-day he'll earn a cent.
> Week in, week out, about the "House" from morn till eve he'll walk,
> he hears the Bulls' incessant bluff, the Bears' alarmist talk,
> and wonders why the Fates his way to "eighths" and "sixteenths" baulk!
> Loafing, regretting, sorrowing, onwards through life he goes,
> with unsoiled page his bargain-book at eve he'll sadly close:
> Something attempted, nothing done, he seeks his night's repose![77]

There was only one conclusion that could be drawn, thought the *Financial Times*. 'The market, in short, is in the hands of Mr. Kruger'.[78]

That this did not always hold good was demonstrated within weeks, when the outbreak of the Spanish-American War in April 1898 caused all markets 'to become feverish and depressed', the Southern African mining market particularly so, as French investors sold Rand shares to cover their exposure in the Spanish market.[79] The broad point held, however, when in May, market prices strengthened significantly. 'There is abundant evidence that the controlling houses, taking advantage of the expected early termination of the [Spanish-American] war and of the clearer state of the political atmosphere

75 *The Statist*, March 19, 1898.
76 *The Critic*, May 25, 1898.
77 *The African Review*, March 5, 1898.
78 *Financial Times*, April 12, 1898.
79 *The African Review*, April 23, 1898.

in general', reported the *Financial Times*, 'have again been giving determined support to their respective stocks. ... The anticipation of real reforms in place of hypocritical devices is now based on the conclusion that the Transvaal must have a loan, and that the required provisions will be made an indispensable condition'.[80]

For the next ten or so months, that is, until the end of March 1899, London's financial press only occasionally criticised the ZAR's Government. Instead, it was generally swept along by the ever-increasing flow of gold and dividends from the Rand as more and more deep-level mines came on stream. An important exception was *The Critic,* whose editor, Henry Hess, had fallen foul of Kruger some years previously and thereafter attacked the Boer government at every turn from exile in Britain. 'There is a feeling among professional men in London and Johannesburg', wrote Hess in June 1898,

> ... that were it not for the distrust inspired by the attitude of the Transvaal government, the prices of the majority of Rand mining shares would advance. Such an unbroken record of technical progress has probably never before been presented by any industry. Monthly returns and annual reports continue to show a continuous decrease in working costs ... Yet the market treats these advances as if they did not affect the value of Witwatersrand mine shares in the slightest. And all because Mr Kruger will insist on sticking by his friends of the dynamite concession.[81]

The African Review, by contrast, was more taken by the fact that the mines themselves 'were never in a sounder or more promising condition'. This, the journal explained, was 'conclusively shown by the dividend list we publish today, for already the sums distributed for the half-year are equal to the amounts paid during the whole of 1896. These dividend payments are the best test of the condition of the mines'.[82] Other financial columnists joined the chorus. Listing dividend-paying mines in alphabetical order, *The Economist* reported that the Bonanza 'pays 50 per cent. in contrast with 25 per cent. for the first half of last year; the City and Suburban pays 7.5 per cent. against 5 per cent; the Crown Reef 100 per cent. against 80 per cent', and so merrily on, 'fully confirming the favourable impression created by the statements of the monthly estimates of profits issued by the companies adopting that highly commendable practice'.[83]

80 *Financial Times*, May 11, 1898.
81 *The Critic,* June 25, 1898.
82 *The African Review*, July 2, 1898.
83 *The Economist,* June 25, 1898.

A mixture of international complications, comparatively dear money and high share prices relative to returns combined from July 1898 onwards to dampen Stock Exchange enthusiasm, the efforts of the biggest mining houses notwithstanding. With the exception of Rhodesia where the suppression of the Ndebele and Shona Risings gave the mining market a temporary boost, the 'inflow of European capital ... practically ceased'.[84] 'The refusal of the public to be drawn into another wild purchase of Kaffir shares at the present juncture is an incident which certain magnates must add to their long catalogue of failures', the *Financial Times* reported with a certain relish. '"In vain is the snare set in the sight of any bird", and particularly of the "oof [money] bird". None but geese could have been enthralled by the palpable nets which some Kaffir "bosses" and their Press organs have been carefully laying during the past few days, and the public who have paid dearly for experiences, are not geese nowadays'.[85]

If investors 'did not find Kaffirs attractive at prices ruling',[86] the reasons were not hard to find. In the first place, the capital of the leading mining houses, the so-called parent companies, had been 'enormously increased' since 1895. This significantly reduced their dividend-earning possibilities, even if 'in them there is always a market'.[87] In all other respects, though, the character of the mining market's control and structure remained essentially unchanged from the heady days of the 'Kaffir Boom'. Vendors' rights and profits continued much as before. 'The preliminary capital outlay [on deep-level mines] has necessarily been heavy, and promoters' profits have been enormous', noted the *Financial Times*. 'Hence the share capital is considerable; and, not withstanding that, the controllers of the companies, who hold the bulk of the shares, have kept them at high market values'.[88] As in the recent past, the market consequences of this were two-fold. Dividends calculated at par, that is, on the original £1 price of shares, served to bait and trap credulous investors, even as they enriched the big mining houses. 'The dividends for the year 1898 will thus be – from Rand Mines, 100 per cent., Crown Deep, 50 per cent., Rose Deep 40 per cent., Geldenhuis Deep 75 per cent', announced the *Financial Times*. But impressive as this appeared, 'to a buyer of Rand Mines at the present market price [of £34 per share] a dividend of 100 per cent. means less than 3 per cent. That is

84 G[eneral]M[anager's] O[ffice]3/2/1/2, 10 August 1898, in Maybin and Conradie, *Confidence of the Whole Country*, 442.

85 *Financial Times*, July 7, 1898.

86 Ibid., July 20, 1898.

87 Ibid., September 21, 1898.

88 Ibid., July 13, 1898.

not much from a mining interest'. 'On the other hand', the paper continued, 'it must be borne in mind that the payment of this 100 per cent. entitles the vendors, Messrs. Wernher, Beit and Co. to 25 per cent. of all future distributions', and that anyway, 'a 100 per cent. dividend only absorbs £332,708 of declared profits. To return the purchaser of shares at [£] 34 ten per cent. on his money – the rate which the buyer into any mining concern is fairly entitled to look for as a minimum – it would be necessary for the Company to distribute in one year £1,414,000, of which the respectable portion of £282,800 would accrue to Messrs. Wernher, Beit and Co. These are interesting facts for the attention of those who talk Rand Mines to still higher prices'.[89]

By the time the dividend distributions for 1898 were published, the international situation had greatly improved. Although the Fashoda Crisis briefly cast a pall over the Stock Exchange as a whole, the situation in Southern Africa, especially following the Anglo-German agreement, was seen as contributing to the 'decidedly cheerful mood of the Kaffir market'.[90] Harry Marks' *Financial News* had in all probability earlier been paid to praise the success of the deep-level mines as heralding 'wonderful prosperity',[91] but there were reasons good enough for the change in market sentiment. Most important was that the gold mining industry's leaders found nothing seriously wrong with prevailing conditions on the Rand. 'I may say that we are by no means ill disposed towards Kruger', Lord Harris, formerly Governor of Bombay and now acting chairman of Consolidated Goldfields, told Chamberlain in November 1898. 'We wish he could establish an honest executive, and then try [to] secure the observance of the provisions of the drink laws: but we don't think that the principle of taxing declared nett profits of mining Cos [is] unfair, or that we are working under a crushing tyranny'.[92]

---

89 Ibid., December 14, 1898.

90 *The Critic*, December 3, 1898. For the Anglo-German Agreement, see Matthew Seligmann, *Rivalry in Southern Africa. The Transformation of German Colonial Policy* (Basingstoke: Palgrave Macmillan, 1998); and Peter Henshaw, "The 'Key to South Africa' in the 1890s: Delagoa Bay and the Origins of the South African War," *Journal of Southern African Studies* 24, no. 3 (1998): 527–43.

91 *Financial News*, October 10, 1898.

92 Lord Harris to Chamberlain, November 20, 1898, as cited in Marais, *Fall of Kruger's Republic*, 228. See also, *The Economist*, December 31, 1898: 'On the Rand, mining has reached a pitch of prosperity that two years ago would have been considered impossible of attainment … it is the deep levels more than anything else that the year's work has so well satisfied those best able to judge the Rand's future … the Government is no more corrupt or incompetent now than a year ago. The 5 per cent tax on dividends recently levied is not a severe measure'. For more on Lord Harris, see Supplement to *The African Review*, April 19, 1902.

However laconically expressed, it was an opinion that rested on hard evidence of expanded output, bigger dividends and reduced working costs. Between 1894 and 1898, annual gold production more than doubled from £7,000,000 to £15,100,000, with dividends jumping from £1,500,000 to £4,800,000. Working costs, particularly in the latter part of the period, fell dramatically, from 38/- a ton in 1894 to 28/- a ton in 1898. This was due to a mixture of technical innovation and expanded production. 'Engineers revolutionised shaft-sinking methods and increased the rate of sinking from 50' a month to 120' a month; continuous-flow cyaniding improved extraction and saved water and chemicals, and the average crushing duty of Rand stamps increased from 3.7 tons a day in 1894 to 4.8 tons in 1899', even as the scale of production increased. 'Prior to 1894, 50-[crushing] stamp mills were the biggest on the Rand, but the 13 deep-level mills and 12 new outcrop mills built after 1894 were each 200-stamp, with a capacity of 24,000 tons of ore a month. These raised the monthly average crushing capacity of all Rand mines from 5.7 tons in January 1895 to 10.2 tons in January 1899'.[93]

Informed opinion in Johannesburg itself was equally sanguine. A confidential assessment conducted during November and December 1898 for the Standard Bank was quite clear that 'the outlook for the [gold mining] industry is more promising today than at any previous period in its history'.[94] 'I see no reason to keep my readers out of sound Witwatersrand Main Reef stocks any longer', ran an editorial in *The Critic*, 'and there appears to be nothing in the political atmosphere to threaten any unpleasantness'.[95]

The New Year saw the mining market improving steadily. Even *The African Review*, never well-disposed towards the Transvaal Government, conceded that the news from the South African Republic was 'fairly satisfactory', noting also that 'the market is disposed to discount very largely the sensational telegrams from Cape Town and Johannesburg that are still being published by the newspapers which act in concert with the [anti- Kruger] South African League'.[96] As regards the political situation on the Rand, the paper was persuaded that 'men's minds at present are mainly occupied with the incipient boom. Revolutions are not made when affairs are prosperous'.[97] By the end of January 1899, 'the upward movement in Kaffirs had continued … practically without a halt'.

---

93 McCarty, "British Investment in Overseas Mining," 91–92.

94 Standard Bank Archives, Johannesburg, INSP 1/1/83, Inspection Report on Johannesburg Branch as at 22nd October 1898, Completed 18th January 1899.

95 *The Critic*, December 31, 1898.

96 *The African Review*, January 14, 1899.

97 Ibid., January 28, 1899.

This could be explained, the paper thought, by the fact that the 'public and the market have been so much worried by politics during the last three years that they seem now inclined to go to the other extreme, and ignore politics altogether'. Money was presently 'much cheaper than it was towards the end of the year, discounts having dropped to 2 per cent, inducing the Directors of the Bank of England to lower their official minimum', and generally politics were 'less calculated to cause distrust than they have been for a long time past'.[98]

From his new vantage point in London, Lionel Phillips was decidedly upbeat. 'The market looks exceedingly healthy, business being extremely active with occasional temporary lulls which are valuable', he wrote to Ecksteins in Johannesburg. 'The tendency, however, is distinctly in the direction of running wild, and if the activity continues, we see every probability of a great boom when, as hitherto, the public will go mad. The present eagerness for shares has of course brought all sorts of new things in the market and a desire on the part of all persons interested in undeveloped properties to seize the opportunity for obtaining working capital'.[99]

During February and March 1899, the Southern African mining market remained buoyant. Something of a 'boomlet' developed in its Rhodesian section, from where it was reported that 'new flotations are being put through apace'.[100] Attracted by a rise in effective yields caused by the fall in share prices from their peak in October 1895 and a big increase in dividends, British investors bought large numbers of shares in established and newly floated deep-level companies.[101] The one sour note sounded at the annual general meeting of the Chamber of Mines concerning the liquor laws and the control of black labour, was ignored by the mining market. It instead chose to play up the news that the State Secretary of the South African Republic had been shown over the Johannesburg Stock Exchange by representatives of Ecksteins, an occasion thought to be 'symptomatic of a better understanding'.[102] Even normally cautious observers were impressed by prevailing conditions. 'It is a matter of common knowledge', wrote *The African Review*, 'that the working mines are in a more favourable position than ever before ... The big houses have given evidence of their belief in the future by arranging for the immediate working of fresh blocks of deep level ground, which will involve a concentration

98 Ibid., January 21, 1899.

99 WB Letters, Phillips, London, to Messrs H. Eckstein & Co., Johannesburg, February 4, 1899, in Fraser and Jeeves, *All That Glittered*, 107.

100 NAZ, A1/5/2, H. Wilson Fox, Secretary, British South Africa Company London, to W. Milton, Administrator, Salisbury, March 4, 1899.

101 McCarty, "British Investment in Overseas Mining," 97.

102 *The Economist*, March 1899, 11.

of capital, attention, and technical skill for a considerable time before results can be shown'.[103] Celebrating the gold mining industry's 'gigantic progress and its extreme prosperity', a special correspondent for *The Economist* explained it as 'essentially a deep level boom'.[104] By the middle of the month, an 'excited' market was displaying every sign of 'a strong upwards tendency'.[105]

Two weeks later, however, Chamberlain dismissed as 'illusory' Kruger's promises of reforms following the discussions then underway with the big Rand mining companies. When these negotiations initially looked promising, Milner had worried that 'the danger is that the big financial houses will think only of themselves and, if they can get the questions, which specially affect their pockets, settled satisfactorily, will give away the bulk of the Uitlander population, and the Imperial Government to boot'.[106] This was the so-called 'Great Deal', but its eventual failure combined with Chamberlain's remarks had an immediate impact on the market. Much to the chagrin of that section of the 'Kaffir Circus' inclined to put its faith in the Transvaal Government, shares began to fall.

'Politics are once again the dominating factor in the Kaffir market', noted *The African Review* at the start of April. 'Although all the mining news is of the most favourable character, there seems little prospect of renewed animation in mining shares until the political situation becomes better defined'.[107] Although the monthly output was 'almost sensationally good, far exceeding the general expectation and establishing an excellent new "record", the share market took no notice, the paper later lamented. 'In fact, the declaration of the magnificent output for March was immediately followed by a distinct relapse in the market, a fact which proves that the political situation … is for the moment a more potent factor than the industrial position'.[108]

'The market opened dull', the *Financial Times* reported. 'There was a story of dissension among the magnates. That a very influential one is at the bottom of the political agitation in the Transvaal, which has culminated in the monster petition to Mr. Chamberlain, is freely believed, and it may be that the objection of others to his action, as calculated to upset the negotiations with the

103 *The African Review*, March 4, 1899.

104 *The Economist*, March 11, 1899.

105 *Financial Times*, March 15, 1899.

106 Milner, Cape Town, to Selborne, London, March 8, 1899, as cited in George Boyce (ed.), *The Crisis of British Power. The Imperial and Naval Papers of the Second Earl of Selborne, 1895–1910* (London: Historians' Press, 1990), 70.

107 *The African Review*, April 8, 1899.

108 Ibid., April 15, 1899.

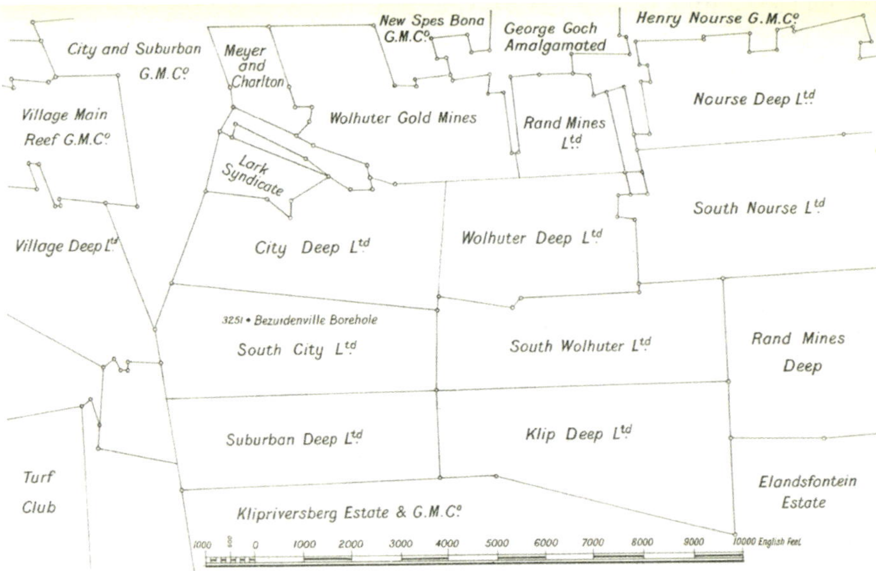

FIGURE 17 Witwatersrand Main Reef: deep level flotations, 1898/9
SOURCE: REPRODUCED FROM JAMES HERBERT CURLE, *THE GOLD MINES OF THE WORLD* (LONDON: WATERLOW AND SONS LIMITED, LONDON WALL, E.C., 1899), BETWEEN PP. 92 AND 93.

Transvaal Government, is the foundation of this rumour'.[109] 'What is still more generally believed', the paper added, 'is that the magnates are depressing the market in the interest of the hoped-for concessions, so as to choke off public buying, as in the event of there being a popular demand for shares, as well as big yields and dividends, the Boers would contend that there could not be much to complain about. It would appear a futile course, as Mr. Kruger is no doubt keen enough to see through such devices; but it is the explanation of the dullness which receives most general acceptance'.[110]

Kruger had never entertained any illusions about the stock-jobbing propensities of the leading Randlords. As far back as 1890, the President had gone to Johannesburg, at the time gripped by depression after the collapse of the first share market boom of 1888–89. There he had been confronted by a large crowd of 'Uitlanders' who, after demanding redress of their many grievances, proceeded to tear down the Transvaal flag from Government buildings and trample it underfoot. FitzPatrick later recalled 'the collapse of the share market and the apparent failure of many of the mines [as having] left a thriftless

109 *Financial Times*, April 14, 1899.
110 Ibid.

and gambling community wholly ruined and half starving, unable to bear the burden which the State imposed … horribly overtaxed … [and aware] that those things that might be their salvation, and are necessary conditions for industrial prosperity – railways, cheap living, consistent and fair government – were not theirs'.[111] Kruger's understanding of the incident was arguably much the more perceptive. Believing that Johannesburg's white inhabitants had only themselves to blame for their predicament, 'yet they would blame the Government', several months afterwards he regaled an audience of burghers with the story 'of the old baboon that is chained up in my yard. When he burnt his tail in the Kaffir's fire the other day, he jumped round and bit me, and just after I had been feeding him'.[112] While FitzPatrick took the anecdote to exemplify Kruger's obstructionist dislike of Johannesburg and the gold mining industry, the author and journalist, Reginald Statham, thought it bore witness to his shrewdness. On Statham's telling, it ended with Kruger explaining 'That's just like these people in Johannesburg. They burn their tails in the fires of speculation, and then they come and bite me'.[113]

Taking his cue from the Government- supporting newspaper, the *Standard & Diggers' News*, that 'the capitalist has the power to move and manipulate markets this way or that way',[114] Kruger eventually contemplated legislation against fraudulent company promotion. In May 1898, he complained that 'companies are being floated here on properties which have not even been properly examined to see if they contain gold. Shares are sold and allotted in Europe to persons who do not know but that the ground is good and who do not discover until they come here that the estates are valueless, and then the blame is cast upon the Government'. For Kruger, the solution was plain. 'Shareholders in Europe are as much entitled to the protection of the Government as the people here. I hope, therefore, that such rules shall be made that no company shall sell or allot its shares before the State Mineralogist or the State Engineer has examined the ground and issued his report, so that the European

111 James FitzPatrick, *The Transvaal from Within. A Private Record of Public Affairs* (London: W. Heinemann, 1900), 65.

112 Ibid.

113 Francis Reginald Statham, *Paul Kruger and His Times* (London: T.F. Unwin, 1898), 95. See also, Montagu White, "The Danger of Personal Rule in South Africa," *North American Review* 170, no. 519 (1900): 232: 'In Johannesburg there was a certain amount of discontent owing to the depression, caused by the inevitable reaction after the great gold boom of 1889. Disappointed speculators, however, generally vent their spleen upon the administration, which in the Transvaal has always been a convenient scapegoat, especially during a slump in the market'.

114 *Standard & Diggers' News*, February 8, 1896.

FIGURE 18
President Paul Kruger
SOURCE: PORTRET VAN DE VERBANNEN PRESIDENT PAUL KRUGER, RIJKSMUSEUM, AMSTERDAM.

public shall no longer be deceived, which then thinks that it is the fault of the Government, and that must be prevented'.[115]

'In its present form, the Uitlander question is only the mask of a financiers' plot, of a piece of Exchange jobbery', insisted Dr Frederick Engelenburg, editor of Pretoria's *Volksstem* newspaper, presenting 'what is practically the view of President Kruger himself'.[116] 'The principal reason why some mines gave no profit and others less profit than the shareholders would have liked to see was to be found in over-capitalisation, in the floating of companies on worthless properties, in the reconstruction of companies whose profits went to the financial houses, and in the speculative fever which drove up shares to such a

115 "De Inzwering van President Kruger op 12 Mei 1898," in Joan Van Oordt, *Paul Kruger en de Opkomst der Zuid-Afrikaansche Republiek* (Cape Town: Hollandsch Afrikaansche Uitgevers, 1898), 850.

116 James Bryce et al., *Briton and Boer. Both Sides of the South African Question* (New York and London: Harper & Brothers, 1900), 123, 119.

height that it became impossible for the purchaser to rely on receiving a good dividend', wrote Kruger in his memoirs. 'The great financial houses had everything in their hands, and caused prices to rise or fall as they pleased … and the public was the victim of their manoeuvres'.[117]

It was a point of view shared in an unlikely quarter. Sir William Butler, newly appointed Commanding Officer at the Cape and Acting High Commissioner during January and part of February 1899 while Milner was briefly back in Britain, was convinced, as was J.A. Hobson writing shortly afterwards for the *Manchester Guardian*, that the Rhodes-controlled local press moved the mining market by manipulating the flow of news.[118] 'The news is first made up here by the syndicate for the transmission of false information, which has such enormous resources at its disposal', claimed Butler, 'and is then cabled to London to produce alarm on the Stock Exchange or unrest in the Cabinet. Here nothing is known about this alarming state of things, and in Johannesburg it is even less apparent. Our Johannesburg has more prosperity in it … than any place in the world. Nowhere is there so much betting, gambling, drinking; so much eating of good things; in no other place are wages so high; nowhere does the lady with the straw-coloured hair reap larger harvests, the publican sell so many drinks … But your *London* Johannesburg is quite another place'.[119]

That certainly appeared to be the case in the first six months or so of 1899. In mid-May, the market for South African mining shares was reported as having undergone a complete change 'within the past few days'. 'Whereas last week all was gloomy foreboding, operators seem inclined now to go to the other extreme. On the somewhat slender basis of a statement that Sir Alfred Milner [the High Commissioner] is about to meet President Kruger, the market jumped to the conclusion that all difficulties and grievances were about to be removed; it laughed at its fears of a week ago, and wondered how it could have been so foolish'.[120] But according to the *Financial Times*, the mining market was not moving entirely of its own volition. Taking issue with the suspiciously large number of signatures purporting to be those of British subjects on a petition detailing 'Uitlander' grievances and recently forwarded to Milner, the paper claimed that despite there being every reason for the boom to continue, once the 'Great Deal' negotiations between the big mining houses and

117 Paul Kruger, *The Memoirs of Paul Kruger* (London: T. Fisher Unwin, 1902), 284. See also, Francis Reitz, *A Century of Wrong* (London: Review of Reviews, 1900), 41–43; and Manfred Nathan, *Paul Kruger. His Life and Times* (Durban: Knox, 1941), 389.

118 John Hobson, *The War in South Africa. Its Causes and Effects* (London: James Nisbet & Co. Ltd, 1900), 206–28.

119 William Butler, *Sir William Butler. An Autobiography* (New York: Scribner's, 1913), 425.

120 *The Critic*, May 13, 1899.

the Government faltered, the market was then brought into play'. 'From the moment of the comparative failure of the negotiations a slump set in, with prices gradually drooping until to-day, precisely on the lines adopted in 1895'.[121]

'To put it plainly', the *Financial Times* concluded, 'the position has been admirably illustrated by a comparison of the political tactics of the principal financial groups here with the tactics pursued by certain people on the race-course. A method not unknown in Johannesburg amongst some owners is to have two horses in the same race, the one being a hot favourite at even money, and another which invariably wins at long odds. To-day Johannesburg is the racecourse, the leading groups are the owners, and the two horses respectively the capitalists and the public. The latter is a very hot favourite – in the Press and on the platform – but on the slightest sign of winning instructions will doubtless be given to the jockey to pull as hard as he can, and the outsider – capitalists – will win at long odds'.[122]

The failure of the Bloemfontein Conference between Milner and Kruger at the beginning of June 1899 caused 'great agitation and severe depression in the Kaffir market'. Up to the very last moment, explained *The African Review*, 'it was hoped that the meeting would lead to some good result, and it was even confidently asserted, on the strength of cabled information, that a solution of all important difficulties was practically assured. So sanguinely was this feeling entertained that the first telegrams announcing that the Conference had proved abortive were generally discredited, and the market presented a firm appearance. As soon as the position came to be correctly understood, however, the market went rapidly worse'. 'If the news we hear is true, that the British Cabinet is resolved to back up Sir Alfred Milner', the paper continued, 'the situation undoubtedly becomes exceedingly grave, and the Transvaal crisis is really only beginning. In that case, the price of gold shares has not by any means touched bottom'.[123]

Always sensitive to prevailing political winds, Wernher, Beit and Company trimmed their sails accordingly. 'I have been down today to Wernher on purpose to learn their point of view, and talked to W. and the others for two hours', Philip Gell of the British South Africa Company told Milner. 'I was surprised considering their financial stake to see how firm they were that the temporary risks and loss of a rupture were to be unswervingly faced. I put it to W. that the City and the Foreign financial opinion would rat directly they felt the slump, inevitable during the progress of hostilities. He allowed for the weak-kneed,

121 *Financial Times*, May 23, 1899.
122 Ibid.
123 *The African Review*, June 10, 1899.

but assured me that the influential Houses would remain confident that you had acted for the best, and would not flinch because the markets went to pieces'.[124] 'I knew that Wernher had been bellicose all the time', Carl Meyer, Rothschilds' confidant and De Beers director, claimed a few months later. 'The City has been only slightly affected by the acuteness of the situation but will become more nervous should an EXPEDITION be sent out which so far is not the case nor imminent, Lord Salisbury being most anxious to give the Boers every chance before resorting to extreme measures'.[125]

In their respective issues for the 10th of June 1899, *The Statist* and *The Economist* came to diametrically opposed conclusions. While the former condemned the situation in the Transvaal as 'a danger to the whole of South Africa ... [which] calls for the firm and effective interference of the supreme Government to bring it to an end',[126] the latter argued that not only did Kruger have a case, but that the motives of the British Government itself were suspect. Emphasising the 'suspicious circumstances which induce one to ask whether the Colonial Office at present is not tainted by the mania for Empire-building by syndicates', *The Economist* echoed sentiments aired in the *Manchester Guardian* by J.A. Hobson. 'Are we fighting for a genuine political principle, or are we acting as the agents of certain private moneyed interests which, by standing in ambush behind a political movement, use that movement to cloak their own designs?'[127] Two months later, its stance had hardened. Not persuaded that the fate of the British Empire depended on whether 'a certain number of miners and capitalists on the Rand are to qualify for the vote during seven years or five', the paper warned against allowing 'an exaggerated imperialism make us ridiculous before the world'.[128]

No other financial paper followed this line of argument, albeit few dealers in the City were convinced that war was inevitable. According to the *Pall Mall Gazette*, nobody expected war. 'All the leading Stock Exchange people are fully convinced that just short of it, if not before, the Boers will climb down'.[129] When Lloyds announced that it had calculated the risk of war at a mere 15–20 percent, the 'Kaffir Circus' breathed a sigh of relief. 'It may be taken as quite certain', reported *The Critic*, 'that the underwriters at Lloyds who do this class

124 Derbyshire Record Office, Gell Papers, D3287 MIL 1/532, Gell to Milner, June 2, 1899.

125 U[niversity of] [Southampton], [Hartley] [Institute], Carl Meyer Letters to his Wife, August 28, 1899.

126 *The Statist*, June 10, 1899.

127 *The Economist*, June 10, 1899.

128 Ibid., August 26, 1899. For *The Economist's* 'strongly anti-war' stance, see Edwards, *Pursuit of Reason*, 420.

129 *Pall Mall Gazette*, June 15, 1899.

of business have taken steps to ascertain the real facts of the case'.[130] There was anyway no sentiment attached to market making. 'Mr. Kruger's avowal that he will make no more concessions, accompanied by considerable selling from Johannesburg, presumably in consequence of that sturdy declaration, caused a feeling of uneasiness in the Kaffir market this morning', reported the *Financial Times*. Nothing daunted, and after a dull opening, 'some jobbers took advantage of the situation to resort to banging tactics. Many dealers who were bulls yesterday turned round and sold bears. Paris, however, still held aloof, and there was no evidence of real holders in this country having taken alarm to any material extent'.[131]

Several days later, the same newspaper dispassionately set out the reasons why war with the Transvaal might be the 'means of deliverance from an exasperating market position'.[132] Under the banner headline of 'WAR AS A BULL POINT', the *Financial Times* lamented the fact that the 'weakness on the Paris Bourse, attendant on the taxation proposals of the Spanish Government, has produced an unexpected complication in our African market'. What had changed, it explained, was that French shareholders had been 'firmly holding their Kaffirs, quite undismayed by the Transvaal crisis; in fact, operators across the Channel had been buyers rather than sellers, believing that any outcome of the present political deadlock must be more or less beneficial to the mining … [until] some French operators, having the prospect of big differences to meet on Spanish and Tintos, have now been selling their African holdings … and the consequent declining tendency of such interests has induced bear transactions here'. If that were not enough, the *Financial Times* added, 'concurrent with the French selling come accounts of melodramatic talk by Boer orators as to readiness to shed their last drops of blood; sensational concoctions by evening papers as to schemes for destroying mines and attacking Cape Town'.[133]

While all this had proved fertile ground for short-lived 'bear' operations, in the medium term it was contradicted by the probability that the Boers would give way. 'Viewing the matter hypothetically, the question arises why the prospect of war with the Transvaal should be represented as a bear point', the paper asked. 'Putting humanitarian considerations aside, and viewing the matter solely in the interest of the mining shareholder, we contend that it would be the best thing that could happen. Nothing could be worse for the market than a prolongation of the present state of things, under which holders have the

130 *The Critic*, June 24, 1899, 481.
131 *Financial Times*, June 16, 1899.
132 Ibid., June 21, 1899.
133 Ibid.

misery of enduring the depreciation of their interests, unable to discern any prospect of conditions calculated to cause a revival'.[134]

Throughout the summer of 1899, the mining share market clung to the hope that war could be avoided. The *Pall Mall Gazette was* unequivocal. 'The Stock markets certainly do not want war and have been disposed all along to take a less bellicose attitude than was sometimes the case outside'.[135] In London, hot weather, two Stock Exchange holidays, and sporting attractions such as Henley and Test cricket matches were greater attractions than 'attendance in Throgmorton-street',[136] while in Paris 'everyone ... [was] taking an intense interest in all South African matters', not least in Chamberlain himself. 'As for Mr. Chamberlain', reported the *Financial Times'* correspondent, 'he is simply the market bogey; his name is in everybody's mouth. It is asserted that he speculates largely. "Il tripote beaucoup," they say, and I know that the rumour is current, and evidently quite credited in some of the biggest houses here, that our Colonial Secretary is largely interested in Kaffir deals, under cover of a firm whose name is freely bandied about'.[137] 'Operators are eager for a settlement of the present difficulties', reported *The Critic*, 'and are ready to clutch at every straw which seems to blow in the direction they want'.[138]

Apart from the occasional nervous *frisson* triggered by City gossip, the Bourse and the Stock Exchange remained lifeless until news reached London in the middle of August that the *Standard & Diggers' News*, presumed to be acting on Pretoria's authority, had proclaimed that the Boers were determined to fight rather than 'permit the capitalist element to rule them'. In the event of war, the mines would be deliberately wrecked. 'By the loss of millions of pounds' worth of mining plant the general body of shareholders in Europe will be irretrievably ruined', the paper pointed out, 'and they should fully understand the price they must pay before authorizing the [British] Government to go to war. One thing is certain – war means absolute ruin to Johannesburg, both as a town and as a mining centre'.[139] But although mining markets initially reacted badly to a threat previously 'considered too wild to be seriously regarded', an equilibrium of sorts soon returned.[140]

'I lunched at New Court', Carl Meyer told his wife, 'but learnt no news, only talk about the Dreyfus Affair, the Paris riots which are nasty & the Transvaal

134 Ibid.
135 *Pall Mall Gazette*, July 10, 1899.
136 *Financial Times*, July 12, 1899.
137 Ibid., July 17, 1899.
138 *The Critic*, July 8, 1899.
139 *Standard & Diggers' News*, August 10, 1899.
140 *Financial Times*, August 12, 1899.

which drags along – but somehow or the other people seem convinced that it will come right as nobody wants war except the soldiers'.[141] Although the London Rothschilds quickly changed tack and sold heavily on receipt of pessimistic telegrams from the Transvaal,[142] the mood elsewhere was more sanguine. 'The Kaffir market continues to mark time', the 'City Notes' column of the *Pall Mall Gazette* recorded. 'On the whole ... opinion in the "House" inclined to the view that war will be averted ... "A day or two must settle this Transvaal business now", say the average dealers with relief, and so long as the prevailing uncertainty is dispelled, that is all the market seems to care about'.[143] With London's mining market inclined to focus on August's record output of gold, and Paris preoccupied by the Dreyfus trial, the conviction hardened in the City that 'the gradual additions to our forces in Natal and Cape Colony will tend to a peaceful settlement eventually'.[144]

The African Review described the Stock Exchange as 'affected with alternate fits of pessimism and optimism. The speech of Mr. Chamberlain in Birmingham on Saturday [when he accused Kruger of dribbling out each reply like a squeezed sponge] caused a moderate slump all round when the Stock Exchange re-opened on Monday. Much as the City likes firm and vigorous talk on the Transvaal question, it always suffers from an attack of nerves when Mr. Chamberlain does speak firmly and vigorously'. The Stock Exchange 'professes to think that the best thing that could happen is that the British Government should "go for" Mr. Kruger and his oligarchy without hesitation and without mercy, yet when a Cabinet Minister does say strong things in a plain way, the Stock Exchange trembles and ... [shares] tumble'.[145] The truth of the matter, explained the *Pall Mall Gazette*, 'is that the Stock Exchange does not want an indefinite prolongation of negotiations. "End it one way or the other, and let us get to business" about expresses the market view'.[146]

'The Market I regret to have to write to you [is] in the middle of a semi-panic', explained Henry Gibbs of Anthony Gibbs and Sons, to a partner living outside London,

> ... but the shrieks for war on the part of the Times, St James and other 'Yellow Press' journals have at last produced a regular scare on the Stock

141 US, HI, Carl Meyer Letters to his Wife, August 21, 1899.
142 Ibid., August 25, 1899.
143 *Pall Mall Gazette*, August 22, 1899.
144 Ibid., September 12, 1899.
145 *The African Review*, September 2, 1899.
146 *Pall Mall Gazette*, September 2, 1899.

> Exchange ... I still don't believe in War, though to read the leading papers, one would think that the Boers had at least occupied the Isle of Wight or massacred every English-speaking person in the Transvaal! If we honestly said we were going to annex the Transvaal & avenge Majuba Hill, I shouldn't mind, but to fight in order to secure a 5 instead of a 7 years franchise & things of that kind for Messrs Neumann & other German Jews seems to me to be quite criminal. If the mining speculators etc don't like the Boer laws, let them leave the country; they have all made pots of money in it, in spite of the 'cruel oppression'.

'The markets close certainly better', he ended, '[and] unless War is declared tomorrow, I expect there will be a scramble back of the "Bears" on Monday. The Stock Exchange is closed tomorrow, which may give people time to recover their senses'.[147]

Three weeks later when share prices had 'dropped to the lowest level of the year', by which point 'depreciation on the Kaffir list cannot be less all round, on the last few months, than between 30 and 40 per cent', *The African Review* merely advised its readers that even if war broke out, the time may have come to buy. 'Investors who can afford to hold to their purchases through all eventualities can hardly do wrong in beginning to pick up shares now'.[148] Sentiment on the Paris Bourse was equally hard-nosed. As reported by the *Financial Times*, 'a leading daily French newspaper' was of the opinion that 'the strengthening of British influence in the Transvaal cannot but have a salutary effect on the security of capital engaged in the mining industry'. 'We are not now discussing the moral aspect of the case', the daily admitted, 'for nothing can justify the interference of the English in a country which is not theirs, ... but looking at matters from the point of view of the investor, we are bound to acknowledge the successful result of British influence. The example of Egypt is there to edify us'.[149]

It was advice that the bigger denizens of the 'Kaffir Circus' were already acting on. Realising that it was never the policy of the big mining houses to buy when markets were booming, but only to intervene when shares could be secured at unusually low prices, close observers of the Stock Exchange were convinced that such 'a course ... [was] now in progress on their part'.

---

147 Guildhall Library, London, MS 11,040, Anthony Gibbs and Sons Ltd, Private letters to partners Volume Three, 1896–99, Henry Gibbs to Frank Keating, September 8, 1899.

148 *The African Review*, September 23, 1899.

149 *Financial Times*, September 18, 1899.

> 'No inside support, the big houses doing nothing', is the exclamation of the market. It is true that the controllers are doing nothing which is visible to the dealers. They do not send brokers in with large buying orders, which make an impression, and, of course, they make no effort to put prices better; but there are numerous selling orders which do not reach the market but are conveyed by brokers direct to the big houses, which quietly absorb shares which the private holders are foolish enough to throw away at less than their intrinsic value, and even at a little less than their market value, an arrangement which often furnishes a comfortable little 'turn' to the broker in addition to his commission.[150]

'A severe fall in prices, due to realisations by some nervous holders and extensive bear operations', the *Financial Times* thought, was 'just what has been awaited by the magnates primarily responsible for the action which has lead up to the present serious political situation, some of whom would be glad to reacquire, at low values, large holdings in prosperous mines'.[151]

Only at the very last moment did the City's attitude harden. 'The feeling now about war', *The Rialto* reported towards the end of September 1899, 'seems to be, "It's a good thing; shove it along"'.[152] Other papers described a sombre acceptance of imminent war with the South African Republic and its Orange Free State ally. 'The Stock Exchange to-day touched a low level of depression', wrote one newspaper. 'War is now accepted in the City as certain, and the general impression is that the sooner it is undertaken the better, for then the sooner it will be over'.[153] 'The Kaffir market took the war prospects very quietly yesterday', reported another, 'and, indeed, after the Cabinet meeting prices showed a tendency to advance'. 'It is noteworthy', the paper continued, 'that there are many waiting to buy, both among the market operators and the outside public. Brokers and others point out that there are far more indications of this desire than any wish to sell. … Provide the Boers do not commence wrecking property … there does not seem much cause for pessimism. The only puzzle with the average investor is to estimate the exact time at which to buy'.[154] Of course, the biggest market makers could make money in the worst of times, and in early October 'considerable purchases [were] effected in the Kaffir market, it is said, by large capitalists who regard the present level of values

150 Ibid., September 28, 1899.

151 Ibid.

152 *The Rialto*, September 23, 1899.

153 *Financial Times*, September 30, 1899.

154 *Pall Mall Gazette*, September 30, 1899.

as sufficient justification for laying in scrip, quite regardless of the possibility of further scares. This has naturally sent a cold shiver down the backs of the bears, and has contributed materially towards the steadying of the markets as a whole'.[155]

Nor was the Southern African mining market greatly troubled by news of the Boer ultimatum. 'Far from it taking the City by surprise, the markets had been waiting for it; weak speculators had prudently stepped aside, and prices had been fairly well adjusted to meet the situation, so that there was no excitement and no pressure to sell', reported the *Financial Times*. 'The course of business was interrupted shortly after three o' clock, when the period of grace granted the British Government by the enemy expired, by one of the patriotic demonstrations for which the House is famous. The incident took place in the Mining market, with Mr. "Charlie" Clarke as the Master of Ceremonies, and, it need hardly be said, it provided an excellent safety-valve for the fervent loyalty of the members'.[156] The 'patriotic demonstration' followed the custom of declaring, or 'hammering' defaulters who could not meet their financial obligations on settlement day. Mounting one of a number of rostrums on the floor of the Stock Exchange, an assistant or 'waiter' would strike the side of the stand with three blows from a wooden mallet before announcing the name of the individual and firm in question.[157] '"Gentlemen!", cried Clarke, having dealt the three dread blows. "Mr Kruger has not complied with his bargains!". The effect was electrical; roar after roar of laughter and applause greeted the sally'.[158] 'The hammering of Kruger at the Stock Exchange', thought J.A. Hobson, was 'a concise and most luminous revelation of this central truth, [viz] ... the power behind the throne in every modern civilised country, is the financier'.[159]

The Stock Exchange's patriotic fervour clearly had not been diminished by the Bank of England's announcements earlier in the month of successive increases in the bank rate. Nor was the financial press unduly perturbed. The prospect of war in South Africa and any interruption to the supply of gold from the Transvaal to Britain was invariably discussed in the context of

155 *Financial Times*, October 6, 1899.

156 Ibid., October 12, 1899.

157 Hubert Meredith, *The Drama of Money Making. Tragedy and Comedy of the London Stock Exchange* (London: Marston & Co., 1929), 252–53. See also, *Pall Mall Gazette*, January 27, 1905.

158 Charles Duguid, *The Story of the Stock Exchange* (London: G. Richards, 1901), 383–84; as cited in Kynaston, *City of London*, 195. See also, Andrew Saint, *London 1870–1914. A City at its Zenith* (London: Lund Humphries, 2021), 192.

159 Hobson, "Capitalism and Imperialism in South Africa," 15.

other pressing needs. When reporting early in October that the bank rate had been raised by one per cent, up from 3½ to 4½ per cent, the *Financial Times* attributed London's move in the first instance to action taken by the Imperial Bank of Germany in raising its rate from 5 to 6 per cent. 'That a rise in the official discount minimum was imminent had been patent for ten days past, and it was fully expected, in view of the Transvaal war preparations', the newspaper commented. 'The position in Berlin has, however, pressed matters forward. The action of the Imperial Bank is hardly to be wondered at, for the note circulation has recently far exceeded the legal limit, and the necessity for calling in loans has become apparent, in order to avoid the tax on its surplusage of paper'.[160]

Thereafter, the *Financial Times* contented itself with congratulating the Governor of the Bank of England for his prompt intervention,

> for this is not a moment at which Great Britain can permit any trenching on the strength of its monetary position. From all quarters demands for gold have been pressing on our central institution, while the arrivals from the Rand have been checked by the disorganization of the mines. Our warlike preparations in South Africa have involved heavy shipments of gold to South Africa to replenish the tills of the local banks; Egypt has made, as usual, considerable drafts on London for the movement of her cotton crop, and South America for the bringing to the seaboard of her harvest; and although the bank has been a steady purchaser of bars and foreign coin, the recent drain has been somewhat exhausting.[161]

A further rise in the bank rate of half a percentage point elicited only the most measured of responses from *The Economist*. 'In ordinary circumstances there would have been nothing in the position of the Bank [of England] to call for further measures of precaution. But at present there is the possibility of war with the Transvaal to be faced. … As a measure of prudence, therefore, and in order that the Bank may be in a position to meet the wants of the Government, it is desirable to seek to attract gold hither from abroad, and it is mainly with that object in view that the advance to 5 per cent. has been made, although of course the stringency of the New York and Berlin markets constitutes an additional reason for the step'.[162]

---

160 *Financial Times*, October 4, 1899. The *Pall Mall Gazette*, October 3, 1899, noted 'disturbed conditions at New York' as yet another reason for the Bank's action.

161 *Financial Times*, October 4, 1899.

162 *The Economist*, October 7, 1899.

Once the war had actually begun, *The Statist* fretted that the situation was worse than the Bank of England had anticipated. 'The outbreak of hostilities in South Africa has stopped, and probably will stop for some months, the export of gold from the Transvaal. If the pacification of the Transvaal does not take place for four months (which is not a very long period to allow for the getting out of the troops, their advance and their complete operations), there will be a withholding of gold to the amount of about six millions sterling – a very serious matter in a market like this', the periodical concluded. If that were not enough, it added, the Indian Government

> has entered into arrangements with the Indian gold-producing mining companies for supplying direct the production of those mines. And, furthermore, a very considerable amount of gold is going from Australia to India – between half a million and three-quarters of a million sterling, we believe. ... Over and above all this, we shall soon have in South Africa, reckoning the colonial contingents and the local levies, over 80,000 men, who have all to be paid, fed, and provided with everything requisite by the Imperial Government. Therefore, large sums will still have to go out to South Africa.[163]

These dire predictions were not widely believed. Nor were they realised. Within a week, the discount rate had dropped to 4½ per cent and was thought likely to fall still further. This came after a speech by the Governor of the Bank of England at the end of October 1899 in which he said that 'he saw no reason at present to anticipate an early advance in the value of money'. Although 'expenditure in South Africa might greatly exceed £6,000,000, they all knew that currency need only be a small percentage of the expenditure. Besides, a great deal of the war expenditure would be on account of freight and other home charges, which would come back to us'.[164] Quietly reassured, *The Economist* reminded its readers that the Bank of England had 'exceptional sources of information at its command'. If the Bank's Court of Directors no longer 'felt constrained to take measures to gain a better control over the market ... in order to counteract a drain of gold for South Africa', and with there being no 'serious apprehensions of gold being taken hence for the United States; indeed, in New York they are talking of the possibility of gold having to be shipped hither', it was 'inevitable that they should relax the precautions they

163 *The Statist*, October 21, 1899.

164 *The Economist*, October 28, 1899.

have hitherto thought it necessary to take'.[165] So little concerned were 'money market' columns in the leading financial daily papers and weekly journals at the prospect of war with the world's leading gold producer, that when *The Economist*, for example, subsequently reviewed the money market for 1899, it devoted as much space to the 'influence of trade activity' as it did to the war in South Africa.[166] While the City as a whole may have pivoted on gold, it did not turn on the Rand.

All that remained, or so it seemed before the 'Black Week' of 10–17 December 1899 brought news of one British military reverse after another at the hands of the Boers, was for the 'Kaffir Circus' to celebrate the close of another highly profitable year, even as it anticipated still better times to come. Clutching an enormous portfolio of properties and holdings worth an estimated £31,000,000, recently augmented by £1,000,000 or so in cash from the sale of shares and dividends, Consolidated Goldfields was believed to have taken advantage of 'the depression consequent on the war to buy back all the shares of the more prominent Companies which have been sold'. Generally speaking, concluded *The African Review*, 'this year's shareholdings exhibit a considerable increase upon those of last year, and if active markets result it is clear that the Company will be ready to take advantage of them as the vendor of large amounts of scrip. In this respect the Company is likely to do well, and before the close of the year the balance in hand should amount to more than two millions'.[167]

Not surprisingly, Lord Harris, Consolidated Goldfield's chairman, was in a relaxed frame of mind when addressing shareholders at the Company's ordinary general meeting in the second half of November 1899. 'It is easy to assert that this war has been made on behalf of capitalists; but let me remind these critics that the real owners of the mines of the Rand are the shareholders', he declared. 'It is absolutely ridiculous to talk of this war as having been made either by or for millionaires. I honestly believe that the indignation of the shareholders ... has to a large measure influenced the feeling of this country,

165 Ibid. This invites reconsideration of the argument that variations in the bank rate as a corrective was 'too disruptive of the home economy, and indeed was often impotent to staunch the flow of gold'; as claimed by S. Checkland, "The Mind of the City 1870–1914," *Oxford Economic Papers* 9, no. 3 (1957): 275. See especially, Richard Sayers, *The Bank of England 1891–1944* (Cambridge: Cambridge University Press, 1976), 51–52; and Peter Cain and Anthony Hopkins, "Gentlemanly Capitalism and Economic Policy: City, Government and the 'National Interest, 1850–1914'," in *The Development of London as a Financial Centre Volume 2: 1850–1914*, ed. Ranald Michie (London: I.B Tauris, 2000), 319–34.

166 *The Economist*, February 17, 1900.

167 *The African Review*, November 11, 1899.

FIGURE 19
Lord Harris
SOURCE: A. HACKER, PORTRAIT OF LORD HARRIS WEARING THE BOW TIE OF THE BAND OF BROTHERS, MARYLEBONE CRICKET CLUB, LONDON, UK, WIKIMEDIA COMMONS.

and their indignation is due to a very strong feeling that without injury to the Transvaal and the Boer community itself, it would have been an easy matter for them to have introduced such reforms as would conform more closely to those conditions of political or municipal life under which those critics are fortunate to live'. When representing these views to Kruger, claimed Harris, 'we put in the background all suggestions made to us as to the advantages which would simply be pecuniary advantages to the mines'.[168]

The Eton and Oxford-educated Harris' emollient remarks were followed by speeches from two Goldfields stalwarts, Hammond, the Company's chief mining engineer, and Charles Rudd, one of its founding managing directors. Neither speaker had any compunction about pointing firmly to the bottom line. They had a better sense than Harris of what the shareholders wanted to hear. Received with cheers, Hammond reiterated his belief that British rule would make possible savings of 6s. per ton in working costs. To great applause, he explained that while this would take some years to put into effect, '6s. a ton

168 "Supplement Company Meetings." *The African Review*, November 18, 1899.

FIGURE 20
John Hays Hammond
SOURCE: JOHN HAYS HAMMOND, PORTRAIT BUST, LIBRARY OF CONGRESS, PRINTS & PHOTOGRAPHS DIVISION, GEORGE GRANTHAM BAIN COLLECTION, REPRODUCTION NUMBER LC-DIG-GGBAIN-00807.

based upon last year's tonnage … [would amount to] £2,199,433 … [and] represent an increase in dividends of 45 per cent'.[169] Rudd, 'who was very heartily received', was more concerned with the bigger picture. Scanning the imperial horizon, Rudd looked forward to what victory in the field and untrammeled rule by financial capitalism might together achieve. Acknowledging that 'we have in power to-day a strong Government [in London]', he deprecated the 'morbid sentimentality among a large section of the community on the question of the natives'. 'If under the cry of civilisation we in Egypt lately mowed down 10,000 or 20,000 Dervishes with Maxims, surely it cannot be considered a hardship to compel the natives in South Africa to give three months in the year to doing a little honest work'.[170]

169 Ibid.
170 Ibid.

CHAPTER 5

Conclusion

By contrast to the many accounts of Southern Africa's gold mining industry that have concentrated on production and working costs, this study has argued that a shift in focus towards financial speculation and market-making illuminates key aspects of the region's mining past previously obscured or largely ignored. Where earlier investigations acknowledged 'windfall' profits accruing from speculation, these were invariably seen as limited either in scope or in duration. 'In 1895, at the height of the boom, there was still a great deal of speculation in shares even by those mining houses which professed a commitment to intensive mining', wrote Elaine Katz. 'All the same, most profits were no longer the result of windfalls resulting from "shady" share transactions, but came mainly from the performance of the mines'.[1] Simply mistaken, both this remark and similar observations made by other scholars, Alan Jeeves' passing acknowledgement that the market operations of Rand financial houses garnered profits that 'probably exceeded – at least for some of the groups – the profits from actual mining' notwithstanding, hugely underestimated the size of speculative gains. Profits secured by production were dwarfed by sums won through speculation.[2]

Noting that the profit on the 1894 output of the Witwatersrand gold mining industry was approximately £2,500,000, *The Economist* drew on the Chamber of Mines own figures to point out that only £1,580,000 was paid in dividends. 'These one and a – half millions sterling were the sole return upon shares ... represent[ing] a market value of approximately £125,000,000', the periodical declared. 'This [is an] absurdly low yield'.[3] In fact, it hardly weighed in the

1 Katz, "Outcrop and deep level mining," 315. A point often overlooked is that Blainey never focused on the travails of deep level mining to the exclusion of other considerations. See his "Lost Causes of the Jameson Raid," 361: 'For the quick overthrow of Kruger's government would loosen the economic yoke that choked deep-level mines and would install a sympathetic government that might revive the confidence of European speculators. In short, a rebellion could bestow the twin prizes of profit from deep mining and profit from the share market' (my emphasis).

2 Richardson and Van Helten, "Gold Mining Industry in the Transvaal," 28; Jeeves, "Control of migratory labour on the South African gold mines," 8–11, as well as his, "Hobson's The War in South Africa," 242; and Kubicek, "Randlords in 1895," 86; and I. Smith, *The Origins of the South African War, 1899–1902* (London: 1996), 163. But see, Phimister, "Frenzied Finance."

3 *The Economist*, July 6, 1895.

 | DOI:10.1163/9789004690790_006

balance against the enormous sums generated through market making. Before the boom collapsed, mining companies 'with a nominal capitalisation of about £50,000,000, were rushed up to a total market valuation of £215,000,000, a sum which barely would have been justified if all the most sanguine estimates of the productive capacity of the goldfields had become accomplished facts'.[4] By the time another two years had passed, *The Economist* thought it entirely reasonable to suggest that the '"bosses" have between them made more by their promoting and share-mongering operations than the whole district is likely to produce in profits for another ten years'.[5]

If the sheer scale of gold mining's speculative dimension has not been fully grasped by most previous accounts of the industry, neither has its systemic, persistent nature been understood. Market making was not confined to share pushing in boom times. Money was made by manipulating falling as well as rising markets. Between 1894 and 1899, the Southern African mining market was as much shaped by bears as it was by bulls. At the same time, its financial operations were invariably bent to accommodate the interests of the big controlling mining groups. 'Enormous fortunes have been made, if not always kept, by inner rings of adventurers, oftentimes by utterly unscrupulous means', *The Economist* claimed. 'By far the larger proportion of the money netted by the millionaires ... has come from the pockets of the gullible or unfortunate investors who have fallen victims to market manipulation, and the most flagrant and systematic puffing of more or less hopeless concerns'.[6]

Market-making took many forms, ranging from inflated claims, to bribing journalists working in the new financial press, to pre-allotment dealing and the creation of fictitious premiums.[7] Long associated with mining shares, the whole business was 'coming to be more and more carried on in the interests of promoters and vendors, and in too many cases outsiders are finding themselves in the position of playing with men who hold loaded dice', *The Economist* insisted.[8] If other sections of the financial press could be believed, the game was very one-sided indeed. 'The Wernher-Beit modus operandi has been to sell a property in exchange for, say, 500,000 shares at par – £1 each. These they allot to themselves. They will then make a market in the shares, and open the ball at, say, 3. Then they raise £300,000 working capital by selling 100,000 shares at 3, and these find their way into the hands of the public through the medium of

4 Ibid., December 28, 1895.
5 Ibid., April 10, 1897.
6 Ibid., October 15, 1898.
7 Van Helten, "Mining, share manias and speculation," 167.
8 "Making a Market in Mining Shares. "*The Economist*, July 4, 1896.

the Stock Exchange', explained *The Rialto*. 'An active market is made in the the shares, which, perhaps, go to 5 or 6. Messrs. Wernher-Beit would probably then unload and get perhaps £3,000,000 for their holding – assuming they were fortunate enough to sell the lot. Perhaps a slump follows, and the price drops. Then in come Messrs. Wernher-Beit to pick up at 2 the shares they sold at 5 or 6. Then they wait for a chance to once again supply the public at a higher level'.[9] Financial art, observed the *National Review*, 'like the black art of the Middle Ages, is protean, and is always breaking out in a fresh place ... Its whole aim and raison d'etre are to create fictitious markets and fictitious values'.[10]

Generally speaking, vendors, that is, sellers, of mining ventures retained a large proportion of the asking price in shares credited as fully-paid. Usually cited as evidence of the seller's confidence in the enterprise being sold, the reality was quite different. In almost every instance, the vendors 'go in for "making a market" for the express purpose of unloading their shares as rapidly as the public will absorb them'. Investors, by contrast, who had subscribed on the basis of the prospectus, were pleased when 'tape' prices quoted their shares at steadily improving prices. Only when they attempted to cash in, did they discover that frequently the market had been 'made' in the fully-paid vendor's shares only, and their partly-paid shares were unsaleable.[11] Better still for insiders were Founders Shares, most notoriously the 2/15ths of the profit made reserved for Rhodes and Rudd by Consolidated Goldfields. Their Founders Shares netted them in excess of £300,000 in 1895.[12] 'You deal in Corners, Concessions, Syndicates', Sir Charles Vandrift was told in Grant Allen's novel, *An African Millionaire*. 'You drain the world dry of its blood and its money. You possess, like the mosquito, a beautiful instrument of suction – Founders' Shares – with which you absorb the surplus wealth of the community'.[13]

These practices were so widespread that they were known at the time as South African methods. 'It is extremely regrettable that an industry of such brilliant achievements, and of such assured promise at that of the Rand should have given rise to a vast amount of over-speculation, and not a little rascality', lamented *The Economist*. 'The conditions under which reconstructions, often

9 "Wernher-Beit's Deep Levels. 'The Curse of the Kaffir Market'." *The Rialto*, September 30, 1903.

10 W. Lawson, "Stock-Jobbing Companies." *National Review* 36, no. 216, 869.

11 *The Economist*, July 4, 1896.

12 The Consolidated Gold Fields of South Africa, Limited, *The Gold Fields' 1887–1937* (London: The Consolidated Gold Fields of South Africa Ltd, 1937), 64. See also, "The Consolidated Goldfields of South Africa." *The Economist*, March 28, 1896, and *The Statist*, March 28, 1896.

13 Grant Allen, *An African Millionaire* (London: George Bell & Sons, 1897), 130.

entirely unnecessary, have been arranged, the plans for raising fresh capital, sham guarantees, and all the rest of it, can scarcely be too strenuously reprobated'.[14] 'The system of enriching the few insiders at the expense of the many outsiders who have to "foot the bill" is sometimes excused, even by people who ought to know better, on the ground that it is the prevailing South African method', the paper explained. 'The obvious reply to such a suggestion is, that where South African methods are opposed to those usually applied to business transactions, where they are subversive of fair dealing and equitable treatment, they are essentially wrong, and they will have to be placed on a juster basis if the industry is to shake off the discredit which these "South African methods" have inflicted upon it'.[15]

As well-informed contemporaries appreciated, 'South African methods' of mining company finance disfigured the industrial prospects of the Southern African region as a whole and of the Witwatersrand in particular. Extravagantly, even recklessly capitalised in a manner designed to yield short-term speculative profits,[16] starved of working capital and poorly managed, large sections of the gold mining industry could not be made to pay in any circumstances. When the blame for this state of affairs was placed at the door of Kruger state by mining industry spokesmen, even those historians who did not take the industry's insistent complaints completely at face value still questioned the ability of the South African Republic to accommodate the legitimate needs of a gigantic industrial complex,[17] 'probably the largest single capitalist development which occurred outside Europe and North America during the last two decades of the nineteenth century'.[18] Evidence of Pretoria's growing ability to do precisely that was occasionally recorded but rarely placed in any wider context.[19] Only a handful of observers saw through the self-serving nature of mining house grievances, not least repeated complaints by Wernher, Beit and Company and their local associates.

'The group comprising the H.F. Syndicate have never been backward in bemoaning the so-called exactions from the Rand industry on the part of the Transvaal Government; but those exactions would have to become very much more excessive to produce anything like the harm which is inflicted upon the industry by the depredations of such bodies as the H.F Syndicate and its allies',

14 *The Economist*, October 26, 1895.

15 Ibid.

16 Kubicek, "Finance Capital and South African Goldmining," 387.

17 Marks, "Southern Africa," 478; and Jeeves, "Hobson's *The War in South Africa*," 242.

18 David Fieldhouse, *Economics and Empire 1830–1914* (London: Macmillan, 1984), 355.

19 For example, Harries, "Capital, State," passim; and Marks, "Southern Africa," passim.

concluded *The Economist* in 1897.[20] 'Now shareholders are being told that their losses have arisen almost solely from the hostility of the Boer Government and the repressive character of the taxation which is throttling the industry', the journal continued. 'We are far from desiring to minimise the real grievances which the mining interest is laboring under, [but] ... the fact remains that excessive as much of the taxation is, it is less excessive than it was a couple of years ago, when, according to the ... [mining houses] and their champions in the Press, the whole district was overflowing with auriferous wealth, existing in practically a unique form of deposit, and giving the assurance of continuing with almost the regularity of the best coal measures, producing untold wealth for everybody concerned'.[21] 'Engineered by the "bosses"', the boom in Rand mining shares was 'almost without ... parallel in the history of joint-stock enterprise, for extravagant hopes and promises', none of them ever 'likely to be fulfilled, even if the Transvaal Government were to become a pattern [sic] of fiscal moderation and of absolute honesty of administration'.[22]

The hugely exaggerated if not entirely baseless nature of the gold mining industry's grievances so far as the Boer administration was concerned became clear after the war when none of Hammond's vaunted five or six shillings per ton reduction in working costs, the alleged difference 'between good and bad government', materialised. 'Before the war there was a general expectation that there was a possibility of materially reducing the working costs of Rand mines, given better conditions in regard to railway rates and living conditions, while the abolition of the dynamite monopoly would, it was clear, bring with it significant economies under this head', commented *The Statist* in June 1905. 'In the light of these anticipations the actual working results of the mines in 1904 are disappointing. This is a mild phrase to express the outcome of an analysis of the returns of 55 of the companies which were producing gold in 1904'.[23] The average working cost in 1898 for 36 companies was 23s 10d per ton. In 1904, the average working cost for 52 companies was actually fractionally higher at 23s 10. 6d per ton.[24]

It was not until 1908 that average working costs fell below pre-war levels, and when they did, it was the result of new technology and improved labour productivity rather than the effects of 'good' British government. 'In the annual statements recently issued by some of the principal Rand gold mining

20 *The Economist*, January 2, 1897.
21 Ibid., April 10, 1897.
22 Ibid.
23 *The Statist*, June 3, 1905.
24 Ibid.

undertakings', reported *The Economist*, 'the feature of outstanding interest has been the general, and in some cases material, reduction which has taken place in the working costs. In many of the instances these reductions follow upon similar economies in some previous years, and ... the substantial fall in operating expenses has practically revolutionised the Rand industry. ... The economies have been mainly due to the employment of heavier [crushing] stamps, the introduction of tube mills, and a distinct improvement in the efficiency of the labour employed, both skilled and unskilled'.[25]

For a man regarded as one of the leading mining engineers of his day and someone perfectly capable of distinguishing between banket and quartz gold reefs, much to Rhodes' fleeting chagrin towards the end of 1894, Hammond's market pronouncements were much less sure-footed.[26] His predilection for speculation had earlier earned him Rudd's censure, while his remarks about the difference between 'good and bad government' on working costs were also designed to boost the market immediately after the outbreak of war. They were not, and could not have been, the result of calculations based on closely observed mining practice. When first adjusting the record to better suit his self-proclaimed part in the Reform Committee and the Jameson Raid, Hammond corresponded with *Harpers* magazine in New York. 'It has also been said that it [the Jameson Raid] was a stock-jobbing operation', he wrote, 'but the personnel of the Committee dispel any suspicion on that ground, as men, many of whom were wealthy, would not risk their lives in a Rebellion for stock-jobbing purposes. Besides this the rebellion was a very costly affair, and how the Reform Leaders could have profited by stock-jobbing I cannot conceive'.[27] Of those contemporaries who thought they knew better, the names of Labouchere and Hobson stand out. They were not the only ones, of course. Less well-remembered names included the *Economist's* special mining correspondent and author of the authoritative *The Gold Mines of the World*, J.H. Curle; the leading jurist, historian and radical, Frederick Harrison; the prominent Liberal politician and author, James Bryce; and tellingly, a former President of the Witwatersrand Mine Employees and Mechanics Union, Edward Rose.

Curle understood better than most that 'the capitalists had no grievances'. As he put it, 'the mining law of the Transvaal favoured them more than did that of any English Colony, there was no direct taxation, three railways were built to Johannesburg from the coast; finally, from 1894 onwards, the public

25 "Rand Working Costs." *The Economist*, December 5, 1908.

26 Van Onselen, *Cowboy Capitalist*, passim.

27 Bodleian Library, Hammond Papers, Folio706, Hammond to P. Bigelow (of Harpers magazine), New York, August 28, 1896. See especially, Van Onselen, *Cowboy Capitalist*, 347–48.

in Europe bought scrip almost as fast as it could be printed. The capitalists wallowed in money'.[28] Recoiling from the sight 'of an Empire scrambling for half a continent', Harrison was in no doubt that it was done 'at the bidding and in the interest of cosmopolitan gamblers and speculative companies in search of bigger dividends and higher premiums'.[29] Bryce, too, was more taken by the gold mining industry's expanding profits than the burdens under which it claimed to labour. 'An examination of the figures', he wrote, 'shows how great has been the development of the industry during the last eight years, how largely the dividends have grown and how much the cost of production has been reduced. Thus in spite of the difficulties mentioned, the profits made have greatly increased, and the shareholder has fared well'.[30] Reflecting on the 'oft-repeated assertion that not only was taxation excessive and oppressive, but that this was largely due to the system of concessions which obtained under the Boers', Rose denied that 'taxation as a whole was of the oppressive nature so frequently asserted'. 'The progress made in the mining industry would alone be sufficient to demonstrate the hollowness of the pretence that the industry was seriously hampered by oppressive taxation', he argued. 'In 1897, there were 106 non-producing gold companies in the Transvaal; in 1898 this number was reduced to forty. It is sheer fatuity to pretend that results like these could have been obtained had the taxation imposed upon the mines been of the restrictive and oppressive nature so persistently represented in England'.[31]

Both Labouchere and Hobson were convinced that market making of one sort or another was the key to unlocking the inner secrets of Southern African mining finance during the 1890s, but neither of them either at the time or subsequently enjoyed much support for their views on 'stock jobbing imperialism'. Apparently knowledgeable individuals brushed aside Labouchere's claims. Writing privately to Milner in 1900, Philip Gell, by then a British South Africa Company director, declared that

> prima facia [I] cannot see that ... Labouchere's publication of the holdings of the Chartered Directors and others before and after the Raid ... proves anything. I know that the holdings of the men mentioned are as a rule very large to-day. I do not believe that there is the least ground for

28 Curle, *The Shadow Show*, 46–47.

29 F. Harrison, "The Boer Republics." *South African Conciliation Committee Pamphlet No. 21*, as cited in Stephen Koss (ed.), *The Anatomy of an Antiwar Movement. The Pro-Boers* (Chicago: University of Chicago Press, 1973), 66.

30 James Bryce, *Impressions of South Africa* (London: Macmillan & co., 1899), 304.

31 Rose, *Truth About the Transvaal*, 69–70.

> assuming that they either bought or sold in view of the Raid. Some of the best friends of the Company now habitually buy if the shares are low, and sell if the market gets speculative, to keep things steady. As you know Rhodes has often deprecated the inflation of prices. I believe the shares were absurdly high in '95, and such men sold them as they would sell to-day. The whole thing seems to me a mare's nest.[32]

But the insider's authority so confidently asserted by Gell was hardly well-informed. He was sufficiently far removed from Rhodes' inner circle that the same letter went on to assume Chamberlain's innocence of any knowledge of the Jameson Raid. 'Looking back at the whole history, it appears to me that the attempt to fix Chamberlain with a complicity which was not the fact, has had results highly disastrous to Rhodes, (who, I believe, is no party to this attempt) to the Chartered Co., and to the whole political situation'. 'It was doubtless evolved for the private defence of Jameson and the Raiders, and very possibly they personally believed in it', Gell concluded, 'but it has not only immensely increased the difficulties of Chamberlain's statesmanlike and straightforward policy, but the constant stirring of the figment by Stead, Labouchere and Hawksley has done more than anything else to keep alive the odium against Rhodes'.[33]

Labouchere's suspicion that the Jameson Raid was driven by share market considerations has generally received short shrift from historians. Contributors to an edited volume marking the centenary of the Raid did not even discuss this aspect of Jameson's gamble. Labouchere himself was mentioned only in the context of two illustrations.[34] An earlier account of the Liberal Party and the Jameson Raid in which Labouchere necessarily loomed large, nonetheless dismissed his information as 'hardly new', without explaining why that was necessarily a point of disqualification. More than this, the same historian pronounced, *de haut en bas*, that 'the gap between fact and inference was very wide, and Labouchere was unable to so argue his case as to force reasonable men to accept a plausible, but by no means inescapable, interpretation'.[35] This dismissal of the possibility that financial considerations were part and parcel of the Jameson Raid, a consequence perhaps of asking the same old questions of narrowly political sources, missed an opportunity to engage with the work of the first scholar in the 1950s to establish Chamberlain's complicity in the

32 Gell Papers, D3287 MIL 1/551, Gell to Milner, March 9, 1900.
33 Ibid.
34 Cuthbertson (ed.), *Jameson Raid*, passim.
35 Butler, *Liberal Party*, 177.

Raid. While conceding that 'the connection of the Johannesburg "movement" with Stock Exchange operations is obscure, for the secrets of the share market are not easily uncovered', Jean van der Poel had been quick to note that 'towards the end of September, that is immediately after the capitalists had met Jameson and agreed to go into the movement with Rhodes, a fall in prices had begun "owing to sales from quarters which remained a mystery even to men who knew every market move"'.[36] There were 'good grounds', she thought, 'for linking the Johannesburg commotions and the Raid with Stock Exchange manoeuvres'.[37]

Two studies devoted exclusively to Labouchere's political life and times were also inclined to give more credence to his claims than is commonly conceded. Making due allowance for Labouchere's own occasionally dubious share market dealings, exposure of which by his arch-rival, Henry Hess, led to his unplanned retirement from the Commons, Richard Hind concluded that 'beneath all his comments about the B.S.A. Company there is an undercurrent of sustained, probably honest, anxiety about the Company and its practices which appear to indicate that the poacher had turned gamekeeper'. Although Labouchere 'made serious charges against the Company without evidence and thus discredited his case', at the same time he was 'a financial expert who had personal experience of manipulating the stock exchange with the help of the press, and so his arguments and allegations were perhaps worthy of more consideration than they were given'.[38] This was especially so, Hind concluded, if the facts he published were correct; that 'Rhodes by March 1896 had disposed of 136,594 shares and Beit 114,880 shares from individual holdings of 166,057 and 122,376 respectively: of shares held jointly they sold 220,891 from a holding of 221,400'.[39]

Eleanor Mabin's detailed investigation of Labouchere's *Truth* and the British South Africa Company was still more favourably disposed towards his findings. Her conclusions placed particular weight on the long editorial, 'How Chartered Shares were Sold Before the Raid', published in *Truth* in January 1898.[40] Listing group and individual share holdings, Labouchere revealed that 'in almost every case either the majority or all the shares held had been sold by March 31, 1896. The sum of the shares held in July 1895 had been something over 900,000. On March 31, 1896, the sum of their holdings was 61,457. Thus over 800,000 shares

36 Van der Poel, *Jameson Raid*, 83.
37 Ibid., 217.
38 Hind, *Henry Labouchere and the Empire*, 35.
39 Ibid., 26.
40 *Truth*, January 13, 1898.

had been sold. Rhodes still held 29,463 shares, a much higher number than anyone else, but he had sold more shares than anyone else, too – 136,594'.[41] Coming from the same source used by Hind, the numbers themselves were never disputed. Labouchere himself admitted that it was 'exceedingly difficult to say whether the shares were sold speculatively for the account. But it is only reasonable to suppose that some of the "patriots" who were unloading their holdings in this wholesale fashion on the public, did also pick up additional money by "Bear" sales'.[42] For Mabin, none of this proved 'conclusively that the Raid was organised for financial gain', but it did suggest that 'those involved in the Raid took advantage of the opportunity potentially to profit, and also to protect themselves from the losses suffered by less well-informed shareholders, when the value of shares dropped after the Raid. … Labouchere showed that the directors of the Company, and their friends, disposed of Chartered Company shares, at high prices, before embarking on the risky enterprise of the conspiracy in Johannesburg, and the associated raid'.[43]

Her findings are supported by this study. The speculative and mining market dimension of the Jameson Raid was obvious to all except those contemporaries who chose not to see it. Even so, its long-term and proximate causes cannot be laid solely at the door of the Stock Exchange. Experienced market-watchers such as *The Investors' Review* and *The Economist* fully appreciated that the credibility of Labouchere's assertions rested on his knowledge of the capital structure of mining markets and the ease with which they were manipulated. They also understood how much his claims were buttressed by his acute sense of the linkages between Rhodes' various enterprises.[44] 'It was Labouchere's belief that the true motive underlying the Raid was a desperate wish to stave off the Chartered Company's bankruptcy by gaining access to the proven wealth of the Transvaal', explained Mabin. 'Matabeleland had proved to be no richer in gold than Mashonaland, and it was apparent that it would be many years before the territory bore significant profit – and the precarious financing of the Company required instant dramatic success. Labouchere considered the Jameson Raid to be just another step in the series of raids undertaken by the Company to enable Rhodes and his associates to engage in stock exchange speculation with British South Africa Company shares'.[45]

41 Mabin, "*Truth* and the British South Africa Company," 127.
42 *Truth*, January 13, 1898.
43 Mabin, "*Truth* and the British South Africa Company," 128.
44 See Wilson, *An Empire in Pawn*, 218–247.
45 Mabin, "*Truth* and the British South Africa Company," 216.

Although Labouchere could not have known that Rhodes had been advised by Hammond as far back as October 1894 that not only was there no 'Second Rand' north of the Limpopo, but that it actually lay underneath the first one, in the deep levels of the Rand itself,[46] he would have been aware of the precarious state of the Chartered Company's finances. Interest on a £750,000 loan taken out by the Company in the immediate aftermath of the Anglo-Ndebele War fell due on 1st January 1896.[47] With the British South Africa Company 'as close to bankruptcy after six years of operation as it had ever been, the sequence of events invoked by Labouchere pointed to a pattern of behaviour all too often repeated'.[48]

If Labouchere's great insight was to identify the transnational dimension of speculative excess, then Hobson's unequalled contribution was a keen understanding of the part played by finance in the fortunes of the Witwatersrand gold mining industry. For Hobson, the South African Republic was 'a country especially adapted to the money-lender and the stock-jobber, a land of hazards and surprises, booms and slumps, where the keen-sighted speculator and the planner of bold complex combinations has unrivalled opportunities'.[49] Randlords, the controllers of the big mining houses, were primarily 'financial speculators, taking their gains not out of the genuine fruits of industry, even the industry of others, but out of the construction, promotion and financial manipulation of companies in which a large number of smaller men are induced to put money, and out of dealing in shares of those companies'.[50]

The Rand, Hobson realised, compared with many other goldfields past and present, was peculiar in possessing underneath this speculative surface

> a sound, substantial property with a tolerably certain profitable future. The early recognition of this fact ... induced this group of financial speculators to secure and retain hold of a prepondering share of this genuinely valuable property, freely selling out and buying in when markets are on the move, but never really giving up their hold upon the sources of wealth. It is important to distinguish the interest these 'capitalists' have in their holdings of ... sound investments ... which may be described as

46 Phimister, "Rhodes, Rhodesia and the Rand," *Journal of Southern African Studies* 1, no. 1 (1974): 83.

47 *African Review*, November 18, 1893. See especially Sarah Millin, *Rhodes* (Cape Town: Central News Agency, 1952), 204–205.

48 Mabin, "*Truth* and the British South Africa Company," 217.

49 Hobson, *The War in South Africa*, 194. See also, Peter Cain, *Hobson and Imperialism. Radicalism, New Liberalism, and Finance* (Oxford: Oxford University Press, 2002), 90–99.

50 Hobson, "Capitalism and Imperialism in South Africa," 5.

> an industrial interest seeking its reward from the profitable working of these mines, and the purely financial interest they assume in the more speculative properties which they use for Stock Exchange purposes.[51]

Of crucial significance was the fact that the speculative interest could and often did come into conflict with the industrial one. 'The forces and interests of the investor and of the financier are by no means always identical', wrote Hobson. 'Even were complete structural amalgamation of the gold mines otherwise advisable, such separation, real or apparent, as favoured the manipulation of and speculation in stocks might counteract the merely industrial economies, i.e., the shareholder might be sacrificed to the speculator'.[52]

In large measure, this is exactly what happened during the period of Southern African gold mining history covered by this study. Ordinary investors suffered far more at the hands of Rand financiers and London promoters than they ever did at those of the Boer Government in Pretoria. Whether in West Africa, Western Australia, or in Southern Africa, the modus operandi was the same: 'They lease, buy, or get an option on a block of auriferous land. Then they parcel it out in claims. Then they sell the claims in lots to companies which they promote, and very likely they take a lot of shares in payment ... [Then] they say, "The borehole on the Kokoloo property has now reached the second level and shows the same excellent results". The excellent result is that small operators rush to buy Kokoloos. And who do you suppose the seller is? That is not very difficult to guess'.[53]

Although acknowledging in July 1894 that 'as an industry, gold mining on the Rand may be considered one of the most successful and progressing economic developments of the period', *The Economist's* special correspondent in Johannesburg made more of the fact that local investors had already been 'completely fleeced ... by ... puissant wirepullers'.[54] 'As a means of wealth production', the report continued, the gold mines have 'only profited a select few'. 'These disappointing results are the more striking when one observes the position of affairs on the spot. The game of reconstructing old mismanaged concerns, and of amalgamating dividend-paying ones with more or less distant deep-level claims, continues in full force. In both instances the process is carried on without the slightest had regard being shown to the direct interests of

51 Ibid.

52 Ibid., 4.

53 *The African Review*, November 2, 1901.

54 *The Economist*, August 18, 1894.

FIGURE 21
J.A. Hobson
SOURCE: MICHAEL SCHNEIDER, *J.A. HOBSON* (LONDON: MACMILLAN, 1996), FRONTISPIECE.

local or European shareholders'.[55] The result, concluded the dispatch, was that South African investors had 'given up gold share speculations wherever the wealthy firms are interested'.[56]

'In the glamour of the boom, and which lasted for many months afterwards', the *Economist* subsequently reflected that

> there is no doubt that directors, consulting engineers, and managers … having lost for the time their sense of the value of money, squandered enormous sums in a most rapid manner. Mines that were unproved or that had been proved failures were supplied with hundreds of thousands of pounds' worth of machinery which was erected in spite of the assays from underground, which, had they been properly scrutinised, did not warrant the spending of a farthing. Everybody was too busy in the share market, or was too ignorant of mining to understand the assays, or was bound by the orders of a millionaire seven thousand miles distant, who had probably never even seen the mine in question.[57]

55 Ibid.
56 Ibid.
57 Ibid., February 6, 1897.

The result was that the gold mining industry had been 'well-nigh suffocated' by the combined efforts of 'a stubborn government on the one side', and 'a group of over-capitalising millionaires, followed by a reckless and gambling public on the other'.[58]

A *Financial Times* article in August 1898 taking at face value grievances voiced by J.B. Robinson at annual meetings of the various companies comprising the 'Robinson Group' was promptly contradicted by a disillusioned and angry investor. As originally reported, Robinson's 'powerful indictment' of Kruger's government claimed that

> over and above the excessive burdens the industry has to bear, in the shape of preposterous dynamite and railway charges, and the dues and taxes on all sorts of necessaries, making the price of labour abnormally high, it is absolutely impossible to work the mines satisfactorily at all without a due supply of labour; that the Government sets all manner of obstacles in the way of the companies obtaining such a supply, refuses to assist them in the many of the ways open to it, and by its maladministration of the law, suffers such labour as is obtainable to be debauched, and, to a great extent, rendered useless by a most nefarious liquor traffic.[59]

This was not at all how some in his audience saw the situation.

Writing to the Editor a few days later, 'A Disgusted Shareholder' was more inclined to blame the Randlords alone for the gold mining industry's woes. Although the letter was concerned specifically with the notoriously speculative and badly managed Randfontein Estates mines of the J.B. Robinson group, it applied much more widely.

> It will be noted that out of the total expenditure of the company less than a tenth was devoted to actual mining operations, the rest being frittered away upon extravagant incidentals and administrative charges. By way of adding insult to our intelligence to the injury of our interests which this remarkable account discloses, we are asked to believe that the unfortunate Transvaal Government is responsible for it all. I venture to think, Sir, that the Transvaal Government has been made a stalking-horse for the sins of London and other company promoters quite long enough. The attempt to father every failure and every humbug upon the unhappy

58 Ibid.

59 "The Robinson Group. Woes of the Rand Mining Industry." *Financial Times*, August 22, 1898.

> Mr. Kruger is now worn so thin that even the veriest tyro in the business can see through it. The plain fact of the matter is that these Randfontein ventures consist of a lot of low-grade, over-capitalised propositions that would never pay to work even if Mr. Robinson, Mr. Rhodes and all the other angels were enthroned in the seats of the Boer Government tomorrow, and the sooner we recognize this to be the case the better.[60]

The mining industry's profitability, as aggrieved shareholders and key sections of the financial press knew perfectly well by the second half of the 1890s, was influenced less by Kruger's much-reviled concessions policy than it was by overcapitalisation, inadequate working capital, incompetent management, company-mongering and market making. Over-speculation, thought one of the industry's leading experts, delayed 'the achievement of the economic results hoped for'.[61]

Very little of this hard-won contemporary knowledge finds expression in the subject's historiography. The materialist *zeitgeist* of the 1970s and 1980s in Southern African studies encouraged an almost myopic focus on production to the exclusion of any other consideration. Most historians analysing the region's gold mining industry, whether putting forward arguments for or against Geoffrey Blainey's emphasis on the importance of deep-level mining, were blind to the significance of the capital structure and control of international mining share markets. Speculation and company-mongering were mentioned in passing only. No-one, as a result, grasped the significance of the prominent role played by George Farrar on the Reform Committee. At a minimum, the presence of such a notorious speculator suggested that the conspirators' motives were not reducible either to those of companies committed to deep-level propositions or to some finely calibrated combination of outcrop and deep-level concerns. Of those historians writing at the time, the present author included, only Robert Kubicek understood the importance of corporate finance, but even he was more concerned with what this might reveal about overarching theories of imperialism than their impact on the fortunes of Witwatersrand gold mining companies. Yet as Kubicek clearly appreciated, the legacy produced by financial speculation of massively overcapitalised mines characterised by high production costs, of companies formed largely for stock exchange purposes and with little intention of ever turning a profit from mining is crucial to understanding the industry's economic dynamics and Southern Africa's political trajectory.[62]

---

60 "A Disgusted Shareholder." *Financial Times*, August 25, 1898.
61 *The Statist*, April 24, 1897.
62 Kubicek, "French Capitalism and British Imperialism," 2.

It helps explain why independently-minded periodicals such as *The Investors' Review* and *The Economist* tended to be much more critical of the speculative, sometimes quasi-fraudulent market activities of the Randlords and other operators than they were of Kruger's Government. They understood that for lengthy periods the biggest profits were those made in the mining share markets of London and Paris, not the ones extracted from mines thousands of feet deep to the west and east of Johannesburg. For a time, those controlling the industry preferred to take their market profits instead of waiting for results in the form of dividends. The so-called burdens imposed on the mining industry by the authorities in Pretoria were of little immediate concern. This being so, there is hardly any evidence before war loomed large in the last six months of 1899 to support the assertion that it 'did not occur to the City that El Dorado might be left to work out its own destiny, only that the City and the British government should overcome such obstacles to profitability as it might pose them. Inevitably then the City favoured a "forward" imperial policy';[63] neither those views of the South African War which have ascribed to the City of London's financial markets 'a thirsty impatience [for war]';[64] nor the claim that, 'sniffing the scent of future profits, the City of London was generally enthusiastic at the prospect of the overthrow of the Kruger regime'.[65]

The same perspective also throws into sharp relief the international dimensions of Southern African mining finance and market making. Here, too, Hobson was quick to grasp the essential point, subsequently obscured by his antisemitic identification of 'men of a single and peculiar race'. 'The names of the chief directors of the leading companies, Wernher, Beit, Eckstein, Rhodes, Rudd, Neumann, Rothschild, Albu, Goertz, Rouliot, Farrar, Barnato, Robinson', he wrote, 'fairly indicates the distinctively international character of this financial power, as well as the closely concentrated form which it has taken'.[66] Whether in Egypt in the 1880s, when it was 'surely European capitalism which triumphed under British leadership';[67] or in China after the turn of the twenti-

63 Jonathan Schneer, *London in 1900. The Imperial Metropolis* (New Haven: Yale University Press, 1999), 79–80.

64 Peter Clarke, *Hope and Glory: Britain 1900–1990* (London: Allen Lane, The Penguin Press, 1996), 15.

65 Denis Judd and Keith Surridge, *The Boer War* (London: Palgrave Macmillan, 2002), 46–47. See also, amongst others, Willie Thompson, *Global Expansion. Britain and its Empire, 1870–1914* (London: Pluto Press, 1999), 43; Victor Leonard Allen, *The History of Black Mineworkers in South Africa. Volume I. The Techniques of Resistance 1871–1948* (Keighley: Moor Press, 1992), 141–42; and Marks, "Southern and Central Africa," 478.

66 Hobson, "Capitalism and Imperialism in South Africa," 3.

67 Guy Palmade, *French Capitalism in the Nineteenth Century* (Newton Abbot: Newton Abbot, David and Charles 1972), 177.

eth century where 'the cosmopolitan character of the entire foreign establishment in China makes it difficult to isolate a particular British factor', financial imperialism 'as a cooperative project under British leadership' is most usefully discussed 'in general terms'.[68] In Southern Africa, the City's financial interests were often international even when registered in London. The transnational connections established between the City, Paris, Berlin, Vienna, Constantinople and Johannesburg put market making by the big mining houses, often acting through proxies, largely beyond detection.

After the Jameson Raid, rumours swirled around Beit, Rhodes and Phillips. 'It was said quite openly that this political action was nothing more or less than a well-prepared manoeuvre on a large scale to bring down prices'; that they 'stood at the head of a secret syndicate formed with the intention of bearing Chartered and other South African shares'.[69] Rhodes, concluded Hobson, was 'essentially a combination of … adventurer and financier … able by his political genius, to give a temporary cloak of political significance to adventures which were *au fond* operations on the stock markets'.[70] 'I am quite sure if you saw the moral and social devastation Rhodes has worked in this country with his money you would feel as I do', wrote Olive Schreiner to W.T. Stead, erstwhile editor of the *Pall Mall Gazette*. 'It's not Rhodes I object to it's his money, which damns him himself in the first place, & causes him to damn others … I use the words with the greatest earnestness & meaning, it's his damnable and damning gold which has first ruined him & is now, through him, ruining South Africa'.[71]

'There is no more nervous man in the world than Alfred Beit, who is growing afraid of his own shadow', darkly hinted *The Rialto* years later. 'It is a nasty feeling after having successfully played the game to win to remember some of the instruments used during the operation'.[72] But because Labouchere's stock exchange informant refused to step up and bear testimony, nothing could be proved. Nor is the considerable circumstantial evidence suggesting that Beit's market making role and speculative interventions were far more important

68 Jürgen Osterhammel, "Britain and China, 1842–1914," in *The Oxford History of the British Empire. The Nineteenth Century*, ed. Andrew Porter (Oxford: Oxford University Press, 1999), 159, 165.

69 Emden, *Randlords*, 199.

70 John Atkinson Hobson, *The Evolution of Modern Capitalism. A Study of Machine Production* (London: Allen & Unwin, 1926), 269.

71 Olive Schreiner to W.T. Stead, [?] July, 1896, in Liz Stanley and Andrea Salter (eds), *The World's Great Question. Olive Schreiner's South African Letters 1889–1920* (Cape Town: Van Riebeek Society, 2014), 67.

72 *The Rialto*, January 2, 1901.

than allowed for by most studies beyond dispute.[73] The *Financial Times* had to content itself with snidely remarking when it published a 'Men of Millions' special supplement in 1898 that 'Mr. Beit is a man of immense wealth and would have been even richer if the revolution he directed from Cape Town had been successful',[74] even if later it insisted that the Jameson Raid was a 'private speculation … planned by Beit and Co.'[75] A verdict under Scottish jurisprudence of 'not proven' guilty but not found innocent may be the safest.[76] W.P. Schreiner, after all, decided that he would not hang Beit on the weight of it.

Of Beit's peers who did come close to being hanged in the immediate aftermath of the Jameson Raid, the two leading Reform Committee members, Lionel Phillips and John Hays Hammond, between them personified the ease with which mining markets were moved, and the hugely destabilising economic and political consequences which could follow. The other side of the coin of Phillips' 'Mene, Tekel' speech in November 1895, deliberately calculated to 'bang' the market and bring Johannesburg's 'Uitlander' population firmly onside with the conspirators, was Hammond's imagination of a reconfigured Boer republic shaped by a febrile mix 'of attitudes and ideas about colonization, expansionism, filibustering, Manifest Destiny, slavery, racial superiority and Social Darwinism', his own experiences of North American mining camps and the emerging outlines of an informal American Empire.[77]

Neither vision was constrained by any consideration of British imperial interests. If, as Juergen Osterhammel observed in the course of surveying the export of capital in the latter part of the nineteenth century, even high finance and international politics 'never overlapped completely',[78] then the money-grubbing proclivities of self-aggrandizing Southern African mining and money markets rarely, and then only belatedly, coincided with Colonial Office concerns. Instead, British politicians faced the alarming prospect not so much of Kruger's Boer republic growing ever mightier, but of it becoming a 'British Republic of such great wealth and so large a [white] population situated at the

73 For example, Kubicek, "Randlords in 1895," 98. But see, Wheatcroft, *Randlords*, 215.

74 *Financial Times*, February 21, 1898.

75 Ibid., November 24, 1898.

76 Margalit Fox, *Conan Doyle for the Defence* (London: Random House, 2018), 123–124: '… "not proven", a verdict that in the sardonic parlance of Scottish lawyers is said to mean "not guilty, and don't do it again"'.

77 Van Onselen, *Cowboy Capitalist*, 466, 470–471.

78 Jürgen Osterhammel, *The Transformation of the World. A Global History of the Nineteenth Century* (Princeton: Princeton University Press, 2014), 738.

geographical centre of political South Africa [that it] would assuredly attract to itself all British Colonies in South Africa'.[79]

Crucially, it was a position shared by Chamberlain himself. Writing in June 1896, the Colonial Secretary declared that he had 'never at any time concealed my opinion that, whatever defects may exist in the present form of Government of the Transvaal, the substitution of an entirely independent Republic governed by or for the capitalists of the Rand would be very much worse both for British interests in the Transvaal itself and for British influence in South Africa'.[80] Rhodes' off-hand remark at the time of the Jameson Raid that 'I was not going to risk my position to change President Kruger for President J.B. Robinson', amplified in a telegram to Rutherfoord Harris in which he made it clear that he would not 'risk everything as I am doing, excepting for British flag',[81] did not go unnoticed in Whitehall.[82] 'I am far from believing that Mr. Rhodes has been moved exclusively or chiefly by purely financial considerations in his politics', conceded Hobson in 1900. 'It is quite likely that some large, indefinite desire to express his personality in what is termed "empire-building" may have fused with, and at times over-powered, the narrower financial aims'.[83]

The political and economic terrain occupied so ruthlessly by Phillips acting under instruction and which Hammond found so congenial was under constant construction and reconstruction by the powerful interests driving international mining markets. For much of the period considered here, it was a space determined less by the production imperatives of cost minimisation and output maximisation than by the manipulation of rising or falling share markets, primarily the City of London's 'Kaffir Circus', but encompassing the Paris Bourse and the Johannesburg Stock Exchange as well. Whatever the grievances of the Randlords were, they were not primarily located in the sphere of production.

79 Bodleian Library, Selborne Papers, Colonial Office Memorandum, March 26, 1896. See especially, Ian Phimister, "Empire, Imperialism and the Partition of Africa," in *Gentlemanly Capitalism, Imperialism and Global History*, ed. Shigeru Akita (Basingstoke: Palgrave Macmillan, 2002), 75–77.

80 *[Extract] Chamberlain's Memorandum. 12 June 1896*, as cited in Drus, "Report on the Papers of Joseph Chamberlain," 49.

81 John G. Lockhart and Christopher M. Woodhouse, *Rhodes* (London: Hodder and Stoughton, 1963), 308.

82 Andrew Porter, *The Origins of the South African War. Joseph Chamberlain and the Diplomacy of Imperialism 1895–99* (Manchester: University Press, 1980), 80.

83 Hobson, "Capitalism and Imperialism in South Africa," 7.

Exuding contempt for what Rhodes once memorably dismissed as 'unctuous rectitude',[84] infused by a pervasive sense of moral if not quite legal fraud, and enveloped by a 'tide of demoralisation which has threatened at times to turn the British Empire into a more or less shady company concern',[85] the portal of globalisation opened to Southern Africa by finance capital had created a world in which 'the company-monger was paramount',[86] and where the influence of 'filibustering speculators' knew no bounds.[87] The challenge this posed to British paramountcy in Southern Africa was paradoxical. Glimpsed long ago by Ronald Robinson and John Gallagher, the 'motive behind intervention was … not the contriving of commercial success. Rather it was commercial success which raised up republicanism and undermined British influence'.[88] 'I see before us the necessity for considerable military effort', wrote Britain's Prime Minister, Lord Salisbury, in August 1899, 'and all for people whom we despise, and for territory which will bring no profit and no power to England'.[89]

---

84 Stutfield, "The Higher Rascality," 75. See also, Millin, *Rhodes*, 209; William Stead (ed.), *The Last Will and Testament of Cecil John Rhodes. With Elucidatory Notes to which are added Some Chapters describing the Political and Religious Ideas of the Testator* (London: "Review of Reviews" Office, 1902), 44; and Vere Stent, *A Personal Record of Some Incidents in the Life of Cecil Rhodes* (Cape Town: Books of Rhodesia, 1925), IX.

85 *Daily Chronicle*, November 10, 1898.

86 Stutfield, "The Higher Rascality," 85.

87 Hobson, *Ethical World*, May 27, 1899, 323.

88 Robinson and Gallagher, *Africa and the Victorians*, 461.

89 John Grenville, *Lord Salisbury and Foreign Policy: The Close of the Nineteenth Century* (London: Athlone Press, 1964), 267.

APPENDIX A

Witwatersrand Gold Production 1888–1893

The output from the Witwatersrand gold fields

	1888	1889	1890	1891	1892	1893
January	7,328	25,506	35,007	53,205	84,560	108,374
February	12,180	22,457	36,887	50,079	86,649	93,252
March	11,976	27,919	37,780	52,949	93,245	111,474
April	14,146	27,029	38,697	56,372	95,562	112,053
May	13,397	35,028	38,836	54,673	99,436	116,773
June	12,773	30,878	37,419	55,863	103,252	122,907
July	16,687	31,091	39,457	54,924	101,279	126,169
August	18,616	30,520	42,864	59,070	102,322	136,069
September	20,242	34,143	45,486	65,602	107,852	129,585
October	27,165	32,214	45,249	72,793	112,167	136,682
November	26,827	33,722	46,783	73,394	106,795	138,640
December	26,784	39,050	50,352	80,323	117,748	146,357
Total, Ounces	208,122	369,557	494,817	729,238	1,210,867	1,478,473

SOURCE: ADAPTED FROM *SOUTH AFRICAN MINING JOURNAL*, OCTOBER 1908.

 | DOI:10.1163/9789004690790_007

APPENDIX B

Witwatersrand Share Prices: 1889 Peak and 1890 Slump

Mine	Highest boom price		Slump price		Issued capital	Market value
	s.	d.	s.	d.	£	£
Aurora	84	6	21	0	50,000	211,250
Bantjes	102	6	8	0	95,000	486.875
City and Suburban	350	0	82	6	60,000	1,050,000
Croesus	100	6	8	6	65,000	326,625
Crown Reef	267	6	90	0	100,000	1,337,500
Ferreira	460	0	190	0	28,000	644,000
Goldfields	140	0	35	0	370,000	2,590,000
George Goch	82	0	10	0	134,500	551,450
Henry Nourse	220	0	35	0	50,000	550,000
Heriot	225	0	35	0	60,000	675,000
Jubilee	230	0	87	6	22,000	231,000
Jumpers	400	0	45	0	49,000	980,000
Meyer and Charlton	215	0	55	0	43,000	462,250
Langlaagte Estate	165	0	60	0	432,000	3,564,000
Moss Rose	130	0	5	0	37,000	240,500
Robinson	122	6	65	0	2,668,750	3,269,218
Roodepoort	195	0	50	0	90,000	877,500
Salisbury	690	0	50	0	24,250	836,625
Simmer and Jack	214	0	80	0	80,000	856,000
Spes Bona	140	0	1	6	70,000	490,000
Stanhope	180	0	55	0	30,000	270,000
Wemmer	320	0	70	0	38,000	608,000
Wolhuter	125	0	20	0	65,000	406,250

SOURCE: HARRY KLEIN, *THE STORY OF THE JOHANNESBURG STOCK EXCHANGE 1887–1947* (JOHANNESBURG: COMMITTEE OF THE JOHANNESBURG STOCK EXCHANGE 1948), 32.

 | DOI:10.1163/9789004690790_008

APPENDIX C

Selected Rand and Rhodesian Share Prices, December 1894–December 1895

	December 1895. £	December 1894. £	Highest price 1895. £
Block B (Langlaagte)	1¾	⅝	3³⁄₁₆
Bufffelsdoorn	3⅛	3¾	9¼
Champ d'Or	2⅝	4⅜	5¹⁄₁₆
City and Suburban (£4)	4⅛	4⅜	8
Croesus (New)	1½	2⅜	3½
Crown Reef	9⅝	10¼	12⅞
De Beers Diamond	22⅞	19¼	32½
Durban – Roodepoort	7	7⅜	8¹⁵⁄₁₆
East Rand	4½	2¾	12⅝
Ferreira	15½	15¾	22
Geldenhuis Deep	5⅛	7¼	4¼
Do Estate	3¾	6⅜	7¼
Glencain	3⅞	3⅞	4⅞
Goldfields Deep	5⅝	4	14
Henry Nourse	4¾	5⅞	8¹⁄₁₆
Heriot	7⅞	8¼	12½
Jagersfontein (New)	8⅝	8¾	12
Jubilee	8	9¼	12⅛
Jumpers	7	6¼	8⅞
Kleinfontein (New)	3¼	3⅞	8¾
Knight's	4⅜	3⅜	11¼
Langlaagte Estate	5⅛	4¼	7¼
May Consolidated	2¾	2¼	4⁵⁄₁₆
Meyer and Charlton	5⅛	7	8¼
Modderfontein	6⅞	10	17⅞
New Chimes	2	2⅞	4⁵⁄₁₆
New Primrose	6	6⅛	8⁵⁄₁₆
New Rietfontein	3⅝	3¾	6⅜

 | DOI:10.1163/9789004690790_009

	December 1895. £	December 1894. £	Highest price 1895. £
Nigel	3⅞	5½	8 7/16
Orion (New)	3⅛	3⅜	5⅛
Paarl Central	1⅛	1½	2⅞
Princess Estate	2¼	2	4½
Rand Mines	21¼	22⅛	45⅛
Robinson	8¾	7¾	11½
Simmer and Jack	20	13½	23
Transvaal Gold	4⅝	3½	10⅞
Van Ryn	5	5	11
Village Main Reef	4¾	6	9½
Wemmer	9¼	6¼	13
Wolhuter	6¾	5⅛	12
	—		
Bechuanaland Exploration	1¼	1 1/16	3¼
British South Africa	4¾	2⅜	8 13/16
Consolidated Goldfields Def.	10⅛	4 5/16	19⅝
Johannesburg Cons. Invest.	3½	2 9/16	6⅞
Lydenburg Estates	1⅛	—	3⅞
Mozambique	1	1⅜	3 1/16
Oceana Land	1 9/16	2⅝	4⅜
South Africa Gold Trust	7⅛	4	12¾
Willoughby Consolidated	1¾	1⅝	2 9/16

SOURCE: *THE ECONOMIST*, DECEMBER 28, 1895.

APPENDIX D

Witwatersrand Yields, Working Costs, and Dividends, 1887–1899

		Yield		Working costs		Dividends	
Year.	Tons. Milled	Total £ sterling.	Shillings per Ton.	Total £ sterling	Shillings per Ton.	Total £ sterling.	Shillings per Ton.
1887	25,000	81,045				12,976	
1888	250,000	729,715				109,052	
1889	575,000	1,447,514				430,666	
	850,000	**2,258,274**	**53.13**	**1,705,580**	**40.13**	**552.694**	**13.00**
1890	702,825	1,735,491	49.38	1,480,940	42.14	254,551	7.24
1891	1,175,465	2,556,398	43.49	2,221,630	37.80	334,698	5.69
1892	1,921,260	4,297,610	44.73	3,418,290	35.58	879,320	9.15
1893	2,203,704	5,187,206	47.08	4,231,848	38.40	955,358	8.78
1894	2,830,885	6,963,100	49.19	5,435,816	38.40	1,527,284	10.70
1895	3,456,575	7,840,779	45.36	5,793,927	33.52	2,046,852	11.84
1896	4,011,697	7,864,341	39.27	6,350,659	31.66	1,513,682	7.61
1897	5,325,355	10,583,616	39.74	7,876,435	29.58	2,707,181	10.16
1898	7,331,446	15,141,376	41.30	10,293,138	28.08	4,848,238	13.22
1899	6,639,355	14,046,686	42.31	11,100,328		2,946,358	
Total	**36,448,567**	**78,474,877**		**59,908,591**		**18,566,216**	
Average	**2,803,736**	**6,036,529**	**44.99818**	**5,446,236**	**35.529**	**1,428,170**	**10**

SOURCE: ADAPTED FROM *SOUTH AFRICAN MINING JOURNAL*, SEPTEMBER 25, 1909.

 | DOI:10.1163/9789004690790_010

APPENDIX E

Flotations: Southern African Mining, Land and Exploration Companies, 1895

1. Mining

Company	Nominal capital £	Working capital £
Abbot's Consolidated Reefs	120,000	
Abercorn Reefs	60,000	
Alder's Consolidated Mines and Lands	500,000	
African Alluvial Gold Mines	150,000	30,000
African and Australian Gold Fields	25,000	
African Gold Mining	100,000	
African Gold Selections	3,000	
African Gold Properties	100,000	
African Metals	400,000	
Alpha (Rand) Gold	100,000	
Anglo-African Gold Properties	200,000	
Anglo-French Gold Mining Syndicate	1,000	
Anglo-Rand Gold Mines	150,000	
Austral-African and General Gold Trust	50,000	
Australian and West African Gold Exploration	75,000	
Auriferous Properties	100,000	
Barberton Gold Fields (South)	100,000	
Barberton Reefs	100,000	
Beaconsfield Diamond	85,000	
Bembesi District Gold	100,000	
Bembesi Gold Reef Development	85,000	
Big Block Gold	200,000	
British Goldfields of West Africa	235,000	40,000
Brand Kumalu Syndicate	60,000	27,750
Buffels Klerksdorp	210,000	
Bulfontein Sun Diamonds	100,000	20,000
Buluwayo Consolidated Gold Fields	250,000	50,000
Buluwayo Gold Reef Development	70,000	

 | DOI:10.1163/9789004690790_011

Company	Nominal capital £	Working capital £
Cape Gold Fields	100,000	
Cariboo Reefs Development	20,000	
Central Lydenburg Gold Estates	100,000	
Central De Kaap Gold Mines	70,000	
Central Panhalanga Gold	130,000	
Chartered Gold Fields	500,000	
Christmas Reef (Rhodesia) Development	100,000	30,000
Clutha Gold Mines	100,000	
Consolidated Black Reef	500,000	
Consolidated Middel Vlei	300,000	
Consort Deep Level Gold	120,000	25,000
Cote d'Or	4,000	
Crescens (Matableland) Mine and Lands	50,000	20,000
Durban Gold Mines	120,000	
Durban Winnie Gold Mines	150,000	
Eagle's Nest Gold	60,000	
East African Gold Fields	60,000	
East Nigel Gold	120,000	20,000
Eastern Rhodesia Gold Reefs	175,000	
Elephant's Kloof Gold	200,000	
English and French Gold Mines Syndicate	120,000	
Fortuna Syndicate	12,000	
French North Rand Estates Gold	150,000	
French Soudan Gold Fields and Exploration	50,000	
Geldfontein Estates and Gold	100,000	
Globe and Phoenix Gold	175,000	
Gold Blocks Gold	150,000	25,000
Gold Explorers	75,000	
Gold Fields of Damaraland Exploration	250,000	75,000
Gold Fields of Matabeleland	500,000	
Gold Fields of Mazoe	110,000	
Gold Reefs of West Africa	90,000	
Good Hope Gold Fields	75,000	
Great de Kaap Moodies Gold Fields	200,000	
Hammond's (Matabele) Gold	200,000	
Henderson's Nigel	360,000	
Hetty Gold	120,000	30,000

Company	Nominal capital £	Working capital £
Ingamsonga Reef	70,000	
Joe's Reef United (Sheba)	90,000	
Jumpers Extended	100,000	
Kaffirs Limited	120,000	20,000
Klerksdorp Gold Farms	30,000	
Klerksdorp Reefs	100,000	
Krugersdoorp Gold Syndicate	5,000	
La Concorde City and Suburban (Matabeleland)	300,000	75,000
Lady Helen Gold	10,000	
Lomagunda Reefs	150,000	
London and Gwelo Reefs	7,000	
Lydenburg Consolidated	150,000	
Lydenburg Gold Fields	1,000	
Lydenburg Minerals	1,000	
Lydenburg (Tranvaal) Gold	150,000	
Marie Rose Gold	175,000	50,000
Mashona Gold Reef	50,000	
Matabele Gold Properties	120,000	
Matabele Mines	250,000	
Matabele Ancient Gold Reefs	80,000	
Mines Selection	200,000	
Middle Black Reef Gold	150,000	40,000
Misgund (Black Reef) Gold	200,000	
Mozambique Gold	100,000	25,000
Mozambique Reefs	50,000	
Nelly and Pioneer Reefs	65,000	
New Randfontein Extension	20,000	
New Golden Koppe	120,000	20,000
New Gold Fields Syndicate	50,000	
Niekerk (Klerksdorp) Gold	150,000	
Nigel Extension	80,000	
Nigel Main Reef	120,000	10,000
Noltzykop Gold Mines	150,000	
Nooitgedacht Diamond	250,000	
North Rand Mines	300,000	
North Sheba Gold	200,000	

Company	Nominal capital £	Working capital £
Oceana Minerals	500,000	100,000
Orion Belt	250,000	
Orion Deep Level	1,000	
Potchefstrom Mining	1,000	
Prince's Gold Mine	130,000	50,000
Prospectors of Matabeleland	200,000	50,000
Rand d'Or Mines	175,000	
Rand Goldfields Syndicate	75,000	
Rand Junction Reefs	200,000	
Rand Minerals	1,000	
Rand Roodepoort Gold	60,000	
Rand Southern Gold	100,000	
Rand Victoria Mines	750,000	
Randt Gold	80,000	
Randfontein Deep	200,000	
Randfontein Extensions	200,000	
Rhodesia Gold Fields	1,000,000	
Rhodesia Gold Exploring	100,000	
Rhodesian Claims	275,000	50,000
Rhodesian Minerals Properties	233,000	50,000
Rhodesian Prospectors	20,000	
Rip Gold Mining	65,000	
Roodekoppen Gold	80,000	
Rorke's Roodepoort	130,000	20,000
Rosenblock Twin Reef	60,000	
Rothery Block	120,000	30,000
Royal Sheba	50,000	20,000
Shazada Mines	60,000	
Sheba Queen Gold	200,000	
Sheba Alliance	120,000	
Simmer and Jack Deep	300,000	40,000
Sneddon Concessions	30,000	10,000
Simmer's Gold Mines	100,000	
South Luipaard's Vlei	175,000	
South Nigel Gold	150,000	
South Randfontein Deep	275,000	
South Rand Proprietary	300,000	

Company	Nominal capital £	Working capital £
South Swaziland Gold	100,000	
Southern Rand Gold	100,000	
Sterkfontein Gold Estates	125,000	
Syndicat Franco-Anglais des Mines d'Or	100,000	
Taylor's Matabele Gold Fields	100,000	25,000
Tigerfontein	50,000	
Tiger (Massi Kessi)	60,000	
Transvaal Black Reef Claims	400,000	
Transvaal Westralians Gold Concessions	50,000	
Umtoli Gold Reefs	50,000	
Ventersdorp Gold Estates	1,000	
Waterberg Minerals	1,000	
Waterfall Estate	25,000	
Waterfall Prospecting	100,000	
West African Consolidated	175,000	
White Rose Gold	125,000	50,000
Witpoortje Gold Mines	150,000	
Woodstock (Transvaal)	200,000	70,000
Wyatt Gold Coast Syndicate	40,000	
Zoutpansberg Consolidated	400,000	
Zululand Natal Gold Fields	50,000	
Total	**31,852,000**	**1,232,750**

SOURCE: *AFRICAN CRITIC*, JANUARY 18, 1896.

2. Land and Finance Companies

Abercorn Mashonaland Development	7,550
African and Australian Exploration and Development	11,000
African Concessions	30,000
African General Development	50,000
African Search	10,000
African Territories	250,000
Africa Trust	150,000
Africana	100
Africana	1,500,00
Albion Transvaal	125,000

Alpha (Rand) Exploration	2,500	
Anglo-Africander	7,000	
Anglo-Africa Exploration	50,000	
Anglo-Dutch Exploration	100,000	
Anglo-French Matabeleland	60,000	
Anglo-West African Concessions	130,000	
Austral-Africa	500,000	
Bechuanaland Exploring	1,000	
Bangwaketsi Concessions	40,000	
Barberton Consols	100,000	
Barberton Syndicate	1,000	
Batley Syndicate	50,000	
Belingwe Development	30,000	
British South African	3,000	
British Exploration	150,000	75,000
British Lomagunda	75,000	
British West Charterland	400,000	
B.S.A. Syndicate	100	
Browne Fairbridge Syndicate	7,000	
Buckley's Rhodesia	5,000	
Cape Investments	10,000	
Cassinga Concessions	300,000	
Charterland Consolidated	200,000	25,000
Charter's Exploration	250,000	
Clark's Consolidated	240,000	70,000
Colenbrander's Matabeleland	280,000	100,000
Concessions Acquisition Syndicate	2,000	
Consolidated Belingwe Development	200,000	
Consolidated Estates of Cape Colony	1,500,000	
Cornubia Syndicate	2,000	
Davies' Selukwe Syndicate	8,000	
Davies' Buluwayo	20,000	
Diamonfontein Estate	60,000	
Dingaan (Nondweni) Syndicate	2,000	
Eastern Rand Syndicate	100,000	
E.J.P. Syndicate	5,000	
Exploring and Development	52,000	
Federated Mines Prospecting	250,000	
Fleming's Matabeleland Exploration	65,000	
Forbes Rhodesia Syndicate	30,000	

Franco-African Exploration	200,000	
Free Estates	7	
Freeman Cohen's Consolidated	1,000,000	
French Exploration	300,000	
Frederick's Matabeleland	50,000	
French South African Development	200,000	
General Rand Company	1,000,000	
Gold Coast Development	30,000	
Gold Coast Exploration and Trading	10,000	
Gold Fields Finance and Development	200,000	
Gourlay's Rhodesia Development	150,000	50,000
Griqualand Syndicate	5,000	
Griqualand West Land and Exploring Syndicate	100	
Grootfontein	125,000	
Gwanda (Rhodesia) Consolidated Development	100,000	20,000
Gwelo (Matabeleland) Exploration and Developing	500,000	
Heidelberg Estates and Exploration	100,000	
Heidelberg Proprietary	80,000	
Heidelberg Roodeport	250,000	
Heidelberg Union Land	120,000	
Holton Land and Mining	75,000	25,000
Imbembezi Syndicate	20,000	
Inca (Matabeleland) Development	120,000	
Investors' Exploration	40,000	
Kaffir Westralian Exploration	30,000	
Kaffirs Consolidated and Investment	50,000	
Kruger Syndicate	5,000	
Laing's Exploring	100,000	
Leechdale Rhodesian Development	150,000	50,000
Liverpool (South Africa) Exploration	20,000	
Livingstone African Exploration	250,000	100,000
Lomatie (Lydenburg) Exploration	150,000	50,000
London-African and General Syndicate	5,000	
London and Buluwayo Syndicate	6,000	
London and Paris Financial and Mining Corporation	500,000	
Lydenburg Development	1,000	
Lydenburg Estates	215,000	
Lydenburg Proprietary	1,000	
Maldo Exploration Syndicate	15,000	
Matabele Central Estates	150,000	10,000

Matabele Development	300,000	50,000
Matabele Exploration Syndicate	30,000	
Mazoe Development	160,000	
Metropolitan Exploration	25,000	
Mines Development (South African Company)	5,000	
Montrose Matabele	100,000	
Moonie Creek Development	100,000	
Moore's Rhodesia Concessions	150,000	30,000
Mozambique Exploring Trading	5,000	
Mullin's South African Syndicate	1,000	
New Transvaal	100,000	
North Charterland Exploration	1,000,000	300,000
Northern Territories (B.S.A.) Exploration	100,000	
Norfolk Syndicate	12,500	
Noycedale Syndicate	20,000	
Panga Company	5,000	
Pardy's Range	120,000	
Premier Tati	300,000	
Prudential Exploration	10,000	
Rand Consols	150,000	
Rand Western Syndicate	10,000	
Rathchine Syndicate	25,000	
Rhodesia Concessions	150,000	
Rhodesia Consolidated (Parent)	100	
Rhodesia Estates and Town Lands	175,000	
Rhodesia Exploration Development	100,000	
Rhodesia, Limited	100	
Rhodesia, Limited	200,000	43,500
Rhodesia Transvaal Syndicate	20,000	
Rhodesian and General Corporation	250,000	
Rights and Exploring of Rhodesia	100,000	32,350
Rosemont Lydenburg Estates	200,000	
Selected Properties of South Africa	100	
Selukwe Consolidated	170,000	40,000
Selukwe Developing Syndicate	45,000	
Senegal S. Syndicate	30,000	
Shangani Development	70,000	
Sherbro and Avery Syndicate	15,000	
Silinda	5,000	
South African Argus Association	50,000	

South African Exploring	50,000	
South African General Development	50,000	
South African Gold Mining Exploration	5,000	
South African Investors' Syndicate	20,000	
South African Territories	500,000	
St. John's River Syndicate	10,000	
Steynskraal Syndicate	16,000	
Tati Concessions	500,000	
Tonkin Exploring	30,000	
Transvaal Exploring	1,000	
Transvaal Mineral Lands	1,000	
Troye Exploration	400,000	
Tyneside African	2,000	
Umtoli (Mashona) Land and Prospecting	2,000	
United Exploration	500,000	
Van Syndicate	20,000	
Van Ryn North Exploration and Mining	170,000	
Vaughan-Williams Rhodesian Development	50,000	15,000
Vincent's Rhodesian Development	75,000	20,000
V.V. (Gwanda) Syndicate	75,000	30,000
Warnford Exploration	10,000	
West African Estates	60,000	
West African Exploration	10,000	
West Rand Exploration	5,000	
Western Transvaal Development	20,000	
Western Witwatersrand Exploration	300,000	80,000
Weston Syndicate	2,500	
Whites's Syndicate	100,000	
Wittkop Exploration Syndicate	1,000	
Witwatersrand and General Development	35,000	
W.R.B. Syndicate	10,000	
Zambesi Rand Investment	250,000	
Zululand Exploration Syndicate	10,000	
Total	53,195,807	2,448,600

3. Miscellaneous Companies

African Saltpetre	300,000	40,000
Barnato Bank	2,000,000	

British African Trading	80,000	
Cape Nitrates	10,000	
New Cassel Coal and Exploration Company of South Africa	200,000	
South African Saltpetre Fields	750,000	50,000
Tyne Valley Colliery	60,000	15,000
United African Collieries	175,000	50,000
International Mining Corporation	750,000	
Johannesburg Mining and General Syndicate	25,000	
Rhodesia Mining and Finance	250,000	55,000
Robinson Bank	3,000,000	
United Gold Field Exploration and Investment	200,000	
Total	60,995,807	2,658,600

[As far as the Editor of the *African Critic*, Henry Hess, was able, the working capital of every concern was provided: 'It will readily be seen how scandalously inadequate this has been in a large number of cases. What chances of success the majority of these companies will have remains to be seen. What I am concerned about is the fact that the British public have subscribed no less than 61 millions sterling with which to float these concerns, of which gigantic sum it may safely be said at least one-half has gone into the pockets of vendors and their intermediaries, whilst of the remaining half probably one-third only will ever return a penny in dividends'.]

APPENDIX F

Control: Southern African Gold Mining Groups, 1896–1897

[Only the largest and / or most influential or controversial Groups are listed. Companies controlled by more than one Group are listed twice.]

Source: compiled from *Financial Times*, September 21, 1896, and *The African Review*, February 8, 1896 and *ibid.*, May 1, 1897.

Messrs. Wernher, Beit, and Company, and Messrs. Eckstein
Bantjes Consolidated Mines
Beira Railway Company
Bonanza
City and Suburban Gold Mining and Estate Company
Crown Deep
Crown Reef Gold Mining Company
Durban Roodepoort Deep
Ferreira Gold Mining Company
Geldenhuis Deep
Glen Deep
H.F. Syndicate
Henry Nourse Gold Mining Company
Jubilee Gold Mining Company
Jumpers Deep
Jumpers Gold Mining Company
Knight Central
Langlaagte Deep
Modderfontein Extension Gold Mining Company
New Heriot Gold Mining Company
New Modderfontein Gold Mining Company
Nigel Gold Mining Company
Nourse Deep
Paarl Central Gold Mining and Exploration Company
Rand Mines
Robinson Gold Mining Company
Rose Deep

 | DOI:10.1163/9789004690790_012

Salisbury Gold Mining Company
Simmer and Jack East
Tati Concessions Company
Transvaal Consolidated Land and Exploration Company
Transvaal Gold Mining Estates
Transvaal Silver Mines
Village Main Deep
West Roodepoort Deep
Witwatersrand Deep
Wolhuter Gold Mines

Consolidated Goldfields of South Africa and the Goldfields Deep
Apex Mines
Banket Gold Mining Company
Belgian Mining Trust of South Africa
Central Nigel Deep
City and Suburban Deep
French Rand Gold Mining Company
Glen Deep
Jupiter Gold Mining Company
Klipfontein Estate and Gold Mining Company
Knight Central
Knight's Deep
Mashonaland Agency
Midas Deep
Middelvlei Estate
New Florida Gold Mines
Nigel Deep
Rand Victoria Mines
Robinson Deep
Rose Deep
Simmer and Jack East
Simmer and Jack Proprietary Mines
Simmer and Jack West
South African Gold Trust
Sub-Nigel
Trust Francaise
Turffontein Estate
Village Main Deep

Messrs. Barnato Brothers

Aurora West United Gold Mining Company
Balmoral Main Reef Gold Mining Company
Barnato Consolidated Mines
Buffelsdoorn "A" Gold Mining Company
Buffelsdoorn Estate and Gold Mining Company
Chimes Mines
Consort Consolidated Gold Mines
Ginsberg Gold Mining Company
Glencairn Main Reef Gold Mining Company
Goldfields of Lydenburg
Johannesburg Consolidated Investment Company
Johannesburg Waterworks, Estate and Exploration Company
Kimberley-Roodepoort Gold Mining Company
Langlaagte Royal Gold Mining Company
London-Paris Financial and Mining Corporation
May Consolidated Gold Mining Company
New Croesus Gold Mining Company
New Florida Gold Mines
New Heidelberg-Roodepoort Gold Mining Company
New Primrose Gold Mining Company
New Rietfontein Estates Gold Mines
New Spes Bona Gold Mining Company
New Unified Gold Mining Company
Orkney Estate and Gold Mining Company
Pleiades Gold Mining Company
Rand Central Mines
Vulcan Gold Mines

Anglo-French Exploration Company and Mr. George Farrar

Agnes Munro Gold Mining Company
Angelo Gold Mines
Anglo-French Collieries Syndicate
Anglo-French Exploration Company
Anglo-French Land Company of the Transvaal
Anglo-French Matabeleland Company
Benoni Claim Gold Mining and Exploration Syndicate
Benoni Gold Mines
Boksburg Gold Mines
Chimes West

Cinderella Gold Mining Company
Driefontein Consolidated Mines
East Rand Proprietary Mines
H. F. Syndicate
Kleinfontein Central
New Blue Sky Gold Mining Company
New Comet Gold Mining Company
New Kleinfontein Company

Mr. J.B. Robinson
Block 'A' Randfontein Gold Mining Company
Block 'B' Langlaagte Estate Gold Mining Company
Langlaagte Estate and Gold Mining Company
Langlaagte Exploration and Building Company
Langlaagte Star Gold Mining Company
Mynpacht Randfontein Gold Mining Company
North Randfontein Gold Mining Company
Porges-Randfontein Gold Mining Company
Randfontein Estates Gold Mining Company
Robinson Diamond Mining Company
Robinson-Randfontein Gold Mining Company
Robinson South African Banking Company

The Bechuanaland Exploration Company
Bechuanaland Trading Company
Charterland Goldfields
Goldfields of Mashonaland
Goldfields of Mazoe
Northern Territories (B. S. A.)Exploring Company
Torva Exploring Syndicate
Umniati Development Company
United Matabele Claims Development Company
Wiltshire Development Company

The Exploration Company
Compagnie Francaise des Mines d'Or et d'Exploration
Consolidated Deep Levels
Geldenhuis Deep
Jumpers Deep
Rose Deep

Oceana Consolidated Company and the New African Company
French Western Nigel
Goldfields of Zambesia
Mozambique Company
New Belgium (Transvaal) Land and Development Company
Oceana Minerals Company
Oceana Transvaal Coal Company
Transvaal Nigel
Van Ryn Gold Mines Estate
Van Ryn North Exploration Company
Van Ryn West Gold Mining Company
Western Kleinfontein

Bibliography

Abraham, Felix. *The Witwatersrand Gold Mines: A True and Unvarnished Account of their Origin and Progress*. London: Effingham Wilson, 1892.

Abraham, Felix. *The New Era of the Goldmining Industry in the Witwatersrand*. London: Effingham Wilson, 1894.

Allen, Grant. *An African Millionaire*. London: George Bell & Sons, 1897.

Allen, Victor Leonard. *The History of Black Mineworkers in South Africa. Volume I. The Techniques of Resistance 1871–1948*. Keighley: Moor Press, 1992.

Ally, Russell. "Great Britain, Gold and South Africa – An Examination of the Influence Gold had in Shaping Britain's Policy towards South Africa, 1886–1914." Unpublished, 1992.

Ally, Russell. *Gold & Empire. The Bank of England and South Africa's Gold Producers 1886–1926*. Johannesburg: Witwatersrand University Press, 1994.

Auchterlonie, Paul. "A Turk of the West: Sir Edgar Vincent's Career in Egypt and the Ottoman Empire." *British Journal of Middle Eastern Studies* 27, no. 1 (2000): 49–67.

Autherman, André. *La Banque Imperiale Ottomane*. Paris: Institut de la gestion publique et du développement économique, 1996.

Blainey, G. "Lost Causes of the Jameson Raid." *Economic History Review* 18, no. 2 (1965): 350–366.

Blake, Robert. *A History of Rhodesia*. London: Methuen, 1977.

Boyce, George, ed. *The Crisis of British Power. The Imperial and Naval Papers of the Second Earl of Selborne, 1895–1910*. London: Historians' Press, 1990.

Bransky, D. "The Causes of the Boer War. Towards a Synthesis." Unpublished, 1974.

Bryce, James. *Impressions of South Africa*. London: Macmillan & co., 1899.

Bryce, James, F. Engelenburg, Karl Blind, Andrew Carnegie, Francis Charmes, Demetrius C. Bulger, Max Nordau, Hans Delbrück, Vladimir Holmstrem, Prince Ookhtomsky, Edmund Gosse. *Briton and Boer. Both Sides of the South African Question*. New York and London: Harper & Brothers, 1900.

Butler, Jeffrey. *The Liberal Party and the Jameson* Raid. Oxford: Clarendon, 1968.

Butler, Jeffrey. Review of *Economic Imperialism in Theory and Practice,* by Robert Kubicek. *Africana Journal* 10 (1979): 75–77.

Butler, William. *Sir William Butler. An Autobiography*. New York: Scribner's, 1913.

Buttery John, and A. Key. *Why Kruger Made War or Behind the Boer Scenes*. London: Heinsmann, 1900.

Cain, Peter. *Hobson and Imperialism. Radicalism, New Liberalism, and Finance*. Oxford: Oxford University Press, 2002.

Cain, Peter J., and Antony G. Hopkins. *British Imperialism 1688–2000. Second Edition*. Harlow: Longman, 2001.

Cartwright, Alan. *The Gold Miners.* Cape Town: Purnell and Sons, 1962.

Cartwright, Alan. *Gold Paved the Way. The Story of the Gold Fields Group of Companies.* London: Macmillan, 1967.

Checkland, S. "The Mind of the City 1870–1914." *Oxford Economic Papers* 9, no. 3 (1957): 261–78.

Churchill, Lord Randolph. *Men, Mines and Animals in South Africa.* London: Sampson Low, Marston & Company, 1893.

Clarence-Smith, William Gervase. *Slaves, Peasants and Capitalists in Southern Angola, 1840–1926.* Cambridge: Cambridge University Press, 1979.

Clarke, Sir Edward. *The Story of My Life.* London: J. Murray, 1918.

Clarke, Peter. *Hope and Glory: Britain 1900–1990.* London: Allen Lane, The Penguin Press, 1996.

Clay, Christopher. "The Imperial Ottoman Bank in the Later Nineteenth Century: A Multinational 'National' Bank?" In *Banks as Multinationals,* edited by Geoffrey Jones, 142–159. London: Routledge, 1990.

Cohen, Louis. *Reminiscences of Johannesburg & London.* London: Robert Holden & Co. Ltd, 1924.

Colvin, Ian. *The Life of Jameson, Volume II.* London: Edward Arnold and Co, 1922.

Conlin, Jonathan. *Mr Five Per Cent. The Many Lives of Calouste Gulbenkian. The World's Richest Man.* London: Profile Books, 2019.

The Consolidated Gold Fields of South Africa, Limited. *The Gold Fields' 1887–1937.* London: The Consolidated Gold Fields of South Africa Ltd, 1937.

Cook, Edward. *Edmund Garrett. A Memoir.* London: E. Arnold, 1909.

Curle, James. *The Gold Mines of the World.* London: Waterlow and Sons, 1899.

Cuthbertson, Greg H., ed. *The Jameson Raid. A Centennial Retrospective.* Johannesburg: Brenthurst Press, 1996.

Davenport-Hines, R., and Jean-Jacques Van Helten, "Edgar Vincent, Viscount D'Abernon, and the Eastern Investment Company in London, Constantinople and Johannesburg." In *Speculators and Patriots. Essays in Business History,* edited by R. Davenport-Hines, 35–61. London: Frank Cass & Co. Ltd., 1986.

Davidson, Apollon. *Cecil Rhodes and His Time.* Moscow: Progress Publishers, 1988.

De Launay, Louis. *Les Mines D'Or du Transvaal.* Paris: Librairie polytechnique, Baudry et cie, 1896.

Don, Charles. *And Having Writ … Memories and Impressions.* Johannesburg: Central News Agency, 1942.

Duguid, Charles. *How to Read the Money Article.* London: Effingham Wilson, 1901.

Duminy, Andrew, and William Guest, eds. *FitzPatrick. South African Politician. Selected Papers, 1888–1906.* Johannesburg: McGraw-Hill Book Company, 1976.

Edelstein, M. "Foreign investment and accumulation, 1860–1914." In *The Economic History of Britain since 1700. Second Edition. Volume 2: 1860–1939,* edited by Rode Floud and Donald McCloskey, 190–226. Cambridge: Cambridge University Press, 1997.

Edwards, Ruth. *The Pursuit of Reason. The Economist 1843–1993*. London: Hamish Hamilton, 1993.

Emden, Paul. *The Randlords*. London: Hodder and Stoughton Limited, 1935.

Etherington, Norman. *Theories of Imperialism. War, Conquest and Capital.* London: Croom Helm, 1984.

Fieldhouse, David. *Economics and Empire 1830–1914*. London: Macmillan, 1984.

FitzPatrick, James. *The Transvaal from Within. A Private Record of Public Affairs.* London: W. Heinemann, 1900.

Flint, J. *Cecil Rhodes*. Toronto: Little, Brown, 1974.

Fort, George Seymour. *Alfred Beit. A Study of the Man and his Work*. London: Ivor Nicholson & Watson, 1932.

Fox, Margalit. *Conan Doyle for the Defence*. London: Random House, 2018.

Fraser Maryna, and Alan Jeeves, eds. *All That Glittered. Selected Correspondence of Lionel Phillips 1890–1924*. Cape Town: Oxford University Press, 1977.

Galbraith, John. *Crown and Charter. The Early Years of the British South Africa Company.* Berkley: University of California Press, 1974.

Garvin, James. *The Life of Joseph Chamberlain. Volume Three 1895–1900. Empire and World Policy*. London: Macmillan, 1934.

Goldmann, Charles. *South African Mines; Their Position, Results, & Developments: Together with an Account of Diamond, Land, Finance, and Kindred Concerns*, 3 Vols. London: E. Wilson & co, 1895–6.

Graham, Wayne. "The Randlord's Bubble 1894–6: South African Gold Mines and Stock Market Manipulation." *University of Oxford Discussion Papers in Economic and Social History*, no. 10 (August 1996).

Grenville, John. *Lord Salisbury and Foreign Policy: The Close of the Nineteenth Century.* London: Athlone Press, 1964.

Gross, Felix. *Rhodes of Africa*. London: Cassel, 1956.

Gutsche, Thelma. *Old Gold. The History of the Wanderers Club*. Cape Town: Timmons, 1966.

Hammond, John Hays. *The Autobiography of John Hays Hammond. Volume 1*. New York: Farrar & Rinehart, 1935.

Harlow, Vincent. "Sir Frederic Hamilton's Narrative of Events Relative to the Jameson Raid." *English Historical Review* 72, no. 283 (1957): 279–305.

Harries, Patrick. "Capital, State, and Labour on the 19th Century Witwatersrand: A Reassessment." *South African Historical Journal* 18 (1986): 25–45.

Harris, Frank. *Frank Harris. His Life and Adventures. An Autobiography*. London: Richards Press,1947.

Harris, John. *The Chartered Millions. Rhodesia and the Challenge to the British Commonwealth*. London: Swarthmore Press, 1920.

Hatch, Frederick, and John Chalmers. *The Gold Mines of the Rand. Being a Description of the Mining Industry of Witwatersrand South African Republic*. London: Macmillan 1895.

Headlam, C., ed. *The Milner Papers. South Africa 1897–1899*. London: Cassell & Company, 1931.

Henshaw, Peter. "The 'Key to South Africa' in the 1890s: Delagoa Bay and the Origins of the South African War." *Journal of Southern African Studies* 24, no. 3 (1998): 527–43.

Hind, R. *Henry Labouchere and the Empire 1880–1905*. London: Athlone Press, 1972.

Hobson, John. *The War in South Africa. Its Causes and Effects*. London: James Nisbet & Co. Ltd, 1900.

Hobson, John. "Capitalism and Imperialism in South Africa." *Contemporary Review* 77 (1900).

Houghton, Rhoades Esther. "John Verschoyle and the 'Fortnightly Review.'" *Victorian Periodicals Newsletter* 1, no. 3 (1968): 17–21.

Hyam Ronald, and Peter Henshaw, eds. *The Lion and the Springbok. Britain and South Africa since the Boer War*. Cambridge: Cambridge University Press, 2003.

Ince, Bernard. "Natural-Born Showman: The Stage Career of Charles Collette, Actor & Comedian." *Theatre Notebook* 63, no. 1 (2009): 1–25.

Innes, Duncan. *Anglo American and the Rise of Modern South Africa*. New York: Monthly Review Press, 1984.

Itzkowitz, David. "Fair Enterprise or Extravagant Speculation: Investment, Speculation, and Gambling in Victorian England." *Victorian Studies* 45, no. 1 (2002): 121–47.

Jeeves, Alan. "The control of migratory labour on the South African gold mines in the era of Kruger and Milner." *Journal of Southern African Studies* 2 (1975): 3–29.

Jeeves, Alan. "Aftermath of Rebellion – The Randlords and Kruger's Republic after the Jameson Raid." *South African Historical Journal* 10, no. 1 (1978): 102–16.

Jeeves, Alan. *Migrant Labour in South Africa's Mining Economy. The Struggle for the Gold Mines' Labour Supply 1890–1920*. Johannesburg: Witwatersrand University Press, 1985.

Jeeves, Alan. "Hobson's The War in South Africa: A Reassessment." in *Writing a Wider War. Rethinking Gender, Race, and Identity in the South African War, 1899–1902*, edited by Greg Cuthbertson, Albert Grundlingh, and Mary-Lynn Suttie, 233–46. Cape Town: David Philip, 2002.

Jeppe, Carl. *The Kaleidoscopic Transvaal*. London: Chapman, 1906.

Johnstone, Frederick. *Class, Race and Gold. A Study of Class Relations and Racial Discrimination in South Africa*. Lanham: University Press of America, 1976.

Judd, Denis, and Keith Surridge. *The Boer War*. London: Palgrave Macmillan, 2002.

Katz, Elaine. "Outcrop and Deep Level Mining In South Africa before the Anglo-Boer War: Re-examining the Blainey Thesis." *Economic History Review* 158, no. 2 (1995): 304–28.

Keppel-Jones, Arthur. *Rhodes and Rhodesia. The White Conquest of Zimbabwe 1884–1902*. Pietermaritzburg: University of Natal Press, 1983.

Klaus, Ian. *Forging Capitalism. Rogues, Swindlers, Frauds, and the Rise of Modern Finance*. New Haven: Yale University Press, 2014.

Klein, Harry. *The Story of the Johannesburg Stock Exchange 1887–1947*. Johannesburg: Committee of the Johannesburg Stock Exchange 1948.

Koss, Stephen, ed. *The Anatomy of an Antiwar Movement. The Pro-Boers*. Chicago: University of Chicago Press, 1973.

Kruger, Paul. *The Memoirs of Paul Kruger*. London: T. Fisher Unwin. 1902.

Kubicek, Robert. "The Randlords in 1895: A Reassessment." *Journal of British Studies* 11, no. 2 (1972): 84–103.

Kubicek, Robert. "Finance Capital and South African Goldmining 1886–1914." *Journal of Imperial and Commonwealth History* 3 (1975): 386–95.

Kubicek, Robert. *Economic Imperialism in Theory and Practice. The Case of South African Gold Mining Finance 1886–1914*. Durham: Duke University Press, 1979.

Kubicek, Robert. "Mining: Patterns of Dependence and Development 1870–1930." In *Studies in the Economic History of Southern Africa. Volume II. South Africa, Lesotho and Swaziland*, edited by Z. Konczacki, Jane L. Parpart, Timothy M. Shaw, 64–86. London: Frank Cas 1991.

Kynaston, David. *The City of London. Volume II. Golden Years 1890–1914*. London: Chatto & Windus, 1995.

Lang, John. *Bullion Johannesburg. Men, Mines and the Challenges of Conflict*. Johannesburg: J. Ball, 1986.

Lauck, William Jett. *The Causes of the Panic of 1893*. Boston: Houghton, Mifflin and company, 1907.

Lawrence, Jeremy. *Buccaneer. A Biography of Sir Joseph Benjamin Robinson, first Baronet*. Cape Town: Gryphon Press, 2001.

Lawson, W. "Stock-Jobbing Companies." *National Review* 36, no. 216.

Levy, Norman. *The Foundations of the South African Cheap Labour System*. London: Routledge and Kegan Paul, 1982.

Lewinsohn, Richard. *Barney Barnato. From Whitechapel Clown to Diamond King*. London: E. P. Dutton & Co., Inc., 1937.

Lewsen, Phyllis, ed.. *Selections from the Correspondence of John X. Merriman 1890–1898*. Cape Town: The Van Riebeek Society, 1963.

Leyds, Willem. *The Transvaal Surrounded*. London: T. Fisher Unwin Ltd., 1919.

Liggett, Walter. *The Rise of Herbert Hoover*. New York: H.K. Fly Company, 1932.

Lockhart, John G., and Christopher M. Woodhouse. *Rhodes*. London: Hodder and Stoughton, 1963.

Lukasiewicz, Mariusz. "Gold, Finance and Speculation: The Making of the Johannesburg Stock Exchange, 1887–1899." PhD diss., Graduate Institute, University of Geneva, 2017.

Lukasiewicz, Mariusz. "From Diamonds to Gold: The Making of the Johannesburg Stock Exchange, 1880–1890." *Journal of Southern African Studies* 43, no. 4 (2017): 715–32.

Mabin, Eleanor. "'Truth' and the British South Africa Company. The Development of a Radical's Opposition to the Development of Capitalist Imperialism in a Southern African Context." MA diss., Simon Fraser University, 1982.

Mabin, Alan and Barbara Conradie, eds. *The Confidence of the Whole Country. Standard Bank Reports on Economic Conditions in Southern Africa 1865–1902*. Johannesburg: Standard Bank Investment Corp, 1987.

Marais, Johannes. *The Fall of Kruger's Republic.* Oxford: Oxford University Press, 1961.

Marks, Shula. "Southern and Central Africa, 1886–1910." In *The Cambridge History of Africa*, vol. 6, edited by G.N. Sanderson and Roland Oliver, 422–92. Cambridge: Cambridge University Press, 1985.

Marks, Shula, and Stanley Trapido. "Lord Milner and the South African State." *History Workshop* 8 (1979): 50–80.

Marks, Shula, and Stanley Trapido, "Lord Milner and the South African State Reconsidered." In *Imperialism, the State and the Third World*, edited by Michael Twaddle, 80–94. London: British Academic Press, 1992.

Marx, Karl. *Capital. A Critique of Political Economy. Volume III*, edited by Friedrich Engels. London: Lawrence and Wishart, 1977.

Mawby, Arthur. "Capital, Government and Politics in the Transvaal, 1900–7: A Revision and a Reversion." *Historical Journal* 17, no. 2 (1974): 387–415.

Mawby, Arthur. *Gold Mining and Politics – Johannesburg 1900–1907*. Lewiston: Edwin Mellen Press, 2000.

Maylam, Paul. *Rhodes, the Tswana, and the British: Colonialism, Collaboration, and Conflict in the Bechuanaland Protectorate, 1885–1899*. Westport: Greenwood Press, 1980.

McCarty, John. "British Investment in Overseas Mining, 1880–1914." PhD diss., University of Cambridge, 1961.

Mendelsohn, Richard. "Blainey and the Jameson Raid: The Debate Renewed." *Journal of Southern African Studies* 6 (1980): 157–170.

Mendelsohn, Richard. "Thirty Years' Debate on the Economic Origins of the Raid." In *The Jameson Raid. A Centennial Retrospective*, edited by Greg H. Cuthbertson, 55–88. Johannesburg: The Brenthurst Press, 1996.

Meredith, Hubert. *The Drama of Money Making*. London: Sampson Low, Marston, & Company, n.d [1931].

Michell, Sir Lewis. *The Life and Times of the Right Honourable Cecil John Rhodes 1853–1902*, II. London: Mitchell Kennerley, 1910.

Michie, Ranald "Options, Concessions, Syndicates, and the Provision of Venture Capital, 1880–1913." *Business History* 23, no. 2 (1981): 147–164.

Michie, Ranald "Different in Name Only? The London Stock Exchange and Foreign Bourses, c.1850–1914." *Business History* 30, no. 1 (1988): 46–68.

Michie, Ranald. *Guilty Money: The City of London in Victorian and Edwardian Culture, 1815–1914*. London: Pickering & Chatto, 2009.

Millin, Sarah. *Rhodes* (Cape Town: Central News Agency, 1952).

Milne, James. *A Window in Fleet Street*. London: John Murray, 1931.

Nathan, Manfred. *Paul Kruger. His Life and Times*. Durban: Knox, 1941.

Osterhammel, Jürgen. "Britain and China, 1842–1914." In *The Oxford History of the British Empire. The Nineteenth Century,* edited by Andrew Porter, 146–169. Oxford: Oxford University Press, 1999.

Osterhammel, Jürgen. *The Transformation of the World. A Global History of the Nineteenth Century*. Princeton: Princeton University Press, 2014.

Palmade, Guy. *French Capitalism in the Nineteenth Century*. Newton Abbot: Newton Abbot, David and Charles, 1972.

Pearson, Hesketh. *Labby. The Life and Character of Henry Labouchere*. London: Harper & Brothers, 1936.

Phillips, Lionel. *Some Reminiscences*. London: Hutchinson & Co., 1924.

Phimister, Ian. "Rhodes, Rhodesia and the Rand." *Journal of Southern African Studies* 1, no. 1 (1974): 74–90.

Phimister, Ian. "'Empire, Imperialism and the Partition of Africa." In *Gentlemanly Capitalism, Imperialism and Global History,* edited by Shigeru Akita, 65–82. Basingstoke: Palgrave Macmillan, 2002.

Phimister, Ian. "Speculation and Exploitation: The Southern Rhodesian Mining Industry in the Company Era." *Zambezia* 30 (2003): 178–89.

Phimister, Ian. "Late Nineteenth Century Globalisation: London and Lomagundi Perspectives on Mining Speculation in Southern Africa, 1894–1904." *Journal of Global History* 10, no. 1 (2015): 27–52.

Phimister, Ian. "Frenzied Finance: Gold Mining in the Globalizing South, c. 1886–1896." In *A Global History of Gold Rushes*, edited by Benjamin Mountford and Stephen Tuffnell, 139–162. Oakland: University of California Press, 2018.

Phimister, Ian. "Markets, Mines, and Magnates: Finance and the Coming of War in South Africa, 1894–1899." *Africa* 2, no. 2 (2020): 5–22.

Phimister, Ian. "Lendy, Lobengula, and London: The 1893 Anglo-Ndebele War Revisited." *Global Nineteenth-Century Studies* 2, no. 2 (2023): 101–41.

Phimister, Ian, and Jeremy Mouat. "Mining, Engineers and Risk Management: British Overseas Investment, 1894–1914." *South African Historical Journal* 49, no. 1 (2003): 1–26.

Porter, Andrew. *The Origins of the South African War: Joseph Chamberlain and the Diplomacy of Imperialism 1895–1899*. London: Manchester University Press, 1980.

Porter, Andrew. "The South African War: Context and Motive Reconsidered." *Journal of African History* 31, no. 1 (1990): 43–57.

Porter, Dilwyn. "'A Trusted Guide of the Investing Public': Harry Marks and the Financial News 1884–1916." *Business History* 28, no. 1 (1986): 1–17.

Regan, William. *Boer and Uitlander. The True History of the Late Events in South Africa*. London: Digby, Long, 1896.

Reitz, Francis. *A Century of Wrong*. London: Review of Reviews, 1900.

Rhoodie, Denys. *Conspirators in Conflict. A Study of the Johannesburg Reform Committee and its role in the conspiracy against the South African Republic*. Cape Town: Tafelberg-uitgewers, 1967.

Richardson Peter, and Jean-Jacques van Helten. "The Gold Mining Industry in the Transvaal, 1886–1899." In *The South African War: The Anglo-Boer War, 1899–1902*, edited by Peter Warwick. Harlow: Longman, 1980.

Richardson Peter, and Jean-Jacques Van Helten. "The Development of the South African Gold-Mining Industry, 1895–1918." *Economic History Review* 37, no. 3 (1984): 319–340.

Rickard, Thomas. *Retrospect. An Autobiography*. New York: Whittlesey House, 1937.

Riddell, Lord. *More Pages from my Diary 1908–1914*. London: Country Life, 1934.

Robb, George. *White-Collar Crime in Modern England. Financial Fraud and Business Morality 1845–1929*. Cambridge: Cambridge University Press, 1992.

Robinson, W. *Muckraker. The Scandalous Life and Times of W.T. Stead*. London: Robson Books, 2012.

Robinson, Ronald, John Gallagher, and Alice Denny, *Africa and the Victorians: The Official Mind of Imperialism*. London: Macmillan 1961.

Rose, Edward. *The Truth About the Transvaal. A Record of Facts based upon Twelve Year's Residence in the Country*. London: E.B. Rose, 1902.

Rosenthal, Eric. *Shovel and Sieve*. Cape Town: Howard Timmins N.D. [1959].

Rotberg, Robert. *The Founder. Cecil Rhodes and the Pursuit of Power*. New York: Oxford University Press, 1988.

Sayers, Richard. *The Bank of England 1891–1944*. Cambridge: Cambridge University Press, 1976.

Schneer, Jonathan. *London in 1900. The Imperial Metropolis*. New Haven: Yale University Press, 1999.

Schreuder, Deryck. *The Scramble for Southern Africa, 1877–1895*. Cambridge: Cambridge University Press, 1980.

Schreuder, Deryck, and Jeffrey Butler, eds. *Sir Graham Bower's Secret History of the Jameson Raid and the South African Crisis, 1895–1902*. Cape Town: Van Riebeeck Society, 2002.

Searle, Geoffrey. *Corruption in British Politics 1895–1930*. Oxford: Oxford University Press, 1987.

Seligmann, Matthew. *Rivalry in Southern Africa. The Transformation of German Colonial Policy*. Basingstoke: Palgrave Macmillan, 1998.

Shenton, Robert. "The Chartered Company, 1889–1898. A Financial and Political History of the British South Africa Company." PhD diss., Harvard University, 1961.

Simons, Jack, and Ray Esther Simons. *Class and Colour in South Africa, 1850–1950*. Harmondsworth: Penguin Books, 1969.

Skinner, Rob. *Modern South Africa in World History. Beyond Imperialism* (London: Bloomsbury, 2017.

Smith, Ian. *The Origins of the South African War, 1899–1902*. London: Longman, 1996.

Stanley, Liz, and Andrea Salter, eds. *The World's Great Question. Olive Schreiner's South African Letters 1889–1920*. Cape Town: Van Riebeek Society, 2014.

Statham, Francis Reginald. *South Africa As It Is*. London: T.F. Unwin, 1897.

Statham, Francis Reginald. *Paul Kruger and His Times*. London: T.F. Unwin, 1898.

Stead, William, ed. *The Last Will and Testament of Cecil John Rhodes. With Elucidatory Notes to which are added Some Chapters describing the Political and Religious Ideas of the Testator.* London: "Review of Reviews" Office, 1902.

Stent, Vere. *A Personal Record of Some Incidents in the Life of Cecil Rhodes*. Cape Town: Books of Rhodesia, 1925.

Stutfield, Hugh. "Investors and their Money." *The National Review* 25, (1895).

Stutfield, Hugh. "The Company Scandal. A City View." *The National Review* 32 (1898).

Stutfield, Hugh. "The Higher Rascality." *The National Review* 31 (1898).

Taylor, James. *Recollections of the Discovery of Gold on the Witwatersrand*. Cape Town: unpublished, 1936.

Taylor, James. *A Pioneer Looks Back*. London: Hutchinson & Co., 1939.

Taylor, William. *African Treasures. Sixty Years among Diamonds and Gold*. London: J. Long, 1932.

Thompson, Willie. *Global Expansion. Britain and its Empire, 1870–1914*. London: Pluto Press, 1999.

Trevelyan, Raleigh. *Grand Dukes and Diamonds. The Wernhers of Luton Hoo*. London: Faber & Faber, 1991.

Turrell Robert, and Jean-Jacques Van Helten. "The Rothschilds, the Exploration Company and Mining Finance." *Business History* 28, no. 2 (1986): 181–205.

Twain, Mark. *More Tramps Abroad*. London: Chatto & Windus, 1897.

Vander Weyer, Martin. *Fortune's Spear. The Story of The Blue-Blooded Rogue Behind the Most Notorious City Scandal of the 1920s*. London: Elliott & Thompson, 2011.

Van der Poel, Jean. *The Jameson Raid*. Cape Town: Oxford University Press, 1951.

Van Helten, Jean-Jacques. "British and European Economic Investment in the Transvaal: With Specific Reference to the Witwatersrand Gold Fields and District, 1886–1910". PhD diss. University of London, 1981, 123.

Van Helten, Jean-Jacques. "Review Article. Mining and Imperialism." *Journal of Southern African Studies* 6, no. 2 (1980): 230–35.

Van Helten, Jean-Jacques. "Empire and High Finance: South Africa and the International Gold Standard 1890–1914." *Journal of African History* 23 (1982): 529–48.

Van Helten, Jean-Jacques. "La France et l'Or des Boers: Some Aspects of French Investment in South Africa between 1890 and 1914." *African Affairs* 84, no. 335 (1985): 247–63.

Van Helten, Jean-Jacques. "Mining, share manias and speculation: British investments in overseas mining, 1880–1913." In *Capitalism in a Mature Economy: Financial Institutions, Capital Exports and British Industry, 1870–1939*, edited by Jean-Jacques Van Helten and Youssef Cassis, 159–85. Aldershot: Edward Elgar Publishing, 1990.

Van Onselen, Charles. *Studies in the Social and Economic History of the Witwatersrand 1886–1914, Volume 1. New Babylon.* Johannesburg: Ravan Press, 1982.

Van Onselen, Charles. *The Cowboy Capitalist. John Hays Hammond, the American West, and the Jameson Raid.* Johannesburg: Jonathan Ball, 2017.

Van Oordt, Joan. *Paul Kruger en de Opkomst der Zuid-Afrikaansche Republiek.* Cape Town: Hollandsch Afrikaansche Uitgevers, 1898.

Van Oss, S.F. "The Gold-Mining Madness in the City." *The Nineteenth Century* 38, no. 224 (1895): 537–547.

Van Oss, S.F. "In Hooley Land," *Journal of Finance* V, no. 21 (1899).

Vindex. *Cecil Rhodes. His Political Life and Speeches 1881–1900.* London: Chapman and Hall, 1900.

Warren, H. *The Modern Bucket Shop.* London: Everett, n.d. [1906].

Webb, Arthur. "Witwatersrand Genesis: A Comparative Study of Some Early Gold Mining Companies 1886–1894." PhD diss., Rhodes University, 1981.

Webb, Arthur. "Blainey and Early Witwatersrand Profitability. Some Thoughts on Financial Management and Capital Constraints Facing the Gold Mining Industry 1886–1894." *South African Journal of Economic History* 12 (1997): 128–52.

Webb, Sidney, and Beatrice Webb, *The Decay of Capitalist Civilisation.* London: George Allen and Unwin, 1923.

Webber, Henry O'Kelly. *The Grip of Gold. A Life Story of a Dominion.* London: Hutchinson, 1936.

Weinthal, Leo, ed. *Memories, Mines and Millions, Being the Life of Sir Joseph B. Robinson.* London: Simpkin Marshall Ltd, 1929.

Wheatcroft, Geoffrey. *The Randlords.* London: Weidenfeld & Nicolson, 1985.

White, Montagu. "The Danger of Personal Rule in South Africa." *North American Review* 170, no. 519 (1900): 225–239.

Wilson, Alexander. *Practical Hints to Investors. And Some Words to Speculators.* London: Clement Wilson, 1897.

Paulet, Henry Marquess of Winchester. *Statesmen, Financiers and Felons.* Abbeville: Imprimerie F. Paillart 1935.

Index

Printed in the United States
by Baker & Taylor Publisher Services